Driving the State

Driving the State
Families and Public Policy in Central Mexico

DOLORES M. BYRNES

CORNELL UNIVERSITY PRESS

ITHACA AND LONDON

First published 2003 by Cornell University Press
First printing, Cornell Paperbacks, 2003

Printed in the United States of America

Library of Congress Cataloging-in-Publication Data

Byrnes, Dolores M., 1958–
    Driving the state : families and public policy in central Mexico / Dolores M. Byrnes.
        p. cm.
Includes bibliographical references (p.) and index.
    ISBN 0-8014-4129-3 (cloth : alk. paper) — ISBN 0-8014-8859-1 (paperback : alk. paper)
    1. Mi Comunidad (Program)   2. Job creation—Government policy—Mexico—Guanajuato (State)   3. Women offshore assembly industry workers—Services for—Mexico—Guanajuato (State)   4. Guanajuato (Mexico : State)—Emigration and immigration—Government policy.   5. Emigrant remittances—Mexico—Guanajuato (State)   I. Title.
    HD5731.A7G833 2003
    362.85′84′082097241

                                                                2002156477

Cornell University Press strives to use environmentally responsible suppliers and materials to the fullest extent possible in the publishing of its books. Such materials include vegetable-based, low-VOC inks and acid-free papers that are recycled, totally chlorine-free, or partly composed of nonwood fibers. For further information, visit our website at www.cornellpress.cornell.edu.

Cloth printing   10 9 8 7 6 5 4 3 2 1
Paperback printing   10 9 8 7 6 5 4 3 2 1

For my sisters and brothers:
Lee, John, Laura, David, and Randy

Contents

Preface

In writing about the Mi Comunidad program, the subject of this book, I sought to create something that my colleagues in Guanajuato could share, that ideally would be both critical of and relevant to their work. I wanted to ensure a careful and clear analysis that would draw from the best of theoretical stances, while remaining grounded to the exigencies of the case. I wondered if the terms of a "radical and plural democracy" (Mouffe 1993) could be framed for people engaged in the process of *being the state*, who could rethink their own roles in enacting power or become part of a project that embraces conflict as "the fundamentally moral choice in a life committed to diversity" (Zabusky 1995, 195). This book is offered in that spirit of dialogue and debate, to my colleagues and to others interested in these themes.

The book would not have been published without the crucial advice and years of cheerful, unflagging support of Davydd J. Greenwood. Friends and colleagues who encouraged me in this project include Jane Fajans, Vilma Santiago-Irizarry, Steve Sangren, Anne Pitcher, Judith Boruchoff, Yemile Mizrahi, Martin Murray, Bob Rothstein (who even gave me an office!), Doug MacDonald, Padma Kaimal, and Andy Rotter. I am especially grateful to my colleagues in Guanajuato, Mexico, in particular my *comadres,* who continue to teach me so much about life and friendship. I can never fully thank two dear friends, José Luis Villar and Rosalía Macias Villar, and their entire wonderful family, Cecilia, Waldo, Pamela, and Eugenio, who have long shared with me friendship, advice, stories, humor, food, and Negra Modelo. They have generously embraced all visiting members of my extended family as well. Friends in Guanajuato include Jane Ashley and her children, as well as Lise Giroux and Yoni Freeman, who nurtured me through lonely times with generous offers of space and companionship.

I also thank the entire staff of the Office of Support to Guanajuatense Communities Abroad (known by its Spanish acronym, DACGE), especially the former office director, for their patience and graciousness over the time of my lengthy presence. My research into the program involved participation and an "inside look" at their office. I learned an enormous amount from all of them and have tried to protect their identities here, while honoring their contributions to this work. Many thanks also to Patricia Begne, Susana Guerrero, and Laura Lozano for their help and support.

Many other people have contributed to my studies along the way, including Maria Cook, Thomas Holloway, the late Dennis Vnenchak, and Dorothy Orofino. My students in Core Mexico and Introduction to Anthropology classes at Colgate University have also been interesting partners in learning. I would never have gone to Guanajuato at all in 1985 without the help of my long-time mentor, Marta Dosa of Syracuse University, who honors me with twenty years of friendship. Publication was greatly aided by my amazing friend and cheerleader, Nancy Ries of Colgate University, and by an excellent and enthusiastic editor, Fran Benson of Cornell University Press. Crucial insights from William French and Susan Tiano helped to improve the book considerably. Bruce Acker made many helpful changes to the manuscript, and Louise E. Robbins greatly facilitated the publishing process.

Institutional support for this project came from Cornell University's Department of Anthropology, through summer funding and four years of fellowships and teaching assistantships, and from Cornell's Mario Einaudi Center for International Studies, which funded preresearch travel to Chicago and Mexico in June and November 1999. The library staffs at Colgate University, the University of Guanajuato, and LeMoyne College, as well as Colgate University's Cindy Terrier and Cornell University's Barb Donnell, have all provided invaluable assistance throughout my research and writing phases.

I also thank my brothers and sisters: Laura for her wit and warmth, Lee for her pride and support in all of us, John for his intense loyalty, David for his wonderful humor and strength, and Randy for his spirit that will always live in us. Finally, I have been impossibly lucky to share so many adventures and experiences with a very special group of people: my kind and generous husband Tim, who never tires of our discussions, and our bright, shining children, Gavin and Brigid, who love Guanajuato as much as I do. Their presence sustains me in every moment.

Las Comadres

Travel (like walking) is a substitute for the legends that used to open up space to something different. . . . Every story is a travel story.

MICHEL DE CERTEAU

On the day of a trip to the *maquilas*,[1] we came at 8:30 or 9:00 in the morning to wait outside of el Archivo, the State Archives, an imposing stone building in the central Mexican city of Guanajuato. My colleague, Rosi, and I would sit on tree-shaded benches talking and waiting for our third companion, holding our bags and papers in our laps, sometimes having bought fruit or sweet pastries to share during our upcoming car ride. Into our discussion eventually came the bleat of a car horn, summoning us to a day of travel with the director of the state government's Mi Comunidad (My Community) program, a job creation policy aimed at rural villages throughout the state of Guanajuato. She dubbed the three of us *comadres*, the female equivalent to *compadres*, or shared godparents.[2] It was an embracing term that I was honored to share, for I had come to Guanajuato to study the program they worked for, hoping to become a part of it in any way that I could. Las comadres is also a term highly indicative of the intensely nurturing work these two women did in running the program.

The Mi Comunidad program was created in 1996 by now-President Vicente Fox Quesada while he served as the first-ever elected, opposition-party governor of Guanajuato. He went on to a stunning victory in the July 2000 presidential election, the first time in seventy years that a non-ruling-party candidate had not only won the presidency of Mexico, but was acknowledged by the ruling party, known as the PRI (Partido Revolucionario Institucional, or the Institutional Revolutionary Party), to have done so.[3] My research interest in this particular program, as Fox's creation, began in 1997, in part because Fox was even then beginning to be described as a noteworthy member of the PAN (Partido de Acción Nacional, or National Action Party), one of Mexico's two major opposition parties. It is said that he began running for the job of president of Mexico as soon as he became governor in 1995.

Mi Comunidad is one of several programs in the state of Guanajuato

1

which have been directed at families affected by the massive social phe-nomenon of migration. The program matches state and private invest-ments, the latter mostly generated by migrants living in the United States, to create jobs in textile-producing maquilas. The jobs were intended to re-duce migration, but have become primarily a source of training and in-come for the women left behind. Thus, the program is a microcase of state paternalism within global capitalism, but also one that has taken place within a national context of momentous political transition. The context and process of this policy—how the program worked—was my primary research subject. My methodological focus was on the everyday practices of the two state employees charged with its implementation in several maquilas across the state and involved a reflective dialogue with them about the program. Aspects of research practice and my own positional-ity are further discussed in chapter 1; relevant changes in the program since the time of my research are noted in the text.

Moving between the multiple sites and relationships of the program were las comadres: two young, professional Mexican women and I. We in-habited a world of "adventure time": full of "random contingencies" and chance, characterized by meetings with others and by "the road" (Bakhtin 1996). Traveling across the state in utter freedom, we sat close together in the intimate space of a silver, four-door sedan. The program director, and our driver on every trip (I drove once, but was found to go too slowly), is named Soco. This energetic, gregarious, and charming woman took me under her care from the time of our first meeting in June 1999. Together with her smart, thoughtful assistant Rosi (who called herself the *co-piloto* in reference to her usual position in the front passenger seat, but this metaphor also applied to her position of essential assistance to Soco), she vowed to teach me all she could about their program.

This book is the result of their instruction. In one sense, it is an ethnog-raphy of our travel, but more importantly, it is a glimpse into and a claim about the disorderly, charming, self-contradictory, personal, mobile, and gendered nature of "the state." These state government representatives produced themselves as "the state" through everyday practices, shaped in part by bureaucratic discourse, but also by their own class and gender po-sitions, their complex hopes, personal experiences, and physicality. For of-ficial power is enacted and embodied: it is comprised of individuals who shape and find meaning in part through the work of being the state.

On one level, this case reveals the differentiating touch of power upon citizens. It suggests an aspect of hegemony which Antonio Gramsci re-ferred to as "contrariety" and which I argue often constitutes a deferral of authority and responsibility. But a close look at the everyday practices of these state employees also suggests an emerging intimacy between the state and the family. Through its migration policies, the state government of Guanajuato has taken on an interdependent and reciprocal relationship with the family, in effect dissolving dichotomous boundaries such as work/home and public/private. Through the ties of obligation which were forged in the program, in the "gift" of work to the rural women, in the program discourse on family and investment, and in the sense of investment as atonement, the state was not so much deified or fetishized but rather became a member of the family. At the same time, families became partners to state authority through business ties.

Caught up in fervent hopes and fears about the future, and reflecting the structural anomalies of the wider political economy, the program's participants were shaped by a state discourse that invoked not only "quality" and "entrepreneurship" but family loss and sorrow. Yet beyond any play of meanings, program participants were also affected by a multitude of everyday practices. In general, these practices of the everyday state followed patterns which reinforced the value of male contributions while dismissing rural female intelligence. However, many practices clearly constituted a *deferral* of government authority, in itself an interesting phenomenon in the context of Mexico. Far from unitary or all-seeing, the "eye" of the state can be distracted; it may wink at times, or wear brightly colored contact lenses. Indeed, the eye of the citizen looks directly back, and each sees and recognizes the other in itself. Thus, this case illustrates the power differences which cut across lived experience, and yet how power itself is always changing ground and being restructured in ongoing relationships. It suggests the sharing and shifting of values across presumably disparate realms such as family and state, even as boundaries like public/private are themselves constructed and maintained by persons in a multitude of everyday practices.

In writing about these mobile and contradictory presences of the state government (*el gobierno del estado*) in Guanajuato, I found little direct, theoretical help from among assorted, abstract reifications of the nation-state in political science, anthropology, feminist theory, public policy analysis, and organizational/bureaucratic studies. Nor has there been much focus on federalism or the relative power of states *within* Mexico: key stories of the state in Mexico have tended to be told about the highly centralized, federal executive forms of power. In other words, power has been described at the level of *el gobierno* (the state in its sense of governance) or *el presidencialismo* (presidentialism, a concept referring to centralized presidential power), but not at the more localized level of Mexico's thirty-one states, that is, of *el estado*. This has been changing in scholarship, reflecting changes in politics in Mexico (for a helpful review, see Ward and Rodríguez 1999). The regional levels in Mexico have been described more as

areas where the power of different sectors of the PRI are centered (Lomnitz et al. 1993). Despite the disillusion of the 1982–1988 efforts at "decentralization by decree," states are gaining new functions, there are stronger
mayors and innovations at the local level, with mixed results in terms of
enduring social participation (Cabrero-Mendoza 2000). Meanwhile, key
stories about "the citizen" in Mexico have been situated either in villages
or urban areas, with relatively less focus on the cities of the interior (such
as the city of Guanajuato), and relatively more on the border cities.[4] Similarly, most work on textile maquilas in Mexico has tended to focus on the
border regions. Thus the focus of this book—the implementation of a program which fosters government-citizen partnership to create work in an
interior state—supplements these other levels of analysis.

EMBODIED KNOWLEDGE

"Our theories of their societies are *our praxis*," Fabian charged (1983, 165).
But as an anthropologist claiming to study the implementation of policy
by *joining with* representatives of state power, while hoping to humanize
mechanistic, dry, or incoherently arch theories and avoid other discipli-
nary problems, I did not want to build a theory of "their" society but an
epistemological understanding of *our* practices in the everyday implementation of the program and the implications of these practices for others in the program. Through this book, I have sought to express the
physicality of our knowledge: the three of us sitting so closely in a car for
hours and months, comparing our bodies and feet when we shopped and
tried on clothes and shoes, wrestling over a ball in a swimming pool one
day when we snuck off from work, eating *gorditas* (stuffed and deep-fried
corn patties) and sampling each others' fruit smoothies, and sharing lip-
sticks, deodorants, combs, bathrooms, and hotel rooms. I was always
aware of inhabiting the taller, paler, relatively thinner, and older body,
with relatively less makeup and undyed hair, dressing like a Swiss woman
Rosi had known once who "didn't show her body either" (in form-fitting
or low-cut clothes, for example). We talked over these comparisons and
which parts of our bodies each would want to change: Soco to be taller and
perhaps a bit less "dark-skinned," Rosi wished her hair and torso were different, while I envied their thin legs and dimpled smiles. The dry heat,
dust, stones, scorpions, sweat literally shining on the faces of the women
working in the maquilas as they sat at the whirring machines, cool tiles
and vast panes of glass at a sewing machine store, whispers in the
cramped office over copies of *Bride* magazine—the perception of these
things, of sensations, also comprises a method of knowing, and must be

woven together with reflections on practices and dialogue to produce a theory of state action that dwells on bodies and personal presences.

This methodological emphasis on the sharing of experience, and thus upon the *physical* aspects of fieldwork and learning, had important epistemological and theoretical implications. First, the patterns of evasion and deferral within the program struck me as noteworthy in and of themselves. They led me to observe and theorize the differences in physical experience which affected citizens involved in the program in relation to the construction of "outsidedness." In Guanajuato, the act of casual, public touching of nonfamily members is very rare. It is unusual to pat someone on the shoulder or touch someone's forearm with the back of the hand to make a point as is done, for example, in the New York metropolitan area. Upon greeting and leave-taking, a handshake and, if one is relatively friendly with the person, a light kiss on the cheek, are normative. Nevertheless, I found that this was a case in which the very *touch* of the state—the everyday, personal practices within the culture surrounding state bureaucracy—were compelling and important pieces of the story, in creating inside and outside boundaries in the program and in determining how some bodies come to "matter" more than others.[5]

Second, the shared aspects of fieldwork led to my emphasis on physicality as a way of knowing, and thus as a way of enacting and embodying the state, understood not exclusively as the nation-state in this case but as one of many possible forms of government authority and power. Such a perspective is certainly suggested by the emphasis in feminist theory on "a taken-for-granted embodiment combined with an understanding of the immense power of the social construction of knowledge" (Rose 1994, 22). But much current scholarship was not useful for my task of explicitly addressing *the state* as constituted by embodied, pluralistic, or contingent presences, in differing relationships with citizens across different levels of government, let alone for my analysis of government in Mexico from such a perspective (see the conclusion for a fuller discussion). Moreover, scholars of bureaucracy have not rethought their own negative characterizations of Mexico's "personalistic" and "irrational government," even though many authors have come to critique the irrationality of First World governments and bureaucracies (Biggart 1989; Ferguson 1984; Herzfeld 1992; Leyton 1978). Therefore, albeit risky for many reasons, I assert and elaborate throughout this work the theoretical importance of "the personal" in government.

In sketching the liminal spaces between macro- and micro-level approaches to the reified entity of the state, I acknowledge that it remains essential to theorize and critique state power in its forms as a mechanistic apparatus of discipline, defining truth, structuring boundaries, certifying identity, and containing futures. But the over-abstracting of both state and body requires fresh approaches and new "local legends" that "permit exits, ways of going out and coming back in, and thus habitable spaces" (Certeau 1984, 106). This work crosses and recrosses a terrain where the commonsense monolith of the State is also understood as an assemblage of personal, everyday practices undertaken by persons who create and discover meaning through the work of being the state. Their interactions with citizens include the constant potential for failure and surprise and for what Carol Greenhouse (1998) calls "the otherwise." These women produced themselves as the state: through their presences and absences, their warm laughter, and their "asides," through their very states of being at rest and reflective *inside of motion.*

THE STATE IN MOTION

In Mexico, "the future . . . is always a substitution project, the future is somewhere else," wrote Guillermo Bonfil Batalla (1996) in referring to the nation's chasm between the elite and the indigenous, or between "imaginary Mexico" and "Mexico *profundo*" (deepest Mexico). Public policies, always oriented toward a future, reveal the "tacit structural anomalies" of a society (Handelman 1981). As a policy and as a set of practices, the Mi Comunidad program exemplifies the complexity within Fox's National Action Party. This party is an important source of political opposition to ruling party power, but it also bears a primarily middle and even upper class, patriarchal, Catholic, and probusiness vision of the future of Mexico.

Ambivalence about gender and class within Mexico came to the forefront in the Mi Comunidad program discourse and practice. The PAN vision which shaped the "substitution project" of the program was manifest in an ideology of forward progress expressed in multiple ways. The everyday practices of the two program directors produced warm, personal relationships across the managerial level, that is, among the people who were seen as bearing potential, and a future. Indeed, physical freedom was itself an index of privilege in the program, for the global market is the place of quality, autonomy, and progress, to which these businesses, and Mexico itself, were said to aspire. It is a mythical space of future possibilities, across which some bodies can move more freely than others. Kinship ties influenced the distribution of value (better jobs, money, mobility) within the program, but gender and class attributes contributed to a kind of emotional mapping of participants onto transnational spaces: from the sorrow over loss of young male migrants, the shameful silences about inside secrets, and the enclosed, seated mass of needy, abandoned women at their machines, to the exciting global market and the male migrants as proud investors and budding entrepreneurs, in motion within and outside of Mexico.

This case illustrates the complex and contradictory aspects of the state. The state can be gendered and gendering, it is mobile and fluid, and disorderly in ways that may empower small businesses or create space for "the otherwise." It is "personal" but not "irrational." In this case also, it reflects the ambivalence of its wider contexts: migration, the global assembly industry, and the family. Weaving through these themes is the story of our travels, so central to the implementation and everyday practices of the program.

¡VAMOS A SALIR!

On our days of visits to the maquilas, we arrived early to wait for Soco in front of the Archives, across the street from the Alhóndiga de Granaditas. The latter is a massive stone structure set back from a wide, open-air plaza which is often filled with school children playing soccer or marching in formation on official occasions. The Alhóndiga is a key site in the story of Mexico's independence. The hero Juan José de los Reyes Martínez (nicknamed el Pípila) is said to have lost his life setting its portal afire in 1810, in the early days of the revolution against Spain. Rebels had marched on the colonial Spanish silver mining city of Guanajuato under the leadership of Padre Miguel Hidalgo, parish priest of the small nearby town of Dolores (now called Dolores Hidalgo). Hidalgo ordered el Pípila to burn the portal, so the latter strapped a stone to his back to deflect arrows, then set the portal afire before being killed by the Spaniards who were hiding inside the former granary, which they used to store weapons. The expression *el grito de Dolores* (the cry of Dolores) captures the passion and rage that began the independence movement. The deeply religious and independent miners of Guanajuato joined the small band of revolutionaries, and violence spread to the city's outlying areas. Later, the instigating rebels were caught and killed; their heads were hung at the four corners of the Alhóndiga for ten years as a warning to their sympathizers.[6] Now the building is a busy museum, an important stop for the many Mexican tour groups which come to Guanajuato, the capital city of the state of Guanajuato, and recently deemed part of the "world cultural patrimony" by UNESCO.

The Alhóndiga's bloody past is depicted in numerous murals, statues, and paintings. A huge sculpture of el Pípila holding aloft a flaming torch towers over the city from a hillside; it can be seen from most points of the city, which is spread like a sparkling blanket through a winding valley in the central mountains of Mexico. The large plaza of the Alhóndiga is also the setting for outdoor musical concerts and political rallies, including two held by presidential candidate Vicente Fox Quesada in 1999 and 2000. Fox, who resigned as governor of Guanajuato to run for president, invoked this fiercely independent history of his home state as part of his call for a great "revolution" at the end of the twentieth century.[7] He specifically invoked the symbolism of doors in a speech in the plaza of the Alhóndiga; after rich references to the role of Guanajuato in the Independence movement from Spain, the Mexican Revolution of 1910–1920, and the Cristero revolt in the 1920s, Fox said: "Guanajuatenses, not in vain are we opening the doors for change" as "we enter victorious in the 21st century" (Venegas 1999).

Fox's new revolution was to be one of overthrow of the long-ruling PRI. The PRI has dominated Mexican politics and the presidency[8] for so long (since its foundation in 1929 as the PNR—Partido Nacional Revolucionario, or National Revolutionary Party) that the government was often referred to as the "PRI-state" (PRI-*gobierno*) during its decades of power. In speeches, campaign appearances, interviews, and debates, Fox continually invoked this theme of revolution, a very powerful reappropriation of a word and concept which has been so central to the name, claims to power, identity, and ideology of the PRI as the party of "permanent revolution" (Brandenburg 1964; Middlebrook 1995).

As Rosi and I waited for our day's travels to begin, school children, university students, and adults carrying babies streamed past us in the fresh, slight chill of the morning air. Many people were coming into the city for the day from the countryside, disembarking at the nearby bus stop and walking to the Mercado Hidalgo (Hidalgo Market) in the Avenida Juárez to sell fruits and vegetables, fresh flowers, embroidered cloth, rugs, and other goods. Vendors selling *tamales* (cornmeal and meat wrapped in husks and steamed) and *atole* (a watery hot chocolate drink) set up shop near the Archives; other vendors sold newspapers and magazines, or plastic bags containing fruit juices or sliced mango, melon, and papaya. Also in this neighborhood one might pass old women sitting in the shadow of a doorway, trimming cactus leaves for *nopales*, a sticky and mildly spicy delicacy. As we waited for our perennially late colleague, Rosi and I spoke of our families and our lives: her mother's illness, my children's experiences in school, her second job as a university lecturer.

As a part of their duties in administering the Mi Comunidad program, the director and her assistant spent a lot of time in a state government office working on paperwork and phone calls, which they perceived as utter drudgery, far less free and fun than when they could *salir* (leave or travel). The cry ¡*Vamonos!* (Come on, let's go!) followed by, "Do you want to go?" marked a joyful moment for all of us, as we gathered up pocketbooks and manila folders and headed out to the car. Other times, a late night call would tell me what time to meet them in front of the Archives the next morning, for those all-day trips which would preclude our going to the office entirely. The routine of our journeys followed the very comfortable, amiable pattern of two people who had been close friends for many years (they met in college and were in their early thirties), sharing heartaches and joys, ideas and secrets, memories and worries, even a conversational style in which each constantly invoked the other, ending or beginning sentences with inclusive phrases: "Isn't that right?" "Can you believe it?" "Don't you remember?" "What do you think?" Their close verbal and personal interdependence was also evident in Rosi's steady role during meetings and phone calls as supplier of names, dates, amounts, phone numbers, and so forth while helping to finish Soco's sentences as needed. We joked that she knew better than Soco the cell phone numbers of Soco's own husband and family.

Trips began with music: plugging a portable CD player into the cigarette lighter slot and selecting one of several different CDs ranging from the soundtrack of *Grease* to current Mexican popsters like Elvis Crespo. We sped through the underground streets (*las tunelas*—some are former silver mining pathways used in the sixteenth century), leaving Guanajuato at its southwest point, passing grand hotels and long public parks along the way. Next we stopped for gas at the Pemex station near the beginning of the toll road, then with a small tip and a smile for the always-interested male attendants and a quick shuffle for the Mex$13.50 needed for the toll, it was out onto the highway and through the flat, sere terrain to begin our discussion of various topics (food, family, personal plans, and the day's pressing work-related topics), or to sing along with favorite ballads. The trips followed these predictable rhythms, with slight variations of tone depending on the events that had passed since the two best friends had last spoken to or seen each other. If there were any worries or disappointments that had occurred, they were discussed and resolved as much as possible, before the two returned to their usual good cheer. In some cases, there was little time indeed that they had been apart, as many evenings they attended aerobics together after work or would get together for a drink or some other outing that I sometimes joined in as well. They were together nearly every weekend as well, when Rosi (and often my own family) were invited to attend the numerous parties held by Soco's large extended family.

Wherever we drove—Salamanca, Yuriria, Irapuato, Celaya, León, Silao, and many other towns and villages of the state—my benefactors and colleagues always knew exactly where we would eat once we were done with whatever meeting or official business we had to attend. At meetings and events, Soco often announced, "Somos comadres" (We are comadres), adding simply, "Ella es Guanajuatense" (She is from Guanajuato), to explain my presence with a confidential smile as a person who, though not born in Guanajuato, was *of* Guanajuato. They possess a broad knowledge of local food specialties such as the *caldo michi* (a seafood broth) of the Yuriria area, the fried fish of a busy, two-story restaurant in Irapuato, the vast open sandwiches of sausage and other fillings served in Moroleon, and then fresh roasted lamb ("killed daily!" Soco assured me solemnly) in the busy indoor market of Silao. There are favorite fruit stands just outside of Salamanca and Salvatierra, beloved restaurants like the Mansion of Mariscos (serving seafood) in Celaya, or a particular street to get the famed strawberries of Irapuato. Hunger sometimes spilled over into meetings that Rosi deemed were going on too long; any impatience Rosi displayed (tapping her fingers or foot, examining the ends of her hair, sighing heavily or yawning) indicated both her boredom at the content of a meeting or the behavior of the interlocutors, as well as an indication that she was hungry and was wondering why we had not left yet and when we would. Over meals, we discussed the events of the day or laughed over stories of the past, childhood, and so on. Someone had to always remember to get a receipt; it was a point of pride that they were the only staff members whose meals were reimbursed.

In addition to food, we also folded shopping into many of our trips: for clothing in Moroleon, for shoes in León and Irapuato, for ceramics, jewelry, and even a window frame during a tour of a cooperative artisan enterprise, and for a sewing machine after a meeting to discuss the equipment for a planned maquila. The new shoes and clothing would be displayed in the dull world of the office the very next day, with knowing winks to me and each other and suppressed giggles over the fact that they had been able to enjoy a day of escape from the office. The directors' extensive knowledge of the shopping and dining available throughout the state did not extend to an ability to find these locations readily, however, and we joked often about their patterns of getting lost. Several times a day we pulled to the side of streets and Rosi would holler out the window, "Excuse me young man! Where is the Avenue of the 20th of November?" or whatever street or town we were seeking at the moment. The always helpful pedestrians would point and explain, and then within a few blocks we would stop again with the same question for another person, since Soco and Rosi accepted as inevitable that most of the respondents did not actually know the way either but did not want to disappoint them by saying so. Rather than admit ignorance, people would make up directions or otherwise bluff their way with a vague set of remarks. Our driver would turn to her copilot, and they would murmur or laugh in agreement: "He doesn't know," and off we would go, asking others until we finally stumbled upon the sought-after locale. For this reason and countless others, we were normally about one hour or more late to nearly every appointment.

On the way back to the city, conversations were more muted: our thoughts began turning toward family and work responsibilities as Soco anticipated picking up her son and Rosi calmly faced the likelihood that she would be late again to teach her 5:00 P.M. international trade class at the university. By then we had analyzed whatever meeting or event we had attended, thus we might become a bit philosophical about the managerial styles of the different *jefes* (bosses or supervisors) in the maquilas, or we might turn to reflections over cultural differences between Mexico and the United States. Soco and Rosi would attempt, with varying degrees of success, to make calls home or to the office on their permanently baffling cell phones, which suffered from dying batteries, mountain interference, various mysterious and unpredictable maladies, or problems at the other end. A tired silence would finally fall over all of us. More than once as we approached the city nestled among its hills, Soco exclaimed, "¡Bella Guanajuato!" (she had studied Italian); once the two of them proudly sang me a traditional song about its beauties.

I begin with this thick evocation of the intimacy and ritual of our journeys to introduce central themes of this work. Patterns in our practices— in daily enactments and representations of state power, in the journeys we made across the state of Guanajuato, in meetings held in the small offices of state-sponsored maquilas—all were important for me in the process of learning about and understanding the program, as well as constituting the major form of practice in the program administrators' fulfillment of their responsibilities. Although I was just a volunteer working in the state government office, I use the term "our" because the three of us traveled, worked, and appeared frequently together in settings in which we clearly represented the state to others. Without having any formal authority myself, I know they view me as a colleague.

In this description, I also emphasize the always-present points of reference to history and to political systems which shape life in Guanajuato. Contextualizing the program within the urban-rural reality of its implementation, the wider geography of its articulation with migrants, and the political aspirations of its designer, who seeks to lead Mexico through a truly historic *sexenio* (six-year term), allows for a fuller understanding of its wider social and political meanings.

FRAMEWORK

Writing and human life are conceptualized in powerfully teleological terms in late industrial societies, as the Mi Comunidad program discourse itself illustrates. Thus, in writing about past and ongoing experiences, I have tried to prevent bad narrative habits from overwhelming this work: to avoid imposing too much "plot," or indulging in the "opiate" of "enclosing narrative" (Banta 1993, 18–21), or forcing a moral or a redemptive cast, upon this writing. Some conventions of textual argument are still valid, notwithstanding charges about inscribing Others or containing identities.[9] A general structure of thesis and support suggests itself, based on trust between the reader and writer, thus I will note at once that I did not understand everything about Mi Comunidad, and even as I write about "the program and its meanings," those things swim in and out of my understanding.[10] Writing this book, I wanted to protect the identity of my colleagues but also to describe important lessons from the case and even analyze problems within it. It was only with time, distance, and efforts at writing about my research that I even began to understand certain aspects of the program.

The difficult and uneven process of fieldwork discovery can often be masked by the coherent appearance of prose about research. Uninvited, but graciously welcomed nevertheless, I tried to be of use to the program during my fieldwork. But I learned many things that were not at all clear until I began to write about them. These aspects of research, to do with physical presence and emotions, do affect the acquisition of knowledge, and as such require some acknowledgement in later analysis. I hope that the following text is both clear in its argument, while also revelatory of my own evasions, ambiguity, and shifting position as an ambivalent fieldworker, straddling the inside and outside of the program.

In seeking to avoid reductionist theories while retaining the power of feminist and anthropological critiques, I have found Michel Foucault's metaphors stressing the movement of power—microphysics, capillary and other circulatory concepts, and his emphasis on the inscription upon the body, like the emphasis on bodies in the work of Hélène Cixous and others[11]—to be of great use in framing this work. The "anti-essentialist" authors, to use Chantal Mouffe's phrase, were also of help in addressing the partiality and tentativeness of knowledge production, for certainly my own narration of events contains as many disruptions and evasions as those I noticed in the program implementation. In Spanish the verbs *contar* and *darse cuenta* mean, respectively, to tell or relate a story and to realize something. Both echo the sound of *encontrar*—to find—or the words *recount* and *encounter* in English, and *raconteur*—storyteller—in French.

These relationships between words suggest that one way to realize something, or to find meaning, is in the telling of a story, and that is what follows. But this story is of course only one of the many possible.

Past and present tenses are mixed here, not to freeze the past into finished products (Fabian 1983) nor to objectify others in the ethnographic present. Tsing describes her "maneuver" between both tenses as, in part, a way to write against timeless constructions (1993, xv). I use both tenses simply to show that some actions and events occurred in moments in the past, while some analytical statements or facts about people and things are simply points that remain true as of this writing. The use of the first person and the descriptions of my own presence are not intended to be egocentric or solipsistic; this stylistic choice is simply a reminder, for my own presence was a part of events. The intersubjectivity and experiences of we comadres have deeply affected my research and life as well as, I believe, it has affected their lives and work. Indeed, the crucial concept of physicality structures this book, underlining the importance of the physical as a source of data and of embodiedness as determinative of the production of knowledge (Rose 1994).

Chapter 1 details the daily production of personal intimacy at the managerial levels of the program and notes my own presence and research plans as a volunteer within the state government office. Ethnographic examples of these practices are given, describing two businesses which were seen, respectively, as a "success" and a "failure" within the official definitions, business processes, and structure of the program.

The program directors' power, made less direct by familial warmth and graciousness, is far from absolute. Chapter 2 outlines examples which suggest that the jefes of the maquilas were becoming more autonomous. As they slowly became more independent of their government consultants, they began to "walk" on their own, in itself an important development for small and medium-sized businesses in the context of Mexico (Mizrahi 1994).

Chapter 3 is a discussion of the ways in which the program directors' personal practices of and values upon mobility resonated in the program's teleological discourse on assisting the fledgling maquilas in their early stages of business operations. The "emotional work" noted in organizational analyses of gender (Gherardi 1995; Hochschild 1983; Macdonald and Sirianni 1996) appears present in this case, as the program administrators produced warmth and intense loyalties in support of program goals, but the case is also more complex. These two young women initially held a great degree of power vis-à-vis the investors and managers (usually older men) who were involved in the business process. The program directors managed this social disjuncture through a kind of deferral of their own official authority and through "female" roles of nurturance. These roles were actually very powerful and freeing, while also allowing the program directors to reproduce the middle-class values they sought to instill in the jefes. Soco and Rosi's middle-class values, business vision, and practices of maternal care have thus far precluded solidarity with the female workers of the program, but their implementation of the program may constitute, in the context of Mexico, an important challenge and reformulation of the practices of government, so long-intertwined with the PRI-state.

A centralized authority seeking to extend dominance over farflung, often geographically isolated territory has long been a theme of governance in Mexico. A sense of this centrality exists even in a relatively small-scale project like Mi Comunidad. Thus, chapter 4 maps the state government office in which I worked (DACGE, the acronym of la Dirección General de Atención a Comunidades Guanajuatenses en el Extranjero, or Office of Support to Guanajuatense Communities Abroad). This office was the central point at which the many disparate threads of the program came together. There was a sense of formality and sophistication in the gracious *palacio* of the capital city, along with the tedium of office work, documentation, immobility, and gossip. The gubernatorial race in Guanajuato created uncertainty within the office; both it and the presidential campaign permeated our work atmosphere. Constant change and restructuring continue as of this writing. Because candidate Fox was seen as particularly "ours," having created the program and met several people in the office, I summarize in that chapter key details of the campaign and provide some historical context on the former ruling party.

Chapter 5 outlines the program's meanings as related to migration. Beliefs about lost or stolen Mexican wealth and potential resonate in the phenomenon of migration. The state discourse on the Mi Comunidad program invoked family, church, and nation in an intimate, emotional appeal, softening and justifying its presence in private lives and families, employing both guilt and pride to evoke patriotic investments in the program. Vicente Fox's recasting of migration counters the symbolic construction of migration in the United States as a statistically validated "problem." Chapter 6 presents the other major context of the program—its articulation with the wider maquila industry—and discusses some of the related ambivalence within the program.

Between the program's teleology of forward, purposive motion and our practice of continual lateness for appointments, there is a metaphor of practice as deferral, or "asides"—shifts in program rationale, evasions, and presentations of the program to officials and outsiders. These practices, reviewed in part 3, successfully maintained the program as a viable government operation, while also constituting differing symbolic uses of the future. Soco rewrote the facts and possibilities of the program according to her vision of business success; her personal charisma, in Weber's sense, indeed "dissolves" the "this-worldly and mundane routines" and ruled domains of bureaucracy (Handelman 1981). Some practices precluded discussion of problems in the maquilas. Chapter 7 reviews program practices toward the working women of the factories, always referred to as *las muchachas* (the girls). I note patterns of exclusion, discipline, and emotion toward these women. Their anomalous presence within the family of the program, and perhaps the nation, led to deep ambivalence in the attitudes and practices directed at them. Seated and silent at the machines, regulated and immobile in time and in the global economy, their female, "rural" docility was both needed and distrusted.[12] Evasive practices also involved the use of data and the concept of "quality," discussed in chapter 8. Quality is part of an evasive discourse of blame regarding the female workers in the program.

Solidarity between these women and the two who directed the program was not yet a possibility, in part because the working women were present primarily as symbols within the program, denied the status of personhood (Chock 1998). Their status as persons in need was seen as inherent and problematic, as opposed to the more temporary and solvable needs of the state's male business partners. They did not share in the full and autonomous, bright visions of the future projected in the program discourse, yet along with these deferrals are always other possibilities, also addressed in chapter 8.

Taken as a whole, these practices suggest a deep ambivalence and skepticism about authority and governance even among state employees, with interesting implications for democratization sketched in the conclusion. The central "eye" of the state is itself distracted in this case, not entirely convinced of its own authority. Documents are stored, and photographs are kept and proudly displayed, yet the promise to which these refer may never have been realized. I use the case to argue for a rethinking of "the personal" in relation to the state and to Mexico, synthesizing an array of literatures and suggesting that concepts like "political culture" and "civil society," stripped of the power of their critique, remain wedged into totalizing prose about the Other's exotic political economies. Some scholarship on Mexico seems to exist in a mutually reinforcing discourse with the rational approach of international finance publications. Fruitful possibilities for cross-disciplinary research are noted in the concluding chapter.

Finally, I suggest that a larger project is needed, of which I can only trace an outline, of analyzing the production of "ethnographic Mexico," a specifically apolitical creation,[13] and of writing against the persistent notion of "ungovernable" Mexico. It is with this particular, important goal in my mind that I have written this work.

PART I

Inside of Motion

CHAPTER 1

Personal Practices

The implementation of the Mi Comunidad program (originally called Mi Familia, or My Family) has been marked in a significant way by personal, everyday practices. Our travel rituals in "adventure time" across the state of Guanajuato, described in the previous chapter, constituted one expression of this intimacy. These journeys solidified the relationship between the program director and her assistant, in particular, and they generously included me within this sentiment as well. Our journeys also reproduced the program directors' personal values on physical freedom and mobility, values based in part upon their own gender and class perspectives. These travels across the state allowed me to witness and experience the gracious, personal warmth which marked "inside," managerial relationships within the program. Before I elaborate the praxis and meanings of this warmth, however, a note about my own situatedness is needed, for an author is "always inscribed in a collective inquiry" (Certeau 1984, 43–44), and theory must "depict the intimate ways in which 'they' and 'we' are imbricated in global contexts that determine all of our identities" (Kearney 1996, 119).

RESEARCH PRACTICES

In this research project, I began with a vague intent to stake out a liminal territory between micro- and macro-level approaches to the state: to understand how the state government representatives in this localized job creation program engaged in the practice of being the state. The anthropological method of close examination over time of practice, language, and symbol in order to understand the production of self and of culture has led to work which also confronts the problematics of theory and of human agency (Bourdieu [1980] 1990; Fajans 1997; Munn 1970; Myers 1991; T. Turner 1982; Weiner 1976). Given the strength and complexity of these works, a focus on practice struck me as important to apply to public policy, that is, to a realm considered to be outside of more typical anthropological interest.[1] Perhaps the workings of business and government can be just as surprising as a stage performance in Bali, indeed, perhaps they *demand* anthropological analysis, as it is through them that cultural differences, imagined as physical, are encoded into official practice and experience (Greenhouse 1998). My framing of research questions took the "risk" of "allowing questions to lead ... to methodology (rather than vice versa)" (Nader 1972). That risk has also meant allowing method and practice to lead back into theory, recognizing that the division of theory and practice is a "radically oxymoronic condition" and a "rhetorical" choice in anthropology (Herzfeld 1987).

Perhaps to avoid having to actually initiate activities to foster social change, activities which may be just as problematic as the act of writing can be, I chose to seek a reflective dialogue with persons involved in a policy aimed at social change that was already in place. One of my research imperatives was an ongoing engagement with the program directors through shared daily practices, reflective dialogue, and efforts to rethink the program together in order to promote pluralistic practices in theory-building (Burdick 1993; Greenwood 1991; Toulmin and Gustavesen 1996). I hoped that this choice would challenge the lure of what Martha Banta (1993) calls "theory desire," or "the culture of theorizing," which posits "the one best way" and thereby seeks to control and contain. Peña (1997) notes that scholars studying maquilas tend to work *with* managers and ignore the "subaltern dimension" of the workplace; a similar charge could be made against my work, but my focus has been on an analytical understanding of the role of the state in the implementation of this program. I tried assiduously to balance the privilege of my access to an "insider" view of power with the need to remain open to the many possible interpretations of the complex forms this power took.

In going to Guanajuato for this fieldwork, I reconnected with many friends and colleagues in a city in which I had lived and worked in 1985 as a visiting professor to the Information Sciences Master's Program. In 1985 I had noticed, but not understood, the usage of the same call number for different book titles during my formal evaluation of library procedures (undertaken at the request of my colleagues). At the time I found it amusing and surprising, but in retrospect, I see that within the cataloging department this practice made sense, as it reflected the use of what was found to be a "good" call number, one which by definition could be used more than once—a usage which thus upset the strict categorization of mutually exclusive objective realities presumed in seventeenth century taxonomies (Foucault [1970] 1994; Handelman 1981). I had already learned at that time that my ideas about helping with development in the library were not relevant to the context in which I was working; simple engagement in everyday, personal relationships within the master's program was of much greater importance than most contributions I or they imagined I could give.

Returning to Guanajuato for my doctoral fieldwork, I was also drawn to be a part of a research project in a state to which I felt linked through the movements of capital, for the new jobs sprouting up around the outskirts of the capital city are only the shiniest new forms of the jobs my father, my sister, and I once held in Ohio. These were the jobs my brothers were prepared for by school and family life, but which were gone before they were old enough to need them. The Taylorist culture of efficiency, which has now left in its wake the devastated communities of the Rust Belt of Ohio and other northern U.S. states, whose members have erected a steel industry museum in Youngstown, is given new forms in the new concrete factories isolated in the middle of fields one hour from the nearest city in Guanajuato. These forms merit the analysis possible from a stance of critical anthropology. Moreover, while many excellent works have been published on the maquila industry as it exists along the U.S.–Mexico border (Fernández Kelly 1983; Kopinak 1996; Peña 1997; Sklair 1993; Tiano 1994, to name a few), few have studied the relatively newer phenomenon of the maquilas of "the interior."

After initial research and a brief visit in June 1999, I offered my assistance to the Mi Comunidad program as a volunteer for several months beginning in January 2000, with a return in May 2002 for a brief additional visit. The program was run from a state government office devoted to the phenomenon of migration; I was graciously welcomed into this office by the staff and by the office director himself. Soon I began assisting with projects such as organizing files, translating documents, and making telephone calls to bureaucracies in the United States on behalf of the citizens of Guanajuato. From the start, my two comadres also welcomed me along on all of their journeys across the state: even some of the most sensitive ones. Their trust and respect was expressed in many ways; I continue to reciprocate those sentiments as best I can. This book records our experiences and conversations in order to elaborate a series of more rarefied points about abstractions such as gender, class, state action, and public policy, but I hope that it also reflects our own shared, intimate commitment to dialogue and to learning from each other. I use pseudonyms for names and places to protect involved parties, as some of the situations described are sensitive and, by definition, "inside."

Our travels across the state were undertaken primarily to attend meetings which were held in the already-operating maquilas of the program, but we also traveled in order to visit the construction sites of new maquilas, to interview a job candidate, to scout out a sewing machine dealer, to attend meetings and workshops held by various other state and federal government agencies which support the program, and to stimulate additional business, for example, with a garment industry dealer representing Wal-Mart and between a local cooperative mine/ceramic factory and a migrant who is a successful businessman in the United States. Many days were spent guiding members of the press, usually print journalists, around the state and, once, a documentary filmmaking crew.

We talked over every experience once we returned to the car or as we ate our midday meal. Our adventures and impressions became a part of a shared store of memories, jokes, and sense-making. For not only did my colleagues hope to instruct me in the ways of their program, but they used incidents and descriptions of the individuals we knew to elaborate many other kinds of issues and lessons. These included their own ideas about Mexico: its strengths and weaknesses, its kinds of people, and its national aspirations and potential. We also discussed topics such as meanings and humor within Mexican Spanish, ways of telling jokes and stories, their theories of physical and personality types, notions of what constitutes a good life, and many other rich themes. Soco especially would push for wider, embracing metacommentaries about life and humankind, a propensity I share, while Rosi cast a keenly analytical eye on life which sometimes obscured her deeply sensitive, trusting ways. In fact, when we were alone together, Soco and I often worried over Rosi's ingenuousness.

These conversations helped to sustain us during the adventurous but long, arduous days of travel and the nagging worries over the businesses. As fun and free as we felt, we each carried our private worries. One of mine was constant: to give something back in return for the many forms of generosity which I received from my colleagues. Perhaps this is why I noticed the emotional shifts within the program that are described throughout this writing, such as guilt and shame or pride and camaraderie. The ambivalence of fieldwork is well known; in my case, it reinforced my own tendencies to be almost too respectful of others' individual privacy and at the same time overly curious and analytical about "wider" patterns in societies. Although I was and, to some extent, even at this distance, remain a relative "insider" to the program through inclusion by my comadres, I am also inherently an outsider as an academic and a citizen of the Unites States, as someone who would even write down the program practices or consider them to be of interest. I know well what a privilege an inside position is in Mexico, a social context in which public-private distinctions are very important and well guarded. From Mexican families which have shared many private topics with me, I have learned through various means how to act in public. Thus, for example, what I at first saw as troubling "shifts" in the self-presentation of the program were not so much evasions or self-deceptions. They reflected a deep discretion about personal relationships and were much more indicative of the personal style of state administration in this case. But learning to understand this was an incomplete and uneven process in itself.

SEATED IN EL PALACIO

Toward the end of the winding, tree-lined, stone-paved street called la Presa, which runs through Guanajuato's Embajadoras (Ambassadors) district, and just before the park which mounts up to a large dam in la Presa de la Olla, is a four-story building of faded pink stone with a small sign to the right of it which states its name: el Palacio de Gobierno. Guards in dark blue uniforms stand outside on the steps holding rifles in their hands, loosely slung across their chests and waists. The graceful Palacio is the location of several departments of the state government. At the time of my research, it was the site of the office which attends to citizens of Guanajuato who are residing outside of Mexico. For a citizen coming to ask about confusing documents received in the mail or to try to locate a relative in the United States, arrival at the Palacio might involve a lengthy journey by a slow bus from the countryside, and then another trek by city bus from the new bus station outside of the city, then clear across the city, mostly by way of underground tunnels, to this imposing guarded structure on a quiet edge of town.

As in many other buildings in Guanajuato, the first floor interior of el Palacio is a cool, open courtyard; the second story offices face out over this open space. In the center of the courtyard is a small kiosk for security. Once a person has left photo identification here or been waved through as an employee, he or she moves beyond this desk to the wide stone steps which mount up to the bright and well-appointed offices on the upper floors. The crowded second-story office in which I volunteered was always buzzing with activity, and here gracious dealings with citizens and callers seemed to be the rule. The phones were answered with a pleasant, nearly sing-song manner and a one word invocation of the lengthy office title: "Comunidades." State power here was represented and enacted by a staff of young women, polite and gracious, often smiling good-naturedly amongst themselves over the actions and orders of the male boss, referred to as *el Licenciado*, but speaking to him in person with a hushed, high-pitched voice of deference. This epithet is a common manner of formal, highly respectful address for those with the equivalent to a bachelor's degree; many of the female staff also possessed such a credential, but he called them by their first names.

The narrow office, with its shared desks, waves of visitors, and constant bustle of telephone and other conversations, was made even more crowded by my chore of organizing the files, because opening the file cabinet drawers stopped egress through the only space that led from the front to the back of our shared office, and from there back to the private office of el Licenciado. The inconvenience caused by my work in the file cabinets was handled with great cheer and graciousness. From these tight quarters, we three colleagues escaped into the world of intense sociality and journeys across the state of Guanajuato.

A brief review of the basic structure of the program will contextualize the discussion of this sociality. According to program records, the Mi Comunidad program was created by Governor Fox in order to diminish the indices of migration through the creation of jobs in textile maquilas in the poorest rural areas of the state of Guanajuato. Maquilas operate with special trade status; machinery, equipment, and raw materials can be imported duty free to create products destined for export. The assembled components can then be reexported without reentry tax in other countries; taxes are paid only on the value added, a minimal cost for the industry because wages range from U.S.$1.60 to U.S.$2.20 per hour (Lindquist 2001). Foreign ownership of this kind of business can be 100 percent, rather than the usual maximum in Mexico of 49 percent. Some of these provisions changed in 2001, as described in chapter 6.

The state government sought through this program to attract the investment of the conationals or *paisanos* (fellow countrymen, but also generally migrants) from Guanajuato who were living in the United States. The state matched investor money: U.S.$60,000 was the official amount each side contributes, but the actual numbers were often higher. The average number of *socios* (investors) who were involved in a single maquila was given as fifty-five. These socios had in most cases left Guanajuato and were living and working in the United States. They often settled in regions where other migrants from the same village also were living.

The program's rationale has shifted with time and conditions, as migration remains high in the state. Program charts note that seven maquilas creating nearly 300 jobs were opened in 1997; since then, fifteen other maquilas entered the program and were either operating or in various planning stages for future operation. All of the program's maquilas were in the textile segment of what is called the global assembly industry.

The presence of maquilas in the interior of Mexico probably dates to the 1970s but is difficult to assess clearly due to changes in legal definitions. Compared to four decades of explosive maquila growth along the U.S.–Mexico border, interior maquilas are clearly on a smaller scale (see chapter 6).

The implementation of the Mi Comunidad program was complex and involved many stages, including the dissemination of information about it, the generation of investment, the legal process of forming an association of investors, the planning and construction of the factories, hiring and training of workers, and ongoing business troubleshooting.

INSIDE EMOTION

Personal warmth permeated all of the stages of the Mi Comunidad program which I witnessed in Guanajuato. This warmth was produced across and among participants at the investment and managerial levels in many forms. The daily work of the two program directors involved verbal and written communications through letters, emails, telephone and face to face conversations, visits, and faxes. Fondness and respect were evident in all such communications, for example in the use of the epithet "Don" before men's names in combination with a nickname, for example "Don Beto," where Beto is short for Alberto. Handshakes, eye contact, the custom of greeting with a small kiss on the right cheek (or merely the placement of the two right cheeks together), joking, listening intently—these gestures reaffirmed the personal nature of relationships with the bosses and investors.

The banter between the managers and program directors also included the exchange of compliments. By phone, Soco once told a boss that they were sending a journalist out to his maquila because, "as you know, one of our favorite maquilas is [yours]." Soco openly praised one maquila (within earshot of its manager) to some documentary filmmakers and on another occasion when conducting visitors around its facilities, called it "a true prototype" for the program. One jefe teased Soco about her "beautiful eyes" after a meeting (she wears vivid green contact lenses), and she laughed merrily.

This everyday production of personal intimacy was a value in itself. As noted, such personal graciousness was highly valued in the office and seemed even to be a wider value within the community of people I knew in Guanajuato, marking relations not only among friends but encounters among acquaintances and even strangers. To some degree, it is related to expectations about women, but also is a personal quality valued in men. It clearly marked relations among staff members and managers, and exceptions to it were noticed and denounced by my comadres as *feo* (rude). This warmth was also present in discussions with those providing outside assistance to the program: consultants from various other government agencies, outsider dealers, salespeople, and so forth.

Sharing food or drink during meetings also added conviviality: cookies and/or sodas were sometimes served and, once, a buffet of cold cuts, salads, and chips. On a few occasions we ate meals with managers or investors in restaurants or homes. Soco and Rosi also recounted stories about good times they had had socializing with some of the program participants in the United States when they had been given opportunities to travel there for business reasons. Sitting together, talking and laughing over tequila and food, listening to music: these were the best times for them. There was never the slightest hint of sexual flirtation in talk of these encounters, although as a single woman, Rosi did have some stories to tell about other men she had met through the office, but who were outside of the Mi Comunidad program. Sometimes these outings were paid for by the government; others by the individuals involved or even the socios. In the program files were receipts that had been saved from program events in hotel restaurants and bars and submitted for reimbursement.

The program directors were offered small gifts of items on hand—sample aprons from a maquila, pastries from the bakery of one investor—which they accepted with polite pleasure and urged me to do the same. Such small exchanges and the seeming politeness in the offer of a cold drink can take on other meanings in the context of Mexican governance. One account of Mexican government bureaucrats noted that officials would not even accept a soft drink on a visit to a rural location, since it was against new policies but also in order to distinguish themselves from the previous state representatives who accepted and solicited cash, meals, gifts of homemade cheese, and other items (Nuijten 1995).[2] But the gestures I saw were very rare and appeared to be unexpected; they never involved the exchange of cash.

FORMS OF SPEECH

Everyday speech genres included the directors' ever-hopeful narratives reflecting upon the program in general and each individual maquila. These optimistic remarks were part of our discussions in the car, in the office, and with outsiders. This optimism was officially documented as well (see chapter 8). These comments were far from naive, however, and often enfolded a sense of problems as well.

Discussion of problems was a key part of the everyday work of fostering the Mi Comunidad family. In the office, Soco was often asked to summarize current program issues for el Licenciado. Depending on the nature of the issue and its outcome, these summaries were either issued breezily from behind her desk in the main office or during private meetings with him behind a closed door, from which she eventually emerged with a rueful smile, a troubled shake of the head, or a furrowed brow. At these times her gifts of communication were a marvel. We glanced up, sometimes rather worriedly, to meet her eyes. She expressed clearly the tone of the meeting to Rosi and I without a word, as the door was now open and el

Licenciado could overhear, as could the other staff members, including one they felt had a private relationship of some undefined kind with the boss. Within seconds of this silent exchange, she almost immediately gave way to a cheery, renewed resolve. Later, out of earshot, the details would emerge, but in the public world of the office, all was well.

Outside the office, venues for problem talk were in the maquilas themselves, usually in the areas just outside of the manager's offices and next to the exits and shipping areas. The liminality of these protected spaces allowed for an interchange which fell between the official formality of meetings held within the offices and the bustling world of the factory. Long, serious conversations in low voices followed many meetings in the maquilas, as the managers drew Soco aside to discuss private issues and problems, while Rosi and I chatted more informally with other attendees or with each other. These "asides" in themselves created a kind of public intimacy, in physically drawing two or more people away from a group to create a more private space for discussion of plans, problems, or secrets, but all within full view of others. Even I experienced these intimate discussions with some of the jefes. These confidential moments, which we comadres discussed as soon as we were alone again, bore performative meaning. The very gesture asserted trust and familiarity, while also carrying an air of professional gravity. I do not remember any of these groups ever bursting into sudden laughter in a way which might be interpreted as impolite to others who were not in on the joke. These "backstage" conversations were an important part of the program directors' work, in gathering new information about problems and providing a supportive ear. The privacy protected the jefes from a too-public discussion of certain problems, such as a dishonest accountant or an irresponsible supervisor.

On the other hand, meetings were marked by much more formal styles of speech, more emphatic presentations of self, and long monologues. At times people interrupted each other's remarks with quick, witty references and lively humor. Problem talk was generally phrased in terms of the group as a whole. The times when it was specifically discussed in relation to one maquila were rare, but they did take place in very grave cases, with a sorrowful tone. While not dismissed, they were glided over relatively smoothly, as described below. Managing these awkward, embarrassing emotions and problems was work in which the whole group participated.

THE PROGRESS OF EMOTION

Through the program, the state of Guanajuato both elicited investment and sought to foster entrepreneurial activities, in a process which policy analysts acknowledge is difficult and risky for private citizens to undertake (Grindle 1988). Indeed, the concept of "midwifery" has been used to describe state–business partnerships, unfortunately without including any mention of gender or female power (Evans 1995).[3] I discuss this aspect of nurturance in more detail in chapter 3. The process requires a great deal of care from the state for its less powerful partners, perhaps especially so in the social context of Mexico, where many people have told me it is extremely sensitive for persons to admit any kind of specific weakness or error.

The "life cycle" of each maquila began with the raising of money for it. Frequent interactions in meetings reinforced the bonds created throughout the long, uncertain process of establishing these small businesses. After the investors were incorporated, the state government dealt with the person or persons designated as their representative(s). Program records stored in the DACGE offices include long lists of signatures and details of donated amounts and addresses of individual investors documenting the kinship relations between many of them through the repetition of family names. Next were site visits by some of the socios to Guanajuato, followed by the process of finding a site for the factory. I saw a few of these groups enter the office, smiling politely at everyone and sometimes shaking hands with all of the staff, then proceeding directly to our boss's office. Sometimes there was only the briefest of introductions to Soco and Rosi, who sat in on some of the meetings. These initial stages were dominated by the authority of the male boss, before the eventual transition of primary dealings to the two female administrators. Soco's forceful personality soon began to dominate these relationships, especially as el Licenciado seemed comparatively distant during meetings of several people (although he could be very engaging in individual encounters).

The investors sometimes had locally based representatives or relatives who oversaw construction of the sites, but we three also made several visits to the maquilas in the early stages of construction, mostly to encourage those in charge and to inquire about their needs of the moment. Nurturing visits throughout the primary stages took place regularly in those maquilas that were constructed and operational, leading up to (and well beyond) the time of the issuance of invitations to inaugural ceremonies. Help with technical and legal details at all stages was available through the directors. For example, at one early meeting with two young men involved in a new maquila, Soco and Rosi arranged to come to the site and help interview job applicants. The state government also paid for "production chiefs" to provide training and consultation to the maquilas. Establishing relationships with potential buyers was said to be primarily within the province of one man (known only as "the man of San Juan del Río"), but contracts also were generated by the two program directors or el Licenciado. The DACGE consultants helped with buying used or new machinery, establishing relationships with other government agencies that were involved in supporting the program, advising on the process of hiring and training workers, and arranging the bureaucratic details of the training *becas* (grants for the women workers).

Communications continued so that the Mi Comunidad staff could monitor business operations and problems. Well after the businesses were fully operating, a high level of personal relationship and knowledge remained. In one simple example of this, I was surprised once to note during a casual exchange between Soco and Rosi the detailed knowledge which they had about the siblings of one jefe.

A BUSINESS SUCCESS

Throughout the period of initiating the small businesses of the program, and then throughout the stages of operation of each of the government-sponsored maquilas, the Mi Comunidad staff was intensely involved in supporting the managers of these factories. One particular jefe moved quickly from the protected, inside status of needing assistance to one of relative public autonomy and success. The rapidity with which this man and his business came to be considered a "prototype" provides a good example of the valued outcomes of the program. His story also shows the astuteness with which the program directors responded to a case where a business was proceeding smoothly to the more autonomous status which was ultimately intended for all of the maquilas.

This maquila had only been open about two months when we visited it. It was located along a highway in a relatively more urban area than others in the program. Hector was both the owner and the onsite manager (as opposed to many of the investors who live in the United States and hire others, usually relatives, to run the business for them). He is a Mexican man who had lived for many years in the United States and had a good relationship with two well-known companies which sell high-end kitchen textiles. These relations provided this maquila with plenty of work, unlike some of the others, although I did visit once during a time when work had slowed down to a halt as people waited for bolts of fabric to be delivered. One frequent visitor was a man who represented one of these companies. Tall, blonde, always dressed in Ralph Lauren chinos, this man told me jovially that "things are getting better all the time" in the maquila. Neither man had ever heard of the Casa Guanajuato (community centers in the United States fostered by DACGE) which was located in the city in which they had met. These centers are the usual site for encouraging investment in the program. I later learned that Hector had become involved in the program in a more ad hoc manner.

This maquila was still undergoing extensive construction at the time of our first visit. Men were painting the management offices (where I noted an expensive new espresso machine and, a month later, a fancy, plush chair on wheels for the accountant's desk). Strong smells from a pig-slaughtering business next door wafted through the open air courtyard, in the center of which stood the small building with large windows on every side that housed the director's office and his secretary's and accountant's work spaces. After a meeting with the director, who has "a Mexican face" in Rosi's words, we stood around in a group behind the seated women workers, who sat on plastic, upholstered kitchen chairs. They were sewing aprons in a cavernous, airy space within the same complex, across from the management building. Soco's pants had ripped in the back during our trip there, so she excused herself as soon as we arrived. As we talked, she returned and reported with a nod of disgust that the bathroom situation there was no exception to the rule of unpleasant maquila bathrooms. One had to cross the courtyard within sight of the small, centrally situated managerial building to get to this bathroom area.

A vast, open courtyard was to the left of the seated women. In later visits, we could see that lunch tables had been constructed in a shaded corner of this courtyard near some soda vending machines, and a huge white sheath was eventually affixed across the open side of the warehouse to block it from the wind blowing in across the courtyard. The women's chairs faced a particularly elaborate shrine to la Virgen de Guadalupe. She is a revered figure in Mexico; the legend is that she appeared in 1531 before a humble indigenous man named Juán Diego who was in a field in Tepeyac (see, e.g., Wolf 1958). She is also said to have appeared in 1557 in Yerbabuena, now a suburb of Guanajuato. One friend told me that the Spanish have admitted she was intentionally created as a myth, but that Mexicans still want and need to believe in her. All of the maquilas had shrines to her, although their level of detail varied widely. December 12 is her feast day, and also a day of obligation for business owners to celebrate her. I was told that on that day the decorations increase. The shrine "makes a little higher the productivity," said Rosi, in English.[4] This one was draped on both sides with long, rich blue curtains and had fresh flowers and lit candles set before it, with blinking lights arranged around it.[5]

On our first visit in February 2000, Soco interviewed some of the production supervisors (one was a young, trim male with a cell phone) and admired the aprons and oven mitts (we were offered free sample aprons as we left, which I declined), while the rest of us from the state office waited, speaking among ourselves. Over the next few days, Rosi was annoyed with the accountant at this factory, which had been in operation about one month when we first visited. The accountant was taking a lot of time giving Rosi the data on the government scholarships, through which the women were paid during their training period. Both Soco and Rosi were more comfortable with Hector, despite their impatience at first with his volubility and their skepticism over his ambitious plans. With time, it became clear that both felt that the energetic and ambitious director of this maquila was not going to need much more help from them, once the details of paying the trainees and the instructor were taken care of, and the April 2000 ceremony of handing out the training certifications was over.

This latter ritual, which had been celebrated in an elaborate feast at another maquila (described below), was performed very differently here. Somehow the director had not even known about the graduation. We government workers and all of the trainees showed up in very nice clothing with some subdued excitement about the ceremony. As we parked our car in the patch of gravel in front of the maquila, we saw the well-dressed workers streaming in on foot along the busy, dangerous highway to their workplace. The boss hastily came out of his office for the ceremony, once he was woken up from a nap at his desk, and told about it by the program directors. The workers, dressed in their high heels and best dresses, had gathered folding chairs and set them up in their lunch area, but as it was too sunny they began to carry these chairs across the courtyard and arrange them in rows in the shade. Some workers even carried chairs for all of us and set them up behind a long table to face the rows of workers' chairs. One key government representative was very late, so we all stood around awkwardly waiting for her. Some exhortatory and vague, unprepared remarks by Hector and Soco were followed by a short pleasant speech by their trainer, who spoke to warm applause and smiles. The workers lined up and received the diplomas and handshakes from the small group of "officials" (including my daughter, who had been unable to go to school that day, was very hungry, and soon grew cross over the inconsistency of the hand-shaking ritual),[6] marked as such only by the presence of the table erected in front of our seats interposed between the workers and managers. The event broke up soon after, with no more fanfare than that. Unlike the feast which Hector spread before the documentary film crew, or the hours-long event attended by many journalists and dignitaries at another maquila the previous year, this ceremony seemed almost an afterthought.

As an urban maquila with a single, onsite owner-manager, and with Governor Fox having resigned to run for president, the act of drawing attention to the gift of training and of work was not relevant or necessary, as it had been for three rural maquilas inaugurated with great celebrations in June 1999. Far from publicly heralding the investment of distant family members into a community, the ceremony reflected the barest outline and meaning of the program, in its sense of the provision of low-wage, no-frills work for those who wanted it.

This maquila, with more money, space, resources, and contacts than the others, as well as a more urban location, not only had fewer of the kinds of problems of the others but soon began to be touted by the directors as a model. It did not seem to require the forms of assistance which the others did. A key advantage it had relative to many of the other maquilas was that Hector, as the owner-manager and primary investor, could make decisions effectively and quickly. Also unlike others, Hector did not appear to have a son or other relative employed in the maquila. Because of its proximity to other employment opportunities and competitive wages, his factory faced a problem of retaining workers, but new replacement labor was plentiful. This factory was even introduced by Soco as "an excellent maquila" when we visited it with a television documentary team which was investigating the impact of migration on those left behind. On another visit with people in the textile business, Soco presented it enthusiastically as "a very beautiful maquila, truly a prototype."

The animated and voluble jefe seemed to embody a classic tale of success. He had left Mexico after people told him it was impossible that he would ever find work in the field he loved, engineering, because he lacked the connections. Moreover, as he explained, during the 1970s, neither the government nor private industry trusted students following the student revolts in Mexico (which had been marked by the killing of several hundred students by the army at Tlatelolco in 1968). He had worked for years in the United States in various difficult circumstances that seemed to have left him very skeptical of people from there (myself included), then had returned to his home region. He told the documentary team that, along with two partners of his in the area, he was genuinely trying to do good and make a profit at the same time, and that between the three of them they had greatly improved the job market in the area. His father invited all of us to his ranch nearby and described to me, over a feast of cold cuts which Hector had provided for the filmmakers, his hard-working life running a small shop with his wife.

Compared to the other jefes, Hector was distant toward all of us, making it clear that he did not really need anything more than the minimum support available from the government in order to get started. As Soco and Rosi saw the success of this maquila, which did not need the worry and attention that the others did, they gradually shifted their approach to the director. He was not involved in the discussions with the other maquilas that formed a part of the Textile Association of Guanajuato (ITG, or Integradora Textil de Guanajuato). The ITG was formed in early 1999 among several (said to be seven or nine) maquilas within the program which are geographically close to each other, pooling resources in an effort to strengthen themselves through unification and coordination. However,

Hector did participate in the wider community of maquilas by sharing work when he had too much and was able to redirect it to a more remote maquila.

In one act of trust, Soco spoke in secret to one of the production supervisors at Hector's maquila about the work called for in a lucrative Wal-Mart contract. She angrily went behind el Licenciado's back to try and spread the work from the Wal-Mart contract out to other maquilas, rather than see it limited to those run by the relatives of el Licenciado. However, she did point out to a government consultant that Hector was not the kind of man who would be able to act as a leader among the maquilas of the Mi Comunidad program. He was *of* the program but not *in* it (i.e., not within the tight family of it) by his choice. The first time we visited, we met briefly with him, and as we left to walk around the workplace, he joked to his U.S. business partner that "the tour" was leaving.

Soco is too smart not to notice such an attitude, and she withdrew from her nurturing role to a much less warmly personal style, even trying to see if Hector could help *her* out rather than the other way around. It is also important to note that she did not seek to exercise any explicit controls over him, or to demand personal favors for herself. Hector exemplified, in a sense, the ideal of the independent small-scale entrepreneur in Mexico, providing local jobs and not beholden to state government officials for "favors," all within a complex context of compromises and personal networks. He may have been involved in more explicitly personal exchanges with local politicians and government officials, for example from the city or county, but this was not evident to us.

Perhaps the directors did not want to have to see this factory as a problem, since so many of the others were. Although some of the female workers at this site had complained to us about their wages during our first visit (chapter 7), the program directors dismissed the complaints and were instead happy to establish this maquila to themselves and to the documentary producers as a prototype. This precluded any pursuit of the information from the workers who had complained to us. Their main complaint, in fact, was that Hector had not ordered food or any celebration around the day of the workers' certification ceremony. They thought that was stingy and, based on our shared food and travel rituals, I had to agree. Overall, it was clear that they thought this business was successful and independent, well on its way in the teleological plan.

TROUBLES IN THE FAMILY

Another rather poignant example illustrates the loyalty and protection which the program directors extended to the managers for as long as they could, and their withdrawal of personal warmth and support once they deemed that management was unworthy of it.

The directors had been particularly concerned about a maquila in Las Cruces for some time. Only one year before, this factory had opened with a joyful inauguration ceremony attended by many of us from the government and several journalists. The smiling, excited group of young women who had just finished their training were in their best dresses, high heeled shoes, and makeup for the event. Walking out from the village to the maquila over a dirt road, they had carried large pots and other vessels of food and brought them to the long tables placed near the door. As we waited for the dignitaries, including Governor Fox, to arrive by helicopter, I read the hand-written exhortations to workers that were posted on the walls and glanced into the nonfunctioning bathrooms. In the main work area, some men were painting the Mi Comunidad and blue and white National Action Party logos on the wall. I spooned chiles into plastic bowls and arranged napkins and plastic utensils on the tables; Rosi and Soco arranged a display of photographs showing the female workers in other maquilas at their sewing machines. Dignitaries arrived and gave speeches; armed soldiers waited outside. After the many speeches and the personal distribution of the certificates by the towering Governor Fox in his trademark "FOX" belt buckle and his black boots, the large group of guests and workers ate slabs of pork or rich servings of chicken *mole*, accompanied by beans, rice, and chiles. All of the food had been prepared by the women who were going to work in the maquila. The socios (originally from this village, but most had resettled in the United States and had been living there for over ten years) had paid for beer, meat, and soda.

During and after the meal, the female employees joked with the young man who was their supervisor and laughed in describing to me the woeful dating situation in the village. Someone asked them to pose by their machines after the meal, and, after a hesitation and some giggles, they agreed. They smiled and sat down, sewing pieces of fabric and explaining how to make simple repairs to the machines. One showed me a homemade, embroidered pillow she used to soften her seat, a metal folding chair. An official-looking woman filmed them with a camcorder.

I had started to help clean up, then noticed that a silent group of people had filed into the hall, had taken seats all around against the walls, not at the tables, and was waiting to eat some of the leftovers from the deserted tables. No one commented on this; we left the food as it was and cleared away only the empty plates and dirty napkins. The waiting, uninvited people, dressed in clothing that marked them as of *el campo* (the countryside), seemed to quietly know that their place at the feast was one of waiting for the scraps left by others. González Casanova has noted the "silent and supplicating" attitude of 50–70 percent of the Mexican population, that is, the indigenous (1970, 134). This moment starkly corroborated his remark and the disparate social levels that coexist in modern economies.

It was the seeming success story of this maquila in an isolated rural village, profiled often in the Spanish and English language newspapers in the United States and in Mexico, and covered extensively in a government-produced film about the program, which was slowly revealed to be suffering serious problems. One hint of this came at a meeting at which the well-connected Hector generously agreed to share work with this other maquila, which was acknowledged at the time to suffer from the disadvantages of not having much work and being in an isolated location, "so far away." At this meeting, with the sounds of pigs squealing next door and Hector's long monologue, the two representatives of Las Cruces did not speak much, but seemed to listen carefully, especially the older man, always addressed as Don Luis. He was always courtly to us and serious in the meetings, keeping his dusty white hat carefully in hand or on the floor next to him, allowing himself a quick grin during more personal conversations. His young (twenty-ish) nephew Gerardo, who actually ran the maquila, listened, but was usually not attentive to the business discussion, sometimes leaving for long periods. During this particular meeting, Gerardo mostly grinned at and exchanged glances with the young woman in attendance who was going to train the workers. After Hector's lengthy presentation, in which he stressed his high expectations of quality from the other maquila, he then offered the extra work to Don Luis, who graciously accepted. Don Luis quietly noted that, unlike other maquilas, they had no problem with workers: it was work itself that they lacked.

Hector's expansive speech was a kind of prerogative of success in this setting, in contrast to the humble, brief remarks of the representative of the less successful business. By his behavior, Gerardo clearly indicated his own lack of seriousness in this public setting.

Representatives of this maquila also turned up at other meetings, although not at the planned government seminars to which all had been invited. They were a part of discussions of the huge Wal-Mart contract, which was being offered by a garment industry dealer. After she pitched this deal at an ITG meeting, Soco allowed herself a vehement complaint about Gerardo in the car on the way home. She said that due to his youth he lacked vision, decision-making skills, and business sense, and on other occasions she excoriated his lack of "leadership." She had been shocked to learn of the low production level at which this maquila was operating, far under its capacity. Usually she did not criticize any of the jefes aloud, but this was clearly a serious case, and she had lost respect for Gerardo's abilities.

Finally, we came to this maquila for a sad, grim meeting attended only by Don Luis, Gerardo, another relative who works in the United States, a man named Tomás hired by the government for general production troubleshooting, and four of us from the government. This was a very serious meeting, as it involved going over the hard facts of poor administration within this maquila. We arrived in a light pickup driven by a government official, as Soco's car was in the shop for repairs. We waited for the others outside of the maquila, observing the half-finished construction of a bull-fighting ring across the road.

The meeting was long and tedious; even with the tension, our hosts were careful to serve cold sodas and water. A cricket climbed the concrete wall behind us. Through the office window, we could see about a dozen women at their sewing machines. I recognized one from the previous year, and we spoke briefly later, but her smile seemed tired and subdued. Gerardo got up to change tapes in the machine or to assist the women if they raised their hands. He sat with his legs splayed and arms folded across his chest, expressing his fears over participating in the Wal-Mart contract, the difficulties of their location, his poor salary and the losses and sacrifices of his whole family, and las muchachas (the girls, or female workers) not "adapting to controls." Soco, referring to the Wal-Mart deal and to the business world in general, urged them: "Take the challenge!" But they worried that with more shirts would come more discord. They even spoke of Gerardo leaving and of renting the maquila. At times Gerardo's tone of sardonic, mocking bitterness toward Soco seemed both disrespectful, and despairing.

As they spoke, it was noted that all of the workers were still making only minimum wage. Soco was openly shocked that there had been no raises in the entire first year of operation; and she made a show of repeating questions to Tomás by way of demonstrating to the others which machines (recta, overlock, etc.) were more complicated and should be associated with a different pay scale. She remarked that if one girl is working very hard on a complicated machine and knows that she is not making any more than anyone else, then she will not feel very motivated in her job. Soco and Rosi then took turns urging the men to carry on, saying that this is how it is for all of the businesses at first. Soco used an organizational structure diagram to chart out the basic management functions for the factory, and also offered a hypothetical business situation to explain another point, but Gerardo interrupted to ask insolently phrased questions which suggested that he had not understood even this simple explanation. Even Don Luis had not understood that some of the management functions could be done by one or two people. Rosi impatiently corrected them. The usual personal graciousness was far less evident in this worrisome environment.

After the meeting, the relative in attendance said that the socios never had a hint of these problems; they are far away and only come home for the baptisms, weddings, and other celebrations held in November and December. The secrets were hidden even from them. He said they were still paying into the maquila and that Don Luis and Gerardo had begun to talk of going to the rest of the socios for help. After the tension and sorrow, we were anxious to escape, but Don Luis graciously offered us a meal prepared by his wife and daughter at the nearby family home. It would have been rude to refuse, but smiles were strained during the meal. Tomás, who was going to take over, temporarily and at government expense, the administration of this maquila, had come with us. He was going to live with Don Luis and his family and try to salvage the business. Some weeks later we heard rumors that even Tomás was goofing off, taking long breaks from work, and so forth, but he was still working there some time later.

As we rode back to the city, the three of us bouncing around in the open bed of the government pickup truck speeding in the afternoon sun through flat, dusty plains, we talked over the worries briefly. Soco said that Don Luis lacked decisiveness and had an old-fashioned, traditional "male" attitude toward women and running things. But then we talked of other things, and laughed and sang and teased male drivers by blowing kisses at them, on the count of three.

Clearly, even her most passionate efforts could not help in this case; Soco herself eventually had to travel to the United States for a difficult and discreet emergency meeting with the socios. This intervention was particularly painful given the deep respect that both Soco and Rosi have for the main representative of this group of investors. The warmth and discretion of side conversations finally had to be put aside in favor of more direct confrontation and action. As of 2002, this maquila continued to be the subject of government attention, with Soco's plans for a new line of baby products and for more support.

The case above was highly unusual in many ways. The following chapter describes in more detail the program workings among the established, fully operating businesses. I return to other aspects of problem-solving within the program in part 3.

CHAPTER 2

Business Deals

The nature of emotional work changed over time as the businesses and their leaders "matured." Sometimes the business managers began to merit treatment more directly as partners and peers, and in two cases, even as leaders among the group of program businesses. A series of incidents and meetings illustrated this development and highlighted the program values on progress within the global market. The members of the ITG (Integradora Textil de Guanajuato) maquila association resisted a particular contract, which was presented as a sure path to future stability and profit. But their decision suggested that another program value was being achieved: growing unity and autonomy of the ITG. The members of this association were beginning over time to proceed to slight degrees of independence from the government. This example also suggests that the program directors were able to shrewdly step back from their own intensely nurturing involvement in the program's internal workings.

LAS CAMISAS DE WAL-MART

One afternoon, a large group of Mi Comunidad program staff gathered in a hotel lobby outside of the city of Guanajuato. Just a few days prior to this, el Licenciado had been excitedly talking to Soco, Rosi, and myself, of course within earshot of the entire office staff, about the millions of dollars worth of clothing business deals to be had with large companies such as Sears, JCPenney, and Wal-Mart. In the lobby, we met with a couple who were in textiles and Robert, an American garment dealer who was hung over from his previous night out ("You have to drink with them if you want to do business here," he muttered to me) and who had worked with el Licenciado on several other deals. Soco and Rosi did not quite trust or like this man, and confided to me that they thought he did not value their program and preferred to make private deals with el Licenciado. Robert soon became more involved in dealings with our office, and I was placed in a position of negotiating with him since he speaks only English. I was able to mediate between him and the program directors, and later el Licenciado, in some interactions which led me to understand even more about certain operations within the program.

The couple turned out to be a cousin of el Licenciado and his wife. We women sat chatting together at first, as the men held discussions at another table. The cousin's wife complained at great length about the troubles of running a maquila in Mexico and the many labor and quality problems she and her husband had experienced in their other enterprises. They were in the middle of planning a new maquila in León but were not part of the Mi Comunidad program.

Soon the men and women joined in one large discussion. El Licenciado was putting the couple together with Robert, who represented Wal-Mart. Robert needed 300,000 T-shirts (with a small appliqué on the front that he demonstrated), to be made over three months for Wal-Mart. He offered a price of U.S.$0.45 per shirt. Although construction on their maquila was not yet complete, let alone machinery purchased, workers hired and trained, and so forth, the couple expressed utter conviction that they would be able to take initial delivery of the fabric in about two months and handle the entire contract alone.

Soco wheedled the sample shirt out of Robert with the promise to give him an answer the next day. For him, timeliness and quality were of utmost importance. He said to me privately that he loved Mexico, but that it was very hard to get the people to work: they take a lot of breaks, forget even to pick up their paychecks, and so forth. He said he had lost half a million dollars on another enterprise, yet he continued to do work in Mexico. He trusted el Licenciado. In later discussions he noted that he was trying to bring good to Mexico through these business dealings, to "help" them. Yet in anger during one telephone call he blurted out: "One of the things about working in Mexico is supposed to be that it is cheaper! Of course they're paying a little bit more here [in the United States] for this work." He claimed this deal would lead to five more years of work with Wal-Mart for the maquilas, with millions of dollars in revenue, yet for himself, he said in a subsequent call, he stood to gain only "pennies" if it went through. He took money and his own family seriously, but little else, even teasing el Licenciado about his vanity in not wearing glasses. I wondered if this fuzzy vision contributed to the rather distant manner the boss brought to most meetings.

We left the meeting and headed with the sample shirt straight to Hector's maquila, the successful case described in chapter 1, to get the opinion of the technicians there about the cost and feasibility of producing such a large amount of T-shirts. Soco was furious with el Licenciado for trying to direct this lucrative contract to his own relatives and their "dream" maquila. She fumed that the couple did not even have an actual maquila that could do the work, while there were many in the program that needed the work and were already operational and ready for it.

Although we went to the maquila at first with the couple, el Licenciado, and a whole crowd of others, after everyone drove off, Soco returned with the sample and secretly negotiated with Hector and one of the production engineers. This visit was the example of trust previously noted, for Soco believed that this maquila's managers would give her a straight answer about the shirt and that she would be able to count on them to be a part of this huge contract. It later developed that they could not help with this contract after all, which led Soco to pursue other maquilas outside of the program.

The next days were frantic, as we searched for a woman, Ana, who had been interviewed for a quality control position, via cell phone and other means to try and get her opinion about the shirt and about the feasibility of this work. Meetings were organized with the ITG maquilas to try and ascertain their opinion about this contract. Soco really wanted them to participate but could not force them. She did, however, use every possible means—logic, pleading, flattering, bullying, and appeals to greed. The jefes were extremely skeptical and hesitant; most of them let their informal leader, Don Alberto Ruíz, express their own doubts. His joking, articulate manner and business confidence were striking.

An intense man with a ready grin, he wore gold bracelets and a chain, and his office bore several "Salesman of the Month" plaques. His business had even hired one of the many expensive quality consultants which bid to assist the program, to help with a computerized quality control system. He described his business as having a very "broad vision." These things indicated his success, and the other managers and owners seemed to defer to him. A verbal and forceful, witty personality like Soco, he argued for more money per T-shirt, while noting that his factory already had plenty of work. At this meeting there were already hints of trouble in Las Cruces, with Don Luis speaking of their disadvantages of distance and lack of work, Gerardo mumbling about things being "his fault," and the others debating with Gerardo. Later, after other announcements, Soco began to summarize issues by way of ending the meeting, as Rosi sat humming loudly and tapping her shoes, and Gerardo sauntered out of the room. Despite their great resistance, Soco went ahead with plans and with a cheerful summary of the path ahead, before the meeting broke up.

The ITG members did hold out for a slightly larger amount (U.S.$0.65/shirt), and Robert finally agreed to a slight increase (U.S.$0.55/shirt, after his first blustering response to the request "You're kidding!"). But we still needed others to help with completing the whole order. We had found Ana, and together we visited an acquaintance of hers who was in textiles.

This acquaintance was another maquila owner, a very poised and self-assured businesswoman. She was not at all a part of the Mi Comunidad program. Unusually, she wore minimal makeup, short hair, a simple black sheath dress, and a single strand of gems around her neck. She was utterly comfortable presenting herself to us in her identity as a businessperson; she explained that two of her daughters assisted her in the business and she came from a family of merchants. She too hesitated about taking a share of the work (50 percent), since so much was needed. Like other jefes in other meetings, she said that she did not like to make promises which she could not keep. But by the end of a long meeting, which she dominated with rather sad life tales and wise reflections, she seemed to be ready to agree. Even Soco could not get a word in during most of the meeting, although she tried standing up at one point. But the woman had talked long enough to feel comfortable with the commitment, similar to the meeting in which Hector had agreed, after a long monologue, to share work with other maquilas. As we made ready to leave, Rosi bought a pair of pants from the woman's small shop at the front of this building (the jefa's office was behind the shop, and behind her office was the maquila itself), and then we strolled out after many pleasantries, planning where to eat the iced, fresh fruit bars that are unique to Irapuato.

With all of this groundwork in place, with meetings, faxes, documents being typed, and plans in motion, it was time to wait for the *contra-muestra* (demonstration) process, in which samples were to be made and returned so that the quality could be checked before the whole deal was assured. But nothing was shipped. Don Alberto Ruíz had waited, some man showed up, but it was not clear who he was (I called and found out that he was just a "representative"), but the fabric did not come. Then Robert said they could skip the demonstration phase. He left for a short vacation, and when he returned, he told us of other delays: the fabric had been produced wrong and would have to be completely redone and would not be shipped until much later, but Wal-Mart was still insisting on the original completion dates for the order. With Holy Week approaching, during which work is simply not done (Wal-Mart is so huge, they "don't want to know" about traditions and these kinds of problems, Robert replied when I pointed out this issue) and the possibility of either overtime or weekend shifts out of the question ("We just don't have the staff," said even Ruíz, with the largest operation), there was great pressure and concern about meeting the deadline.

Then abruptly came the news that the contract had been cancelled by the man who had been setting it all up with Robert; Wal-Mart had decided to do the work in the United States as they were running out of time because of all the fabric delays. ("These huge companies can do whatever they like," said Robert.) There might still be a chance of work with them in the future, but this particular T-shirt segment of it was gone. I had to break the news to Soco and Rosi, who seemed crushed. They each insisted on making separate phone calls in their halting English to explain to Robert how upset they were about the turn of events. Then Soco also got on the phone with Victor, Robert's Spanish-speaking partner in his leather cutting business. There followed a long lamentation about all their dashed hopes and how well trained the women workers were, with over one year of experience, and if there was any way they could send other work to make up for this loss, they should. She noted how ready the women would be for the future work which Robert now had an obligation to find for them, to replace what was lost. She sadly explained how the maquilas had even turned down other contract possibilities in order to gear up for this order. Listening, I grew concerned that I had been too calm about the news, but Soco laughed merrily after the call, saying that all of the maquilas had plenty of work, and began to plan how she might break the news to the jefes by saying that it was *she* who had decided to cancel the deal.

We continued to deal with Robert, whom both Soco and Rosi were now confirmed in mistrusting. Mostly he made airy promises to us about additional work, but confided to me that his leather cutting business and his own plans for further operations in Mexico, with government help via el Licenciado, were now taking up more of his time. In particular, he was expected to be heavily involved in operations planned for the northeast region of the state of Guanajuato (see chapter 7).

This series of events suggested the growing autonomy of the jefes in resisting government pressures. Even the most intense pleading and advocacy on Soco's part did not succeed in enlisting the ITG members. It also indicated the various promises, flatteries, and manipulations in which Soco was involved as she negotiated with the world outside of the program. The issue of how much work the maquilas actually had was clearly subject to multiple uses; through it, Soco pressed a claim against el Licenciado, Ruíz projected power in negotiating with big foreign companies and in being able to turn down new work, managers from Las Cruces made excuses about their own situation, and Soco solicited future work through guilt over lost, past work. The concept of "workload" was vague enough to permit differing visions and framings of time.

Gerardo's blunt, discouraged remarks were also notable in the public setting of the meeting with the other jefes. His disaffection from the values of the group was clear over the course of many meetings in such acts as not paying attention, grumbling, and leaving meetings before they were over. Although they were in part excused as due to his immaturity, these behaviors also suggested the deep crisis of his situation. Another meeting (discussed below) illustrated the jefes' great potential for supporting each other and him.

THE QUALITY PLAN

We met one June morning with representatives from all of the members of the ITG, gathering in a maquila with a huge PRI banner along its outside wall and some trucks bearing PAN and PRI bumper stickers sitting in the gravel driveway. The election was to take place within a few weeks. Inside, the gray concrete structure was brightened somewhat by many large mounds of dark gray and purple velour fabric which were to be sewn into long-sleeved shirts. The women workers watched us curiously as we mounted a set of open, concrete steps up to an office with large glass windows looking out over the workshop floor. Plastic bags in an adjoining room were filled with white cloths and bore masking tape on which had been written "Defectos." Soco passed out copies of a new quality control plan she had devised, giving everyone time to read them. After a while, using a marker and erasable white board to note details, she began to summarize some of the problems facing the ITG, often seconded and supplemented by the articulate and successful jefe, Don Beto Ruíz. She framed the choices.

First, there was staying as they were: functioning at a low level of production, "solitos" (small and alone), not growing, just surviving, "waiting for the Holy Spirit . . . or Robert," in an ironic reference to the recently cancelled Wal-Mart deal. People soberly admitted how low their production levels and profits were, and the slowness of their staffs. One said that knowledge of workers—how to hire, train, evaluate, fire, and so on—did not exist in Guanajuato or even in Mexico. In terms of their own association, two jefes, Ruíz and another named Antonio Avila, stressed the importance of unity and faith in each other's word.

Soco let this discussion unfold, then situated herself: "From the outside, then, I see problems," and proceeded to detail the need for astute, "well-prepared people" to help solve the problems. This claim of distance belied her own decisive role in devising the second choice—the quality plan—in controlling its dissemination within the group, and in having already selected the job candidate for one of the two planned positions. In a sense, her actions here paralleled one description of the pre-*dedazo* (or "finger tap," as the PRI ritual of naming the next presidential candidate is known) announcements of a sitting president in Mexico. "Analyses of 'the problem' that the new president will solve are therefore also read as subtle allusions to the precandidates" (Lomnitz et al. 1993, 363). However, Soco had already introduced, to widespread agreement, the idea of the quality candidate at an earlier meeting.

This kind of stylistic formalism occurred in several other official settings I witnessed, and within the values on graciousness already noted. In meetings and formal presentations, official presenters tended to read word for word from prepared texts, with some minimal ad hoc elaboration using visual aids. In grade-school classroom settings, there was an emphasis on printed texts as important bases for reading aloud, memorizing, or copying by hand word for word. While such formalities of authority may have helped to set an official tone for the Mi Comunidad meetings, they certainly did not control the overall flow of discussion or the outcomes of meetings.

Soco skimmed briefly over the problem of hiring relatives and moved on quickly to other issues of competence needed from the "outside." She stressed that, for the government, it would be easy to say that once the investment is made our role is over, but she felt they needed to do more to help the maquilas "advance." Up to this point, Rosi had been clicking her pen idly, taking some calls on her cell phone, but also making copious notes about the meeting. Don Tonio began to pass out sodas and to open a box of cookies.

The vague hint of a vacuum where the government had been was the space presented for the ITG to strengthen itself through further integration, as envisioned in the new quality plan. People were mostly in favor of going ahead with the plan, except for Gerardo. Rosi turned rather harshly on him, noting his obvious needs and problems with production and personnel. Others tried to speak, but Soco and Rosi interrupted several times, clearly emotional about the topic. But soon Avila and Ruíz began to counsel Gerardo more directly, telling him to not be afraid, to be more decisive. Soco tried to lead a review of the problems and advantages of Las Cruces, bringing up the issue of leadership, as Gerardo said in a low voice that they were "down," adding sorrowfully, "because of ourselves." Then Avila said, "We have the same problems as you," to the young man, who was by then standing and leaning against the wall.

The older men, their kind faces bearing small smiles at times, had a gentle manner with Gerardo, and some teased him a bit about why he came at all to the meetings, and told him he had to decide if he was going to work together with them. Even the sole female jefa quietly noted the importance of taking care in learning and of taking opportunities. Avila added how they had all started out thus; others agreed, adding, "We didn't know how to do anything either . . . and *now* [*y ya*]," using the common expression (also used in Vicente Fox's campaign) for describing readiness and completedness. They noted that they needed Gerardo, or else integration did not really make sense. Finally, after other pressures, he acceded.

At last Soco could move through the document and plans. By now, people were a bit bored, and Gerardo strolled around, as the meeting headed into a second hour. Soco's method was to ask questions to which she already had the best answers, giving an impression of agreement to the "outside" plan but really persuading them to accept an already-created plan. Nevertheless, disagreements with her and side conversations among the jefes showed that her role was not taken to be one of supreme control. Gina, the only female boss, even gently teased about how much the government had done for them and asked with a smile if even more could be done. After Soco's lengthy review of other issues, Rosi stood up to take over the financial discussion, including what the jefes would need to invest, as the government had already given a lot. As they went through the estimated costs of the new plan (including a centralized office which would be located in one of the maquilas, a vehicle to be shared, etc.), people became concerned once they understood that they were paying for it also.

Other news was shared, along with a short statement about my interest in working with the women, which was met with polite encouragement. Unusually, there was even talk of the low salaries and high turnover, and the relation between them, which was notable in a setting dominated by management problems of sales and profits. After other interruptions and hesitations in the discussion, Soco issued an affirming, summarizing statement: "Together, you are stronger." We all slowly filed out past some giggling workers who were lounging on large bags of fabric. Their boss smiled too. We stood talking in the shady area outside of the workshop, and here Soco learned of more problems at Las Cruces.

The directors in the ITG rallied around Soco in the expensive quality plan; she convinced them it was in the interests of their businesses. But the joking and other behaviors at this meeting showed more distancing of the jefes from the government representatives and signs of solidarity among themselves. They intervened and overruled Soco's impatience toward Gerardo, and instead gently drew him into their inside group through their admissions of past mistakes and flaws. His obvious sense of personal crisis and alienation, expressed in such a public setting, elicited support and warmth from the group members, not rejection. The meeting suggested that a project of fostering entrepreneurship among individuals and as a class was being realized within the program in a humble, relatively unheralded way.

It is also significant that when the program directors referred to official power, they said "el gobierno" (the state or the government) rather than "el Gobernador" (the governor). This in itself is a key difference from government proceedings described in other rural settings in Mexico. For example, federal agricultural officials meeting with *ejidatarios* (members of an *ejido*, or collective land parcel) buttressed their discussion of policy with constant references to the desires and plans of "el Presidente" (who at the time was Carlos Salinas de Gortari) (Nuijten 1995).[1] The absence in the Mi Comunidad program practices of such references is discussed further in the conclusion.

SUMMARY

Although Soco wielded a great deal of power in most of her personal dealings, she moderated her will around the jefes according to each one's specific situation, pressuring or getting angry in some cases, flattering in others, seeking help from them in still others. She presented ideas forcefully, but was willing to graciously cede power as the managers developed their own strength. She projected visions of hopeful futures, and the managers were included within her vision of the future as a place of progress. But these visions were not cast in terms of her own personality or through demands of loyalty to herself. There were hints of her pursuit of "her own project" by one staff member who was angry with her, but these hints do not diminish the larger points of the case.

Soco's personal warmth was part of her overall efforts to foster individual, entrepreneurial success. She reaffirmed and enacted the wider, cultural value of sociality in order to achieve her own success and to promote her program, but she stopped short of a fusion between herself and a totalizing power of the state. Moreover, she criticized instances of dishonesty by her boss. She allowed discussion of other possibilities, of critique and failure, within the family of the program. In these and other ways, her form of state power seems to constitute an important shift away from many accounts of government in Mexico. Among the multiple levels of state bureaucracy in Mexico, theorists have noted processes such as the "fetishization" of the president and the union of "personal gain and national interest" (Lomnitz-Adler 1992). Guillermo de la Peña (1981) has analyzed the PRI's maintenance of dependency relationships through a pyramid of patron–client connections, suggesting that at any point in this hierarchy, from the village to the federal government, "government representatives are present." These kinds of connections did not seem to be the case in the everyday implementation of the Mi Comunidad program.

The differences in state warmth and visions of the future tended to favor management over las muchachas, as will be seen in more detail below,

while the deferral of authority may foster the "clandestinity" or even ille-
gality of practices associated with the wider maquila industry (Wilson
1991). But the fact that program practices were not monolithic or co-optive
of the entrepreneurs suggests that the program directors did not, through
their practices, inscribe a heavy, disciplining mark of the "synoptic" state
upon its citizen-partners. Statistics and documents were kept and taken
seriously, but they were almost incidental. Nothing was irreversible. Perhaps in practicing new roles of government, shaped in part by PAN discourse and in part by their own backgrounds and experiences, Soco and
Rosi were also exploring an important, new terrain of state responsibilities which lies between the ideals of formal encouragement and informal
control. But the forms of power which *were* at work bear examination in
more detail.

CHAPTER 3

Social Work

The Mi Comunidad program directors often noted to outsiders that their office fell under *social service,* not economic, programs in the state organizational structure. They also described their work as assisting the women of poor areas through the creation of jobs. Although they did assist and succeed in creating jobs, in fact the direct sense of being in a helping or social service profession was primarily in the support given at the managerial level, as noted above. And in fact, this emphasis on entrepreneurs is important in the state of Guanajuato and throughout Mexico.

Federal-level, centralized policies in Mexico have more typically been aimed at directly or indirectly encouraging large-scale domestic and foreign-based private capital over the decades of PRI rule.[1] More recently, in state-level policy, fostering small and medium-sized businesses and strengthening local economies have been identified as important social and economic needs in Guanajuato. Governor Fox's state government plan included several overall economic goals for the state which are relevant to the Mi Comunidad program, specifically: (1) the creation of work in both urban and rural areas with special emphasis on marginal areas; (2) the fostering of small and medium-sized businesses; and (3) the attraction of investment from citizens and foreigners (*Plan* 1996, 5–6).

Even beyond these internal policy goals for the state economy, support for the entrepreneurial class in Mexico may be important to the organization of opposition to the PRI. "Business" is not one of the official sectors of the PRI, and business organizations are officially banned from political participation. Although large-scale businesses are closely tied to the party, small and medium-sized businesses have tended to be more politically autonomous, and are seen as having the potential to preserve domestic economic sovereignty (Heredia 1992). Jorge Castañeda (then President Fox's foreign minister) wrote that it would be important for business in Mexico to be a part of a leftist constituency and to "act as an entrepreneurial class" (1994, 475). The business class in Chihuahua has already fostered political change through its activism in support of the PAN, and through an insistence on "free and fair rules" in business, which is actually a "radical" call in the context of Mexico (Mizrahi 1994). Similar ideas have been noted elsewhere in Latin America, for example in the case of Nicaragua (Babb 2001). However, the Chihuahua businesspeople's "pragmatic" definition of democracy is based more on rules than on social justice (Mizrahi 1994). Cabrero-Mendoza (2000) has suggested that "change agents" in Mexico are "generally preeminent local businessmen who, once included in the local government, are not generally interested in extending political participation to other groups."

In the case of Mi Comunidad, the very process of establishing a business is a crucial form of practice for these small-scale entrepreneurs. "Practices" in two senses are relevant in the program: (1) everyday practices of intimacy matter deeply in this case, and (2) the managerial-level participants in the program are in a sense practicing being entrepreneurs, and even being "the government." For nothing was assured in the evolution of the program and its maquilas; the process was fraught throughout with uncertainty. The Mi Comunidad program reflected this uncertainty and ambivalence in many ways, as will be noted in subsequent chapters.

If the PAN, or more broadly the business class, does bear the potential for political change and democratization in Mexico, its growing significance also bears many other implications for society that are not as easy to assess. One illustration of this is found in the very structure of the program. By definition, the main impetus for investment in the factories is *outside* of Mexico and outside of Guanajuato. There are exceptions to the outside locus of planning—for example, when the investors are living in the state of Guanajuato. But even in that case, they work directly with the state and not with the citizens of the community in planning the business. Another exception which was in the works in 2000 was the Northeast Project, which was being planned by el Licenciado in a joint venture with Robert, the garment industry dealer. Of course, generating capital from outside of the area may be necessary and reasonable, but this process is problematic.

The communities of origin of the investors were usually the intended sites for the maquilas, but initial conversations took place far from the site where any given maquila was actually to be constructed, and did not involve many of the persons living in those targeted communities, beyond some of the relatives of the investors. Institute of Women Director Laura Lozano told me that government planning in Mexican rural areas involves "a paternalistic relationship, but the community does not participate in taking these decisions," although the community is aware of its own needs. She argued that construction of the maquilas should be integrated with the communities, not imposed upon them.

The "donor–recipient" orientation of Mi Comunidad would be considered by policy analysts to be "traditional" rather than "participatory"

(Wight 1997). Wight's dichotomy is based on development projects between *countries,* but problematic assumptions regarding the use of outside "experts," short-term project goals, and so forth can mark a case of internal development as well. James Scott (1998) also critiques projects which subordinate local knowledge, or *"mētis,"* as he terms it. In a sense, the use of "my" (*mi*) rather than "our" (*nuestra*) reflects this lack of direct participation in the Mi Comunidad projects by all members of the targeted community. Indeed, the program name, in the use of the singular possessive, validates a personal claim to the program which differs from the reality of its collective aspect, given that the average number of investors in each maquila is over fifty.

Another problem generated by the outside locus of investment is that the privilege of participating in planning is earned with the contribution of money. This is also the case in another migrant-based investment program in Guerrero, in which investors viewed the contribution of money toward building a road as the key to earning a right to a voice in the town (Boruchoff 1998). This linkage between money and participation or responsibility began early on in the program and continued throughout its implementation. While not an unusual linkage in many societies, this focus can be problematic if it excludes other possibilities for participation. Moreover, perhaps inevitably, this linkage has become intrinsically related to gender.

SUPPORTING ENTREPRENEURS

The Mi Comunidad program fell under the internal, DACGE office category of Economic Promotion; the program directors' business cards, giving "Economic Coordinator" as their position, also asserted an economic function. Far from a *social* project, in fact the state government staff clearly assisted the Mi Comunidad maquilas with all stages of business planning and economic operations. The government even intervened on the demand side, guaranteeing a market for the output of the factories. Support for this form of business was also available through federal-level agencies. The plan for Guanajuato was eventually to convert the maquilas so that they could manufacture under foreign brands or under their own label, and to develop manufacturing plants for products like furniture and leather. They would then be able to enter the manufacturing market without the full protection of the state government.

Interestingly, one scholarly description reminiscent of the Mi Comunidad program examines direct sales organizations (DSOs) like Amway and Mary Kay Cosmetics. Family terminology and emotions were used to foster entrepreneurship in the far-flung distributors as being less about what they *do* than *"who they are* as being entrepreneurial" (Biggart 1989, 163). The author writes that the lack of security and salary within the DSO industry is presented instead as a sign of the distributors' strength of character and willingness to take risks. Through the implementation of the Mi Comunidad program, as in the discourse toward its investors, there is a similar kind of flattering and nurturing, which takes economic, legal, technical, and emotional forms.

Patterns in the program's emotional intimacy for the most part reinforced an unsurprising program-wide bias toward management-level thinking about problems and solutions. To each other and myself, the two program directors frequently expressed their worries about the financial health and viability of the factories of the program. They worried over the issues of maintaining and improving quality, retaining workers, and other internal affairs of each maquila. Much of their daily work was toward these ends, in addition to shepherding other groups through the process of establishing new maquilas. Our travels were almost always marked by the excitement of a new plan which Soco had devised to solve one or more problems. I witnessed the almost missionary zeal with which they worked to get new contracts for the maquilas, to arrange purchases and loans of sewing machines, to hire coordinators and trainers, and to elicit additional government grants for the hiring of quality and other kinds of consultants and managers. Determining who was in a position to provide support to the program was a constant enterprise.

They were also concerned explicitly with safeguarding the capital investment made by the faraway *paisanos*. Soco told me that, as representatives of the government, she and Rosi were responsible for the money of these investors. They had to help to ensure that the sincere act of investment was rewarded or at least that investments were taken care of properly.

This family-style warmth, energy, and concern were extended beyond actual kinship ties for, as noted, the most intense and personal relationships were those which were fostered and maintained among those at the investment and managerial level. With skillfulness and winning personal charm, the program directors balanced many roles: consultant, coordinator, cheerleader, sales and marketing associate, and caretaker. These powerful women were in paid positions to provide a great amount of fairly technical support to the managers/entrepreneurs in Guanajuato: financial and managerial advice, logistical and procedural details, not to mention channeling financial support from the government to the businesses. But their practices and self-descriptions as representatives of the state were primarily cast in terms of their role in partnering and nurturing the businesses, downplaying and deferring their own centrality and authority.

For example, regarding their own power, Rosi went so far as to state

that the state government, embodied in herself, had no power at all to enforce even the laws regarding the minimum wage and work schedule, let
alone to encourage the maquilas to provide better conditions, incentives,
pay raises, and so forth. She seemed bemused at one of my suggestions:
that any profits could someday be funneled back into the maquilas in order to improve certain conditions and, thereby, morale. When I mentioned
using the sites as central locations for classes or meetings, she joked, "Why
not tennis courts and swimming pools?" Ana, a woman whom Soco interviewed for a job planned in part to boost productivity and morale, also
noted that the program directors function primarily as consultants, without decision-making authority.

In addition to this deferral of power, support for the businesses was also
cast in maternal, nurturing terms. It is important to examine these two related ways of expressing state power.

LEARNING TO WALK

Soco once described the difficult period of late 1999, when several maquilas at the same time were in the early stages of operation. She used the
analogy of a newborn baby to describe the way in which she and Rosi
maintained daily, even round-the-clock telephone contact with all of the
new maquilas, likening it to the time when the two of them had cared for
her infant son while also attending classes at the university together. She
explained that soon, however, the businesses had begun "walking" (*cami-
nando*) on their own, and there was far less need for daily calls or for as frequent visits. The familial intimacy of the program is captured by such
nurturing verbal descriptions and proud evocations of memory, echoing
the sense of family evoked in the official discourse about the Mi Comunidad program. And indeed, the production of intimate emotion paralleled the realities of kinship of many of the program participants.

But this is more than a family metaphor. The sense of maternity here is
a powerful one: not passively nurturing the businesses, but truly protecting them from harm, enabling life. The business process, even once it was
set in motion, was by no means smooth and inevitable. Many serious problems arose to impede or stop the plans of a given maquila. Documents in
the files showed correspondence between the socios and the local government authorities regarding issues like water, electricity, and road
paving to the new sites. In the office was an album which Soco often took
along to meetings in order to illustrate the program. Photographs in it depicted groundbreaking and other ceremonies at sites that were still incomplete more than a year after the initial excitement. The life cycle was
not secure; it required the close monitoring that a pregnancy might, or

even the first year of life in the city of Guanajuato, where friends of mine worried a great deal over the dust, the wind, and even the many trees shading that part of the city where their infant granddaughter lived. This maternal metaphor of nurturance may well evoke a notion of female power that threatens patriarchy (Jay 1992), or a female "ethic of caring," but these broader meanings were not as relevant to this case.[2]

Instead, I tried to make sense of these nurturing metaphors within the unique context of the program, as part of everyday work. For the directors' power stemmed from their position: linking the program to the wider global market, embodying the potential for success of Guanajuato. They did not need to threaten "patriarchy." Instead, they were in charge of and at the center of this highly patriarchal program, with its male office supervisor, its male investors and managers, hierarchical planning and management style, its "outside" impetus for investment, and its linkage with the problematic maquila industry, which is often associated with the exploitation of female labor.

There is a complex intersection of gender and class in this program which is significant to this analysis. The program directors were young women, while most of the program's investors and managers were middle-aged men. The discomfort of this sensitive situation—of young females in Mexico holding a degree of state power and business knowledge relative to older men—was alleviated by the emotional and familial practices of the program, by references to the social and maternal aspects of their work (which also distanced the program from the exploitative meaning of maquilas discussed in chapter 6), and by the habits of respectful graciousness on all sides which helped to keep relations smooth. These practices produced the "insiderness" of the managerial level. This personal and familial warmth was forged *across* and despite differences in age and gender; insiderness was based instead upon the reproduction of middle-class and probusiness values.

In their deferral of their own power, the program directors reinforced the value of *male* contributions to the program—real and potential—as investors, managers, and entrepreneurs. Within the family of the program, male involvement was foundational and essential. The needs and problems of the male entrepreneurs were valid, important, temporary, and ultimately soluble. The initial stage of male neediness was metaphorized within the program in terms of progress forward, from the early "toddling" and onward toward success in the "global market." This differed from the depiction of the female workers. This distinction was doubly determined—by the PAN's patriarchal, middle-class values and by the delicacy of gender relations within Mexico. The emotional style of administration allowed a kind of parenting which was suited to the sensitive situation in which the male maquila bosses and investors needed advice and help. Ironically, it allowed the power of the two young, female administrators to be smoothed over with the very ideology of maternal nurturance that has often been used to subordinate women across cultures.

"Emotional work" is a concept used in many studies to address gender roles and norms, work expectations and sex-typing, and women's forms of resistance to patriarchal work settings (Hochschild 1983; Macdonald and Sirianni 1996). But the program directors' discussions with me about gender relations in Mexico and at work, in combination with their nurturing practices, indicated that their "feminine" work with emotions was distinctly *not* understood as a form of resistance. This work was crucial to maintaining the delicate relations and the gender disjunctures noted above, especially during the tentative early stages of the program. But it was also quite effective and powerful in terms of their own goals and values, including those of having fun and freedom.

FEMALE IDENTITY

The encircling cultures of family, home, and church, especially in the rural areas of Guanajuato, are marked by strong pressures on women to value and identify themselves exclusively as mothers and housewives. Some of the single women I knew in Guanajuato faced family pressures on this point and had internalized them to some extent as well, worrying over their age and marital status. The first time I met Rosi's father, I remarked on how hard she worked. He replied at once, and within her hearing, that "of course she works hard, for she has a lot of time, being single." Soco worried a great deal over how lonely Rosi was and always included her in any social outings and events at which she might meet men.

Both Soco and Rosi believed strongly in the separateness of gender roles and the importance of each gender within the family as parents. Strongly held gender beliefs were expressed in many settings in Guanajuato. Two gender conferences included group exercises on what constituted female and male characteristics. Even in these relatively well-educated professional groups there were many stereotypical ideas: alcoholism was attributed to males but not females, while different notions of values, strength, level of interest in sex, and so forth were asserted for each sex. In our discussions of the feminist movement, Soco stressed her opinion that for women, the family should be the first priority. She said that it is fine to help and to encourage everyone, yet each sex has its role in society. She also felt strongly that women should not verbally attack men as a group. Other friends held very specific notions about the differences between men and women (baby boys are hungrier than baby girls, women are more emotional and men more rational). One professional woman said her brothers had teased her as a child because she liked to read, repeating the common saying that her eyelashes would fall out from too much study. One female student believed that homosexuals and women had the same chromosomes.

Female identity in the state of Guanajuato, usually described as a conservative Catholic state, is understood as "maternity," which is stressed and even sanctified (del Refugio Ortega et al. 1999). Emphasis on sexualized images of the female body in mass media, comic books, and everyday fashion, along with a normative expectation of marriage and motherhood, was combined in Guanajuato with silence and widespread ignorance about sex. On one shopping trip, we passed block after block of streets filled on both sides with clothing stores, with racks of polyester dresses and pants spilling out into the streets. Throughout this sprawling area (a delight for my coworkers and two other government workers who were with us), stores used wire forms of the human torso to display the clothing. Even those which were made to display clothing for girls had been shaped in such a way as to simulate breasts; and many of the shirts for little girls also had frills and flounces sewn across the chest, further highlighting this area of the body. But one friend told me she and her boyfriend had no idea where to even put his penis the first time they had sex. Planned Parenthood estimates that 23 percent of Mexican adolescent girls are sexually active, and of these about 6 percent use contraceptives. These things cannot be discussed, as knowledge of anything, especially sex, makes a woman more "suspect," as Paloma Bonfil noted during a gender and poverty workshop. Silence can have serious consequences: Mexican rural women may have eight to ten children, and poorly performed abortions are said to kill 140,000 Mexican women per year, which translates into 110 maternal deaths per 100,000 live births.[3] Although a state official noted in 2002 some reason for hope on the topic of abortion, these issues remain urgent.

Bonfil, coordinator of a Gender and Poverty workshop for state employees held in June 2000, also noted that physical control is still very much a part of the life of rural Mexican women, evidenced in values such as that placed on virginity. The ideology of the "traditional rural family" has long included a value on female "seclusion" (Wilson 1991)—staying in the house or yard and acting as the symbolic heart of the home and hearth—while the man tends to the wandering animals and distant pieces of land or to business dealings in faraway villages. A house lot (*solar*) in villages is usually managed by women and children and includes small orchards, cornfields, and a yard for animals (Zendejas 1995, 31).

The public appearance of females has been controlled and even linked to the "honor" of a family and of both men and women in many cultures (Abu Lughod 1986). Female physical freedom and mobility can become associated with imputations of immorality: participants in a gender workshop said that women who migrate are often, when they return, considered *usadas* (used, as in sexually soiled), and that their own *suegras* (mothers-in-law) call them *putas* (whores). This gendered and moral sense of mobility is evident elsewhere. Mexican male migrants resent the disciplines imposed on their use of public spaces in the United States; they interpret subtle physical constraints which force them to go straight from work to home and back again as specifically making them "effeminate" (Rouse 1992).

But Soco and Rosi overcome the gendered physical controls upon women in Guanajuato by way of many class-based privileges. Such a degree of physical freedom for women, not only in mobility but in professional choices and opportunities, clothing and other self-presentational styles, especially in the rural areas of this conservative state, is a recent and significant phenomenon in itself. Although as females the program directors are subject to various constraints within the context of Mexico (but also entitled to certain privileges, which they would be the first to point out), they are of a professional and urban class which has cars, money, cell phones, clothes appropriate for travel and circulation in the business world, and many other markers of physical freedom and power. From their point of view, far from being inferior to the men of the program, Soco and Rosi were luckier and much better off than the male jefes in at least one sense: in their own physical freedom to drive away from the maquilas, to shop, and to dine in nice restaurants at government expense.

The program directors embodied and reproduced the values they were seeking to instill among the male jefes of the maquilas—including the emphasis on freedom through personal mobility, stylishness, and consumption. They themselves modeled the middle class, the envisioned future of the program.

DRESSED FOR SUCCESS

Specific clothes worn by young professional women of Guanajuato clearly indicate economic success and attractiveness. One early evening, about 7:00 P.M., I sat with a friend in Guanajuato's central square (el Jardín) for the always-available pastime of watching people stroll by. Many small groups of women passed; in each group, all of the women were dressed in the same outfit, usually a tailored blazer over a blouse, with a snug, short matching skirt and matching shoes. Like the teenagers in their tight, far more revealing clothes, the women were clearly promenading, not just hurrying home from work. My friend noted that they worked in the banks and were proud of their uniforms and liked to display them: for them, clearly, the uniforms were a special way of looking attractive and sexy, as well as asserting financial success and savvy.

During our visits to the maquilas, my colleagues were usually dressed in dark suit jackets with skirts or dress slacks. Rosi also wore dresses— usually brightly colored and snugly fitting. They wore the latest shoes of León, and their hair colors and styles, jewelry, and makeup showed signs of relative wealth, as they bustled in importantly carrying folders and papers, laughing, and talking loudly. All of these behaviors and self-presentations were markedly different from those of the less-educated or lower-class women of Guanajuato. Far from the deferential or shy manners of many women, my colleagues were confident, proud, and physically comfortable with their power.

The program directors hoped to partner the jefes into this wider world; indeed, that was part of their responsibility. In discussions and meetings, Soco and Rosi made reference to this idea of becoming participants in a larger market, according to the teleology noted above, in which the businesses will grow more independent and self-supporting, someday able to manufacture their own label. But privately the directors worried about the ability of these businesses to survive in the global market as they saw it. Even I could see that there was a wide variation among the jefes whom I met, in terms of skill and experience, ease of manner regarding employees, and other characteristics. Of the men who ran the maquilas, most were open and friendly, and some appeared to be very sincere and hard-working, although not as sophisticated perhaps as Soco and Rosi, who live in the capital city, hold university degrees, have traveled outside of Mexico, and have friends who are foreign. Some managers, like Hector, had traveled, lived in the United States, and knew a bit of English. Others were extremely shy and humble; two arrived by public bus for an initial meeting with us.

Unlike my stylish comadres, these small business-owners and managers tended to dress simply in plain, open-collared, and buttoned shirts, with dark pants or jeans; among them, there were some variations in quality and flashiness expressed in choices about belts, boots, and hats. Indeed, one staff member said that "the jefes themselves are also humble," in other words, like the women workers. One staffer said she used her old and less-nice outfits when on trips out to the maquilas and to the remote villages, and in other subtle ways she made clear her slight distaste for this rural world: boring, not full of very handsome or interesting men, and so on.

On many occasions when the jefes had been asked to attend important all-day courses or morning meetings, most would show up without even pen or pencil for taking notes and signing documents. Some did not attend at all. Technological proficiency, cell phone or email usage, and business card exchange seemed to be widespread markers of professionalism in the capital city, thus the act of attending a business meeting without even the crudest form of writing or communication equipment was striking. Las Cruces did not have a computer or even a phone line. It was located in a village where calls were put through (and overheard) by an operator located in a small building in the center of town.

However, even my relatively sophisticated comadres might on the surface be considered "unprofessional." I noticed some curious glances at meetings outside of the program when they pulled items from their bags like a large yellow, pencil-shaped and zippered plastic children's pencil case, an appointment book featuring big photographs of puppy dogs, or a child's backpack to carry government papers.

CLASS MOBILITY

Values of physical freedom or mobility were reproduced in the program discourse about and the warm encouragement of increased autonomy for the young businesses, as exemplified in the successful maquilas. Forward motion within a wider, internationally validating space, symbolized by the global market, was reproduced in the practices of the Mi Comunidad program. First, personal warmth was directed at managerial-level participants, those with potential for entry into the global market. Second, travel or mobility was a professional requirement and a class privilege, as well as a form of identity.

For the two program directors, as best friends, work meant a day of freedom, out of the office and onto the highway, with a meeting to endure (and some friendly conversations before and after it with the managers) and then a good meal: in short, a day spent together, enjoying laughter, music, jokes and shopping, meeting new people who might prove useful in business contacts or just in generating new ideas. Every morning as we left for a trip, we were buoyant as we drove away from the city. We were not yet hungry, dusty, or windblown in the late afternoon's dry heat: we had all just eaten breakfast at home, everyone's hair, makeup, and clothes were still fresh, the air was cool and the vistas crisp. To some extent, our joy was also in part because we left, for the day, personal and professional worries behind us. Like the migrants whose money was sought as an investment in the program, we left behind our needy, comparatively immobile family members in our pursuit of other adventures, opportunities, and responsibilities. We would never have wanted to leave permanently behind those who elicited our concern and weighty feelings of obligation: ill mothers, needy children, or doting husbands. And indeed as we traveled, we also absorbed the new worries of each day.

Our ritualized adventures of travel were central to our work life, our relationships with each other, and our identities in the office and among friends. We were always about to leave (*salir*), or we were just returning from a trip, or wearing things purchased in other localities, and so on. Our physical mobility was cherished and an emblem of pride; the state-reimbursed mileage and tolls, not to mention meals, only reaffirmed our physical freedom. Enacting the state in this case thus meant embracing the opportunity to pursue individually and officially cherished values although, of course, not at the cost of forgoing family responsibilities.

Other patterns of physical freedom and movement that were structured by the program followed a more predictable model. These patterns extended far beyond the villages, through linkages to the physically free males who live in the United States and invest money in the program, returning when they can or when they desire to visit home. The gendered aspects of physical freedom are captured in a government-made film about the program, as the camera travels far away to interview the investors as they relax together in various settings or stroll through a winery, while all of the footage of the women workers shows them within the confines of the maquila—either seated at their machines or standing at a table cutting fabric or folding garments. Unfortunately, these images of freedom enjoyed by the distant males are not often borne out in reality. Life in the United States entails discipline and oversight for migrants, as well as hardship and violence (see chapter 5).

The program values on mobility were distinctly related to the aspirations of the middle class in Mexico, aspirations which have become a part of the revolutionary change in government. In recent years there has been a growing sense of dissatisfaction with the PRI among many members of the middle class, for example over peso devaluations and crises, the government's mismanagement of the 1985 earthquake relief effort, and other problems (see chapter 4). Some analysts have suggested that high levels of migration from Mexico must be seen in part as a rejection of the PRI. As many as 10–30 percent of Mexicans living in the United States may be "political" migrants: the middle class and university trained in whom Mexico has invested, people who "represent the contemporary failures of the Mexican state" (de la Garza and Szekely 1997). Candidate Fox often touched upon these themes in campaign speeches, simultaneously blaming the PRI for high migration levels while lauding the migrants themselves for their courage and hard work.

During the presidential campaign period, I heard expressions from friends inside and outside of the office of great hope for change. Some people noticed with pleasure the high level of international interest in the elections. When Fox referred, during the second debate, to "building a bridge to democracy" and cited other examples "like Poland, like Spain, like Chile," he captured an important theme for many of the Mexicans I know. Later, just before election day, I detected among some people a slight annoyance or sensitivity about the presence of foreign observers of the election. Some friends expressed a kind of anxious pride that Mexico be seen as taking its rightful place in the world, to be compared with nations other than the United States, for example in signing a trade agreement with the European Union during the spring of 2000 that signaled a step into the global economy. The orderly conduct of the election and its historic result were seen by many as an important validation, even among opponents of the PAN, of Mexican democracy in the eyes of the world.

During our car rides, Soco and Rosi sometimes reflected on another theme that was not limited to the office: usually expressed as "the problems we have here in Mexico" or, another variation, "what we lack." As examples, they cited the lack of a professional culture or a culture of work, not valuing women, and not knowing how to organize in civil and fund-raising organizations. Among the many conversations we had with people in the course of work in the Mi Comunidad program, this topic also arose. One employee in the federal government complained to us of her problems with businesspeople (*empresarios*), citing "this culture of ours" in reference to environmental pollution. A relative of el Licenciado who was involved in managing maquilas indulged in a lengthy narrative on this topic during the hotel lobby meeting with the dealer representing Wal-Mart (see chapter 2). Even the sewing machine salesman held forth on the lack of work culture and professionalism in Mexico, as Rosi and Soco nodded in agreement. I also heard these kinds of self-critical reflections during my stay in 1985, suggesting a wider narrative of problems, but one expressed within a context of pride and patriotism.

SUMMARY

Program discourse and practice suggested progress toward an exciting, moving "future." Within this sense of valued progress, Soco and Rosi successfully navigated many domains, integrating work, family, responsibility, fun, and faith. As daughters, wives, mothers, and sisters, they fulfilled multiple responsibilities. They used the context of their professional work, their income, and their time on the road primarily to pursue middle-class consumer freedoms for themselves and their families. As young professional women, they bought new things, discussed the latest movies and music, tried new foods. As administrators, they envisioned and enacted a warm, free-market-based future for the program, without losing a sense of the importance of personal relations. While they promoted a teleological vision of Mexico's future with crucial implications for the lives of all program participants, yet they were always late for appointments. It is in the complexity of such everyday practices that "the state" is understood best as both personal and self-contradictory, and as embodied and enacted by persons who are engaged in many other roles.

PART II
Bridging the Program Contexts

CHAPTER 4

The DACGE Office

When we were not traveling through the state of Guanajuato, we spent many hours sitting in the cramped rooms of the Office of Support to Guanajuatense Communities Abroad (known by the Spanish acronym DACGE). Office life included a quiet assessment of each visitor to the office, raised eyebrows, witty repartee, and utterly public work. The combination of a calm but bustling atmosphere even within these tight quarters was in part a result of the consistent graciousness of all of the staff members. As a person with a great need for privacy, I was struck by the apparent comfort of every staff member with the fact that no remark or telephone conversation would go unobserved or even unheard. Even a relatively low-voiced discussion I had with an intern about this person's grades was overheard and laughingly interrupted by teasing. When el Licenciado was out of his office, some of the staff did go in to use his desk or telephone, but the door always remained open. On this very public stage of state assistance to citizens, there was a sense of openness to any newcomers, but as in any office, "backstage" life was vividly present at all times. Personal relationships were complicated, with the mostly female staff engaged in various cliques and gossip.

Office morale was intentionally targeted as part of the meetings on "quality" and as part of sessions such as an all-day workshop in which the staff participated in various group activities. The office staff was commonly referred to as a team (*equipo*).[1] Yet many divisions existed across the staff, one of which was the intentional distancing by the program directors from others in the office. Their freedom to leave the office, their education, and their important positions were some of the factors in this distancing. I was aware of these tensions, but tried hard to maintain friendly relations with all of the staff—downplaying my own good fortune in being one of those who was able to leave the office so often. As an outsider who was clearly not so well schooled in the prevailing rules of self-presentation and social decorum, I was accorded a certain tolerance behind the smooth graciousness extended to all newcomers.

During the first months of 2000, the presidential and other campaigns began to intensify across Mexico, and some office workers were discussing the possibility that their department might be shut down by a change in state government after the July election. As noted, leadership of the state government in Guanajuato was at this time in the hands of the National Action Party (PAN). This national political party, founded in 1939 by Manuel Gómez Morín and originally made up of conservative professionals, merchants, and pro-Church intellectuals (Hamilton 1982), constitutes one of the two most prominent rivals to the Institutional Revolutionary Party (PRI).

In the 1995 election for governor in Guanajuato, Vicente Fox Quesada of the PAN won with 58.1 percent of the vote. Fox also may have won the 1990 gubernatorial election; many believe that fraudulent practices granted that election instead to the PRI candidate, Ramon Aguirre Velázquez. A report by the Instituto Electoral del Estado de Guanajuato (the Electoral Institute of the State of Guanajuato, or IEEG) notes that there were "mutual denunciations . . . over . . . alleged irregularities" (*Memoria* 1997, 1) among the three main parties involved in the 1990 election (the third party is the Partido de la Revolución Democrática [Democratic Revolution Party, or PRD]). Eventually, an interim incumbency was agreed upon and filled by the PAN's Carlos Medina Plascencia. This was seen as corrupting for the PAN, in striking a deal with the PRI. Kathleen Bruhn suggests that a stern *New York Times* editorial urging President Carlos Salinas de Gortari to "correct" the situation in Guanajuato led to this move, because prior to the article's publication, Salinas appeared to accept the problematic results without question (1996, 313n). As a result of this agreement, Fox stated he was quitting politics in disgust with his own party, but eventually he returned to run for governor again.

The IEEG, created in the wake of this problematic election as part of other reforms, is housed about one block away from el Palacio. IEEG radio broadcasts during the 2000 presidential campaign stressed its role in the constant oversight of laws and promotion of civic culture, while its educational materials spread ideas about elections and democracy to school-age children. The organization published a carefully detailed account of changes in procedures in Guanajuato prior to the gubernatorial election which Fox won, including lists of campaign costs, information on election day logistics and location of the voting booths, and details on ballot design and supplies used. The process was "innovative and meticulous," representing "the new concept of a state electoral organ" (*Memoria* 1997, 1).

The third major party in Mexico, as noted, is the PRD, founded by a group including Cuauhtémoc Cárdenas when the Democratic Current split off from the PRI to form a "leftist" variant between March and October 1987. Cárdenas, the son of former President Lázaro del Río Cárdenas (1934–1940), was sworn in as the first elected mayor of Mexico City in

1997; he made unsuccessful attempts at the presidency in the elections of 1988, 1994, and 2000.[2] Fox joked that the only way Cárdenas was going back to Los Pinos, the presidential home, was to look for his teddy bear. A brief summary of these national contexts will further situate the Mi Comunidad program; the full history of Mexican politics and government is absorbing, but obviously beyond my scope here.

NATIONAL POWER

The PRI-state has been highly successful during its decades in power at dividing or co-opting its political opponents, be they political parties or segments of society such as labor, intellectuals, and peasants (Bruhn 1996; Middlebrook 1995; Stevens 1977). In fact, many journalists and observers, as well as friends of mine, were enraged at Cárdenas's stubborn refusal to withdraw from the 2000 presidential campaign, fearful that the PRI would win yet again via the strategy of dividing its opposition.[3] Labels for the form of government wielded by the PRI-state vary, from authoritarian, bureaucratic-authoritarian, *dirigiste*, hybrid, "symbiosis" between state and party, co-optative/clientelist, activist, and corporatist to simply one-party system (Castro Escudero 1995; Cornelius 1996; Dubbs 1996; Grindle 1977, 1996; Middlebrook 1995; Teichman 1995). "Secular authoritarianism" by the PRI has also meant centralized control over the Church, the military, and the universities (Stevens 1977, 230). Executive power dominates the judicial and the legislative branches of government.

Relations between local citizens and government power have been channeled through three sectors of the PRI—the Confederation of Mexican Workers, the National Confederation of Popular Organizations (including bureaucrats, teachers, shopkeepers, etc.), and the Confederation of National Campesinos/Peasants (respectively: CTM, CNOP, and CNC).[4] These sectors were meant to represent labor, the popular sector, and peasants. They balance each other in "manipulating and inhibiting collective demands in exchange for personal favors" (de la Peña 1981, 247). Indeed, Roberto Varela (1984) suggests in his detailed review of local politics and practices in Morelos that conferring the "permission" to be corrupt, and the resulting corruption, are themselves a form of control.

The PRI has also co-opted the past, forging national myths into its own history, so that its evolution as an institution is presented as entwined with the nation.[5] It even uses, illegally, the symbolic power of the Mexican national flag's colors—red, white, and green—for its party colors, hence the references in the press to the party simply as *el tricolor*.

Linda Arnold argues that the modern Mexican nation-state is linked to its colonial past through its faith in Enlightenment ideology and through its federal executive structures (1988, 55, 129). She asserts that the colonial-era bureaucracy—made up of professional employees and implementing consistent policy—was replaced by national politicians as the intervening structure between state and society during the first decade of the first Federal Republic of Mexico (1824–1835). Postindependence government agencies were marked by favoritism, jockeying, the sale of positions, and decreased morale. Civil servants became dependent on politicians for work, made official in a May 1833 law which made secretariats of state the "personal confidantes of presidents" (ibid., 96, 126). The entrenched nature of government power is seen in the current bureaucracy of the large federal state, which numbers twenty-one ministries. One estimate is that there is one government employee for every forty-two inhabitants in Mexico (*La Nota*, 17 November 2000).

The size of the Mexican bureaucracy reflects a long and complex relationship between the state and private capital. Nora Hamilton, in an examination of banking structures in Mexico, argues that dominant private and foreign capital during the period prior to the 1910 Revolution and through the Cárdenas years limited the progressivism of the revolutionaries and led to the regularization of the processes of their "self enrichment," as the state itself became "an important source of the capitalist class" and of capital accumulation, leading to "inherently contradictory" state policies to both promote and control capital (1982, 86, 87, 187). Anderson also asserts the development of "banks as political institutions" (1963, 165). The 1917 Constitution was the basis for the proliferation of state enterprises (parastatals), which went from being "important national symbols" to "mammoth" organizations during the period 1940–1970 as the interventionist state was consolidated (Teichmann 1995).

Authors debate the degree to which these bureaucracies wield power in and of themselves (i.e., separately from the PRI) or simply function to rubber stamp presidential decrees (Benveniste 1970; Centeno and Maxfield 1992; Purcell and Purcell 1977) as the congress and judiciary have done (Ward and Rodríguez 1999). Within state government, there are signs of a developing "tradition of a career civil service," which has been lacking in Mexico (ibid.), as well as indications that the composition of the "technobureaucrats" is beginning to reflect changes in the political elite (Centeno and Maxfield 1992).

With the 1982 debt crisis and external pressures from the International Monetary Fund and the World Bank, Mexico began a process of privatization and other efforts to reduce bureaucracy and decentralize. As a result, the number of federal employees dropped from 1,456,800 in 1987 to 918,500 in 1996 (Rose 2000). The national government still controls an estimated 74 percent of public expenditures (Arellano-Gault 2000), but even macro-level and neoliberal economic analysts fear that the cuts may have been too deep, hurting both infrastructure productivity, while the worsening position of the poor and marginalized is also widely discussed in other venues.

The stability and continuity of the modern political economy in Mexico have often been noted, sometimes with a sense of the social costs of these characteristics. The 1910–1920 Revolution was "but a chapter in the longer historical process of elite-directed modernization and reform" (Benjamin 1996, xx). "Conservative modernization" is Alain Rouquié's term for the maintenance of tradition *through* industrialization (1982, 28–29), and Horcasitas wrote of PRI elections that should be seen not as "stability without change, but as continuity through change" (cited in Bruhn 1996, 53). This stability has been achieved through repression, social inequality, and violence, especially in rural areas, where promises of land reform have been staved off for decades as foreign capital, agribusiness, and wealthy family powers hold on to the best lands in states across Mexico. As Nora Hamilton writes: "The evident success of the control and cooptive mechanisms of the Mexican state has led to a tendency to regard the Mexican population as passive and acquiescent and to ignore the repressive mechanisms which underlie the authority of the state" (1982, 37). For those who prove "unco-optable," harsh measures are the response (Cornelius 1996).

The countryside has been considered a political stronghold for the PRI, but "peasant" trust in the PRI-state as the mechanism for land reform has decreased, especially since the 1991 gutting of the important Article 27 of the Constitution on *ejido* lands, an act which triggered the revolt of the Zapatista Army of National Liberation (EZLN) in the still-unresolved Chiapas issues. Local strongmen (*caciques*) and patronage systems still dominate many political and landholding relations, continuing patterns which many trace to the cruel practices under Spanish colonization, reproduced through the "societal memory" of violence (Rouquié 1982; Wasserstrom 1983). Although the military has been relatively weak in national politics and small in size since the 1920s, it continues to be repressive in rural areas. Supplementing official power, the "white armies" hired by Chiapas landowners are much like the system of private guards which President Porfirio Díaz (1876–1910) thought necessary for the haciendas to maintain "order in the country" (Bazant 1977, 106).

The revolt in Chiapas is also feeding a long national debate over indigenous people (*la indígena*), part of a wider discussion of the effects of neoliberalism. The control exercised by the Catholic Church hierarchy (and, by implication, the PRI) over the appointment of a bishop to replace the proindigenous Samuel Ruíz in the spring of 2000 led to this charge: "The Vatican is continuing the capitalist policy of letting all those who do not produce or consume disappear. And those who do not produce or consume do not have the right to live; then they do not count" (Corro y Vera 2000, 9–10).

The army's massacre of demonstrating students in 1968 at Tlatelolco is also invoked in public debate, included in graffiti on the walls of university buildings in Guanajuato, and remains an undercurrent of the continuing student restiveness at UNAM, the Universidad Nacional Autónoma de Mexico. Carlos Fuentes now points to the crucial incident at Tlatelolco as the beginning of the end for the PRI; Rouquié also links it to the "erosion" of political legitimacy (1982, 219). The recent problems undermining the legitimacy of the Mexican state thus have included: economic crises; the disaffection of unions, business leaders, students, peasants, and the middle class; the 1985 earthquake in Mexico City which provoked civic protest over inept government responses; and the broader loss of credibility for the PRI following political violence, the 1995 peso devaluation, and overt electoral manipulations like the fraudulent 1988 election of Salinas (Grindle 1996).

Along with these challenges, political openness has been slowly increasing in Mexico in recent years: PRI candidates have lost gubernatorial races in several states, as well as losing the majority in 1997 in the lower house of the National Legislature. Electoral reforms have been instituted and President Ernesto Zedillo (1994–2000) showed signs of "letting go" of centralized power, thereby providing political space for governors and local government initiatives to flourish (Ward and Rodríguez 1999). The federal bureaucracy itself may be a key to change. For years it has been a factor in the PRI's successful practices of "change within continuity" through the periodic "fracturing" and "internal recomposition" of the bureaucracy, which takes place around the change of each president (Lomnitz et al. 1993). Some see the transition to democracy as entailing three simultaneous processes: the end of single-party rule, economic liberalization, and "professionalization and decentralization of public policy making" (Cabrero-Mendoza 2000).

The year 2000 marked the first time that primaries were held for the PRI candidate for president, although many felt that the old system of *el dedazo*, or the "finger tap" (in which the incumbent handpicks his successor), was still in use. Former President Carlos Salinas de Gortari visited Mexico in June 1999 from exile in Ireland; many observers suspect he influenced the selection process within the PRI during this visit. There was open outrage in the press over his presence, ostensibly for a relative's graduation ceremony. Editorials criticized him; one cartoon depicted the former president skulking through town with his suitcase, while two of the always-beleaguered citizens of Mexico City complained to each other about the problem of security in the city (looking at Salinas), what with so many unsavory characters in the streets.

Along with the other reasons for political openness advanced above, the role of neoliberal restructuring of the Mexican economy under the Salinas technocrats has been debated, paralleling the international debates about the linkage between liberal free market economies and democracy which Albert Hirschman (1982) elucidated decades ago. Clearly, a widespread momentum for political change has been building for some time in Mexico, and has now in part been accomplished with Fox's election. But Fox has been hampered thus far by many obstacles, including the lack of a PAN majority in the 500-member Chamber of Deputies (each of the three major parties lacks a majority there). Fox's term as of this writing has been uneven.

FOX'S LAND OF OPPORTUNITY

Vicente Fox's historic election was far from inevitable. During the time of my fieldwork, a great deal of uncertainty surrounded his campaign. In examining the daily implementation of the Mi Comunidad program, which he designed at a time when he was also considering a run for the presidency, I kept in mind his role as a critic of PRI policies and PRI ways of thinking, and his claim to represent Mexico. His speeches as reported in the media, campaign appearances, and themes invoked a very powerful message built on a point which could not be refuted: "Ya cada vez somos más" (loosely translated, "We're growing all the time," but also with an impatient meaning, as in "Let's get on with it already!"). This was repeated on bumper stickers, tequila glasses, bedroom slippers, and T-shirts. *Ya* in itself is an interesting word in Mexican Spanish usage, because depending on the context and expression, it can mean "ready," "already," or even "OK, let's go." My colleague Rosi once described getting ready to go out: her choice of a dress, her shower and makeup, hair preparations, "¡Y, ya!" she smiled and shrugged at the same time, spreading her hands wide to show her readiness for action.

Fox employed the open-ended theme of *having already won,* by virtue of the fact that he was in the race at all, let alone enjoying a lead in the polls. The slogan was a powerful discursive move in the era of post-logocentrism, when notions of the "always already" are refuted. For the PRI has so clearly always been already there, defining themselves *as Mexico.* Like his reappropriation of the PRI theme of revolution, Fox's optimistic characterization of his own political position was a remarkable, damning refutation of PRI dominance, since never before had a candidate been seriously considered who had not *already* been selected from within the ranks of the PRI elite by the sitting president. With this preemptive slogan, he also undermined the legitimacy of any possible PRI victor in the election.

Many tactics were employed in the national media to undermine Fox's candidacy, including an "exposé" in the final days before the election of "foreign" contributions to his campaign. This charge was ironic given that James Carville, who is known for his work on the campaigns of Democratic politicians in the United States, was a paid consultant to PRI candidate Francisco Labastida Ochoa. Within Guanajuato, one long-term demonstration against the PAN became part of our everyday office life. Members of a national protest group called the Antorchistas camped outside of el Palacio for a demonstration against the state government in June 1999. They recast the PAN's state slogan, *Tierra de las Oportunidades* (Land of Opportunities), in a banner which read *Tierra de Corrupción* (Land of Corruption). Between March and June 2000, the final months of the presidential campaign (and in some states, including Guanajuato, the gubernatorial, senatorial, and mayoral campaigns), they returned more permanently. They set up mattresses and tents virtually on the steps of el Palacio, blocking all traffic on one side of the street. Loudspeakers blared music, speeches, and chants in front of the building and the sound echoed throughout the inner courtyard and offices. The Antorchistas claimed that the PAN government had not honored certain promises made regarding schools, higher education funding, and rural services. Government workers picked their way through the crowds sitting on the steps, while children played and the taco and seafood stands nearby profited from additional clients in this normally rather sleepy end of town. The Antorchistas occasionally marched through the entire city with banners and chants, escorted by government vehicles, shutting down traffic through the vital downtown area for hours. Although their group encampment appeared permanent, it was rumored that the individual people participating in the demonstration changed every week or so. The press soon began to discuss what most suspected: that the PRI had founded this group and was paying them to disrupt and embarrass the PAN state government.

The bus to DACGE rattled through patches of shade and sun and over speed bumps and cobblestones, passing the massive red structures of the national PRI headquarters. The PRI acronym and symbols are carved into the stone facade of the sprawling complex; across the street from it is a square dedicated to Luis Donaldo Colosio Murrieta, the political leader who many believe was assassinated by fellow members of the PRI (*priistas*) because he was rising too fast within the ranks. The square is dominated by a large bust of him looking intently across the street at the PRI headquarters. A popular television soap opera, entitled "The Candidate" (El Candidato), was loosely based on the story of this young reformist leader, who was killed in 1994. Many character and plot details of El Candidato were similar to actual events in recent Mexican political life, and friends of mine enjoyed unraveling the references. The airing of the show, essentially a critique of the PRI, was seen by many as another exciting and hopeful sign of new political openness. The show was also unique in that it was interactive, with a website for viewer suggestions, and a plot that incorporated daily the current news events in Mexico City. Selected episodes taken from the course of the entire series were broadcast on the night before the historic 2 July 2000 election. The last scene showed the handsome candidate hero and his beautiful girlfriend. They have just voted, and he teasingly asks her if she voted for him. She smiles without reply, and they embrace passionately. This scene was followed by images of Emiliano Zapata and other heroes in Mexican history, and then a text stating "Your vote is for the love of Mexico," linking romantic passion, patriotism, and the act of voting.

In coming to or leaving work, the only possible route was past these symbolic buildings and groups: the PRI structures, Colosio plaza, the demonstrators, and armed guards. They were daily physical reminders of state presence, authority, and co-opted resistance. Yet some signs of possible change were also visible. On the other side of the street and around a curve in the road from the PRI headquarters is the humble edifice of the PRD. There were few signs of activity there until the weeks just prior to the election, when a handful of people began to appear in and around the door of the offices. Guanajuato is known to be largely supportive of the PAN at the state level, but the PRD candidate for mayor was a popular former mayor and well-known candidate whom many of my friends expected would win, and who did in fact do so. Meanwhile, at the busy PRI headquarters, well-dressed men and women could be seen climbing out of shiny new Suburbans and mounting the high steps. The PRI was gearing up to regain the whole state with its gubernatorial candidate, Ignacio Torres Landa, the son of a former governor of Guanajuato. "Yes, we can continue with the change," intoned his advertisements, cynically claiming Fox's campaign theme of change. The press reported some confusion among voters mistaking the son for the father.

Throughout the campaign, television, radio, and billboard ads reminded citizens of the importance of voting and of the fact that the vote is free and secret. These messages were intended to prevent the manipulation and abuse of voters. In the local mines that still operate in Guanajuato, some of the bosses are said to lie to workers by saying: "I know who you voted for, it is all here in my computer." At the Goodyear service station where friends of mine voted, a long banner stating that the election observers are not authorities was taped on the rear bumper of a car which was up on a hydraulic lift, and all voting booths had white privacy flaps on the sides, on which were printed the reminder: "Your vote is free and secret." Across the front of the second story of the Electoral Institute of the State of Guanajuato was a large sign asserting that it is citizens who make elections happen. These and many other public announcements reinforced civic rights and responsibility through nonpartisan messages, making the time prior to the election both exciting and poignant. A few public personages in particular used television appearances to spread civic information and to foster an imperative that every citizen vote: newscaster Javier Alatorre, Federal Institute of Elections Director Jose Woldenberg, and even President Ernesto Zedillo himself. The soothing baritones and handsome features of these three men assured viewers in many appearances on television that their vote mattered and that it would be respected.

Full-page explanations of the procedures for voting, how to read one's voter credential card, how to find the correct voting booth, how to fill in the many forms, and so forth were available in the local newspapers the week before and the day of the election, as well as being posted near polling places. On election day, a local television station in Guanajuato was on the air live throughout the entire day providing telephone numbers for voters to call with any questions they had about procedures. In one example of increased transparency at the local level, and perhaps even an emblem of pride for each neighborhood, large pieces of paper bearing hand-written breakdowns of the votes cast at each polling place were posted near the entrances of each site after the votes were counted; the tallies were left up for several days. During a 1985 election which occurred during an earlier period when I lived in Guanajuato, printouts of data for entire districts were simply mounted on large boards in the town center, a blizzard of unindividuated totals bearing no connection with a human count on a block-by-block level. Perhaps the notorious "glitch"-prone computers of the PRI will finally be of the past in Mexico.

OFFICE CULTURE

In working with these employees of Fox's state government (although he resigned to run for president in late 1999), I hoped to understand something of the ways in which workers in a state bureaucracy run by an opposition party might envision themselves as distinct from previous administrations. I was interested in how they interpret and embody the hopes of the PAN, as the Catholic, conservative, and middle-class party of Mexico, to create change in Guanajuato and throughout Mexico.

Events in the campaigns for president, governor, and mayor were discussed in the office, along with party platforms, parents' views, and so forth, but ultimately party allegiances did not play an explicit or key role in the program practices. Within the office, there was fairly open debate and some joking, with rising tensions as the elections drew nearer. One employee, whose *priista* father had been an official in the party, had inside knowledge of PRI tactics and thus was cynical about the party. This staff member described the way that people of the country, *los campesinos*, must bring their voter credential card along when they want to get other services, like water and food. English-language newspapers have been drawing more attention to such manipulations in the countryside by the PRI, describing the gifts of food, beer, and even washing machines to voters, but this is old news in Mexico. One friend told me of a common saying that translates as: "The PRI gives you a free meal on election day, then robs you for six years." Another staff member was a *priista* with the possibility of obtaining work through her father's connections; she refused to take advantage of that benefit, but felt that the PAN was not "used to power" and was therefore even more greedy and corrupt than the PRI.

One political theme in the office was Fox's handsomeness; we all referred to him as Soco's *novio* (boyfriend). Many women I know teased about wanting to join the list of potential wives for Fox (who was unmarried at the time), and to become the first lady. There was even talk of his pairing up with Lucia Mendez, a well-known star of a telenovela. A female friend of mine who works at the university referred to Fox's "all-female fan club." His attractiveness to women, and his kind of earthy virility, which was also celebrated in the press (e.g., his large belt buckle, high boots, thick moustache), may even have inspired the PRI to use male strippers from a group called Sexy Boys at a campaign rally in Chimalhuacán, at which the backs of the men's underwear spelled out "V-O-T-A P-R-I" (Ambriz 2000, 30–35). Sex appeal was clearly seen as part of Fox's many strengths, and his quick, bawdy sense of humor was enjoyed by both men and women I knew.

For the office workers, the state gubernatorial election results would most directly affect their own jobs and lives; there was often discussion of this election in the office. The PAN gubernatorial candidate in the 2000 election was Juan Carlos Romero Hicks. He was well known and widely admired as "noble" in the city of Guanajuato due to his successful period as rector at the university, but many people feared he would be seen by some voters as too much of a gringo, or at least as not truly Mexican. This fear was also expressed regarding Fox, some of whose ancestors are from Spain and Ireland. Romero's PRI opponent, Torres Landa, had the advantage of full Mexican heritage and a family background in local politics, but his own experience was limited to governing the small city of San Juan d'Iturbide. Despite Romero's family ties to the United States and his appearance (pale skin and blue eyes, also widely acknowledged to be a bit too serious and unsmiling), the mustachioed, youthful-looking man was known to be smart and honorable, to have ten children, and to have a wife who, although away frequently, was very active in philanthropy in Guanajuato.

Although Soco and Rosi felt that their program would probably be maintained even under a PRI governor, others in the office wondered about the future of their jobs and of the office (which has since been restructured). As of this writing, the office is still functioning under the Romero Hicks administration, but el Licenciado has left his position.

MISSION AND POSITION

Official records, publications, and pronouncements are key texts for analysis, with many possible levels of interpretation. They may document confusion, failure, cynicism, or change in political priorities. Benjamin Orlove (1991) uses the rhetorical concept of prolepsis, or "the assumption that future acts are preordained," such that "the state anticipates its own future actions" to analyze maps created by the state in Peru. He found that the series of maps reflected the planned teleology of state laws more than they charted the actual terrain. This degree of planning was far from the case in the DACGE office, however, further challenging the notion of the hegemonic state.

In records which assert the office's organizational mission, one can trace official identification of migration as a problem for Guanajuato. DACGE was created in April and May 1994 by Carlos Medina Plascencia, the interim governor appointed after the 1990 election irregularities in Guanajuato previously noted. At the same time, a companion project to study migrant networks was created, based at the University of Guanajuato. These offices are described as the state government's response to high migration from Guanajuato, which has long been termed by migration scholars one of four "sender states" (the others are Michoacán, Jalisco, and Zacatecas) that have the highest migration levels in the country. This initiative in Guanajuato followed federal-level policy: President Salinas began the first Program for Mexican Communities Abroad, intended as a permanent link of communication between the government and migrants (Boruchoff 1998). In 1992, an agency headed by Roger Díaz de Cosío was created to address migrant communities. He invited all of the states in Mexico to initiate such policies. Guanajuato is said to have had difficulty instituting a program, because it lacked the information and infrastructure that its neighbors had (González Martínez and Hernández Hernández 1998).

The office was originally given a rather high profile position under the direct oversight of the governor. It was established specifically to support all the citizens affected by the phenomenon of migration, those who leave and those who remain (DACGE 2000). A report on quality within the office (written by a staff member who is a lawyer hired to be in charge of quality), states that "our migrant society is our principal client." The text notes that the staff works with Mexican consulates and other organizations in the United States and generally assists citizens involved in all phases of the migration process. According to the quality report, DACGE also has ties with mayoralties and intermediate organizations, as well as an office in Dallas, Texas, which increases its span through the Casas Guanajuato (ibid., 1). This is the name for the community centers which have been created in thirty-two different regions in the United States.

One source refers to DACGE simply as "the state migration office" (*Economist* 2000), somewhat oversimplifying its far-flung operations. Besides coordinating the Mi Comunidad program, the office staff are involved in providing assistance directly to citizens involved in migration cases, support for the Casas Guanajuato, and "social communications"— radio and television broadcasts to the communities in the United States and a print periodical called *Pa'l Norte*. The title is a reference to the expression *para el Norte* (for/to the North) as a destination for those who migrate. Some members of the DACGE team worked at a branch office in nearby Silao, run by the brother-in-law of el Licenciado. I did not study these other aspects of the office beyond noting their articulations with the Mi Comunidad program.

The director of the office has noted that at any time up to 30 percent of the population of Guanajuato is in the United States (*Economist* 2000). The state population of Guanajuato was about 4.5 million in 2000. Documents from a state government seminar in 1999 estimate that there were two million Guanajuatenses living in the United States, of whom half were born in Mexico. Of those who have crossed, 500,000 are without documentation and are paid an average of 30 percent less than the legal minimum wage. El Licenciado told me that Guanajuatenses can be found in every state in the United States. Other documents note the issue of those left behind by migrants. Abandoned children, widows and orphans, the problems of AIDS, family disintegration, loss of family identity, and destructive behaviors of the wife in the absence of the husband (alcohol and drug abuse, extramarital sexual activity) are all cited as migration-related problems (Guerrero Reséndiz 1999).

Thus, the organizational mission of the office was clear, if incredibly broad: to support all state citizens involved in migration, those who leave and those who are left behind, which might conceivably include all of the state's citizens, and to seek to ameliorate the multiple social and economic effects of migration losses. A description from a 1977 account of a federal bureaucracy in Mexico has an echo in the state government documents relating to the DACGE office, in that the guidelines of policy were so general as to provide little guidance to decision-makers (Grindle 1977, 171). In the 1977 example, Grindle suggests that this left resource allocation open to "political" pressures and was perhaps "intentional." Leaving aside the possibility that all resource allocation is open to political pressure, one could argue instead that the open-ended generality of the policy statements in the DACGE case left space for a flexible stance toward citizens, and demonstrated an unwillingness to preestablish conditions upon which citizens will be required to approach the state.

The relationship of DACGE to the wider state hierarchy in power at the time of my research was unclear, perhaps in part because the office predates the 1995–2000 PAN administration of Governor Fox. By 1998, the office had been moved from its original, direct supervision by the governor's office. The above-mentioned internal report on quality presents only one organizational chart—for the office itself. There was no chart depicting the location of DACGE within the state hierarchy, and references in various texts to its linkage with the state government are so broad as to be irrelevant. Predating the Fox administration, the office apparently had no "natural" place within the state hierarchy. It was transferred from the direct supervision of the executive office of the state, "but its objectives continue to be the same" (González Martínez and Hernández Hernández 1998); it seemed to have been simply left in existence without any more specific external linkages than the general government of the state.

The shifts of the DACGE office over time, from a position within the governor's direct oversight to an office without a clear tie to the state hierarchy, run by a businessman and then for a short time by a person considered by some to be an unqualified inside hire, suggest significant changes in the political priority of this office. Some of these changes may have been related to Vicente Fox's political ambitions and his awareness of migration as a crucial political issue on both sides of the border. As president, Fox has a new forum for his ideas on migration, but the issue continues to draw attention from within the state government of Guanajuato. By 2002, a lawyer was in charge of DACGE and committed to its mission, but Fox's national office on migrants had been closed.

Some documents regarding the office's functions and relations to the state government were unclear. A chart defining "Goals and commitments" for the state government in 1999 linked three of the DACGE functions to the concept of "Indicators affecting the development and competitiveness of the state." The three functions were the Casas Guanajuato, the Mi Comunidad program, and general communications with migrants. The document asserted a link between these outreach programs and the overall development and competitiveness of the state, even though they all operate within the context of *migration*—by definition a phenomenon of movement *away* from the state—and two of them are directed to clients based outside of the state and even the country. The awkwardness of this logic and phrasing suggests that a staff member was using a predetermined set of concepts and attempting to squeeze DACGE work into them. Further, a letter from an economic development department notes that a resource transfer to the Mi Comunidad program had the following "intended benefit": "To give better services to migrants from Guanajuato in the U.S.," which is an interesting assertion as well, given that the other two programs are much more explicitly directed at such a goal of support *in the United States*, while the service aspect of the Mi Comunidad program is supposed to be entirely focused inward, within the state. In the office organizational chart, the Mi Comunidad program is not specifically listed but simply implied in the Office of Economic Promotion under Soco's name. One of the most important functions of the office, described in Chapter 5, involving assistance to those with relatives in the United States, is not specified at all in this chart, simply assumed under the name "Pati," a DACGE employee who is in charge of this service.

Governor Fox's state plan did not specify relations with migrant populations in any of its statements of vision, objectives, and strategies for the state's development. Instead, it focused all of the plans for social, economic, legal, and civil development *within* the state. The state government aims which *were* relevant to DACGE functions could be said to fall under some of the overall economic goals for the state. As noted, these were the creation of work with special emphasis on marginal areas, the fostering of small and medium-sized businesses, and the attraction of investment (*Plan* 1996, 5–6). These three policy goals did have an echo in the Mi Comunidad program rationales. This connection makes sense, and was often noted explicitly as a program goal. However, Soco usually asserted to outsiders that the program fell within the sphere of *social* aims of the state hierarchy.

The Weberian concepts of "mission" and "vision" were echoed in posters on the walls and in office documentation, workshops on quality, and signs within the maquilas of Mi Comunidad. The report on quality notes the following aspects of the office's mission, vision, values, and policies. The mission: to offer a service which fosters the integration between citizens abroad and in Mexico, improving communication, organization, and established ties. The vision: to be the leading government office at the national level to call attention to any Guanajuatense community abroad, thereby improving its development. Values were detailed: commitment, responsibility, sensitivity, tolerance, respect, efficiency, and effectiveness, while the policy statement was simply stated: quality in attending to the phenomenon of migration in all its contexts—a repetition of the DACGE mission with the inclusion of the word "quality."

SUMMARY

On paper, then, the DACGE office was situated within a very broadly defined intersection of organizational missions having to do with both economic development and multiple forms of social outreach to migrants. Sweeping phrases explained and justified it, as in similar kinds of documents presented by any organization, but the shifting connection between it and the wider state structure had not been clearly documented in the records which I found. In general, office documents confirmed the variety of missions pursued within the office, but without articulating a direct connection with other parts of the government bureaucracy and without always clearly describing and promoting some of its key functions. The office was and is being successfully maintained and funded within the state government.[6] The broad, loosely defined missions of the DACGE office and the Mi Comunidad program reflected several wider contexts and had important implications in practice.

CHAPTER 5

Pa'l Norte

The Mi Comunidad program was intrinsically linked to the geographically far-flung, complex phenomenon of migration, both in its official intent (to reduce migration) and in one of its primary sources of funding (migrant remittances). Many of the emotional meanings of migration that were specifically invoked by the program also came to the forefront during the 2000 campaign in Mexico.

THE POLITICS OF MIGRATION

As events and debate proceeded within the presidential campaign, the magical concept of the international market arose in the powerful issue of migration. Migration to the United States is seen as necessary and inevitable by many in Mexico, a sorrowful loss for the families involved and for the nation, but basically a part of life. Migration was a key issue in the campaigns of both presidential hopeful Vicente Fox and PAN candidate for governor of Guanajuato Juan Carlos Romero, because both men were suspected of hiding *gringo* sympathies and of lacking true Mexican heritage. There were suggestions that, if elected, both would favor the U.S. position on the issue of migration (such as more policing of the border) over the Mexican position. Newspapers in Guanajuato and throughout Mexico track this issue carefully, noting proposed legislation in the U.S. Congress regarding border militarization, amnesty for migrants, and other legal changes. PRI candidate Francisco Labastida Ochoa and his wife spoke publicly about Fox's likelihood of supporting border controls and questioned his national loyalties; the word "traitor" was even mentioned. After his election, Fox intensified an emotional appeal that is popular to many Mexicans by calling for an open border and through constant references to those who cross as *laborers*. This emphasis draws attention to their hard work, rather than to their status as "illegal aliens" or "immigrants."

The approach of the 2 July 2000 election date led to increased demand from journalists, state government officials, and other callers for information about the Office of Support to Guanajuatense Communities Abroad (DACGE) and its programs. There was heightened interest in defining and elaborating the achievements of the state government under the PAN as the party faced the gubernatorial election. Within the state government, there was demand for information in order to plan for the next cycle, regardless of the victors. Soco and Rosi were certain that their program would continue even if the PRI regained the state. Several times, the directors of the Mi Comunidad program were suddenly ordered to summarize information for their boss within the space of a night or a weekend for meetings to be held with officials in the government. At these meetings, el Licenciado was called on both to highlight the results of programs and to help in planning future budgets. But in addition to this reason for curiosity about the office, journalists and others were calling for data on migration in relation to the ongoing violence against Mexicans which takes place along the U.S.–Mexico border. Existing tensions were further incited by the press coverage of vigilante and other forms of violence against Mexicans in the United States, an ever-present issue that took on deeper urgency in the rhetoric of the presidential and gubernatorial campaigns. All of these factors led to more outside interest in migration and thus in the work of the department: in individual cases, statistics, and related job creation issues.

TRACKING MIGRANT BODIES

When we were all present in the office, the two directors of Mi Comunidad were often on the telephone arranging meetings with the maquila directors or investors or tending to myriad other details of the program. A few feet away, another woman would be arranging the transport of a corpse of a dead Guanajuatense back from the United States for burial, or trying to help a bereaved family find information on their rights to the Social Security funds contributed by their deceased family member who had worked in the United States. A major component of the office's work was handling the requests of citizens for help in locating those who had left or dealing with cases such as divorce petitions, illness, and relatives dying alone in foreign hospitals. As a part of my efforts to foster a participative form of fieldwork, I offered to help the woman charged with this work, so that when we were in the office I often was involved in her case load rather than solely working with the Mi Comunidad directors.

The shipment of bodies is an expensive and complex process. In one case in which I helped by making phone calls in English, a body was being sent to Mexico. With a rosary service, paperwork, and shipping, the charges amounted to U.S.$3,200. Sometimes specific Casas Guanajuato in the United States help their fellow villagers with these costs. Pati, the woman in charge of this office function, told me that the families often hope to be able to see the deceased because they have not laid eyes on them in so long, and they do not realize that once the casket is sealed and shipped, it cannot be reopened.

Bureaucratic situations involving citizens in or from Guanajuato were handled primarily by Pati herself. She listened with bottomless sympathy to various pleas—by phone or in person—of those who had ridden the bus all morning to come and stand or sit, carefully holding documents and sometimes a small basket containing their lunch wrapped in cloth, next to the small desk in the back corner of a long, narrow, intensely crowded office bustling with phone calls, faxes, photocopying, and conversations. One day a woman waiting in one of the two available chairs fell fast asleep, and no one disturbed her, thinking she had come to see Pati and would get to her business eventually. About an hour later the boss finally noticed her and woke her up. As she had no business in the office that she could think of, he courteously escorted her out, accompanied by many giggles from the staff.

In late June, the office was rearranged when new furniture arrived. Pati's desk was moved to the front, where she had a much more convenient position for direct dealings with these citizens. Soft-spoken, with warm brown eyes and a ready smile, she brought a gentle mediation to the humble or frightened citizen facing confusing forms and legal situations.

On election day, I watched news coverage with friends and waited at the polling place as they voted. At their home, they had agreed to allow a young woman and her son from the countryside to wait for a call from her husband. He had left home just weeks ago, and she knew very little of his whereabouts or work. I mentioned DACGE to her, and its availability to help persons like herself, in part because I knew that Pati's manner was so gentle as to soothe even the most hesitant supplicant. In exchange for the use of my friends' telephone to receive the call, she cleaned the kitchen, dishes, and all the floors of the house as she waited. Slowly, over the course of the day, my friends drew her little son out and engaged him in some fun activities in the garden. As most of the country was riveted by the process of the election, this young woman waited with the utmost patience and virtual silence for nearly twelve hours, and finally received the weekly call from her faraway husband at 10:00 P.M.

Pati told me that of all her tasks, the most difficult was helping local citizens to find their relatives in the United States. These migrants do not often have formal addresses, telephone numbers, or work arrangements through which they can be traced. She described the reluctance many have to seek help in the United States, even at the Mexican embassy or consulates. Due to their "mistrust of their government," they hesitate even to

approach their own nation's official contacts. The history of PRI dominance and corruption throughout all levels of Mexican government, as
well as the undocumented nature of many Mexicans' residence in the
United States, creates a situation charged with fears of detection. This
leads to isolation and greater vulnerability of migrants to unscrupulous
people of all kinds; thus most migrants are involved in "passage rituals"
and extensive personal networks which help them to negotiate the dangers and risks (Cebada Contreras 2000; Chávez 1992; Lomnitz 1977).

Pati's cases illustrate the absorption of these general risks by individual people. For example, one undocumented Mexican man, working in
construction after arriving in the United States about two weeks earlier,
fell and injured his spinal cord, becoming a quadriplegic. Lacking insur-
ance through workers' compensation, he and his parents face a lifetime of
hardship. Another man returned to Mexico to visit his children and wife,
then died in Mexico of lung disease related to an excavating job he had
held in the Southwest United States for twelve years. He had paid into the
Social Security system in the United States this entire time. Many families
are unaware of their rights or hesitate to press claims upon the intimidating foreign bureaucracy. These and many other cases of occupational risk
being absorbed by the bodies of vulnerable migrants in the United States
demonstrate the personal and physical costs of this massive phenomenon,
so often pathologized as an "invasion" from the south.

While sympathetic in all personal relations, Pati was also realistic and
pragmatic. She could be quite stern in describing those she judged to be
dishonest or manipulative. When I expressed sorrow over one case, she
shrugged and noted that the deceased person had virtually abandoned
their children and was not a very good parent anyway.

During May and June 2000, reports of vigilantism and other tragedies
befalling Mexican citizens in the United States were widely covered in the
Mexican press, bringing additional attention to DACGE and to the multiple and ongoing senses of loss of these migrants. Hundreds die along the
border every year from dehydration, hypothermia, drowning, violence
and other causes (Thompson 2000a). The always-political issues of migration and violence were raised in a particularly ugly fashion, showing
the racism of many in the United States, especially Arizona, just at the time
of the already-heated exchanges between the three top Mexican presidential candidates of that time. A campaign advertisement by one local candidate was dominated by a full-page photograph of the funeral of one of
the recent victims. A newspaper covering an exhibit in Mexico City on
racism in the United States reproduced only one photograph, which depicted a 1950s lynching of an African American.

Pati was not moved by the press coverage of vigilante killings in Arizona, saying that violence happened "all the time" and that the incidents were just being exaggerated for political reasons. She was angry that the media coverage led to many donations for these few cases, while the people affected by the many other cases that happened at other times languished for lack of money. She pointed out that plenty of violence in the United States involves Mexicans fighting each other: for example, next-door neighbors getting into drunken arguments. One afternoon I had just hung up from a call to a funeral director and shook my head sadly over the case of this particular death. Pati nodded in agreement, but then noted in a whisper that the deceased had been a very bad person, and, like all of his brothers, a violent drunk, and that his Mexican enemies had finally simply murdered him. Where I was often ready to blame situations vaguely on "life" in the United States, Pati tended to blame the persons themselves for getting into the situations in the first place.

Pati's work expanded across a wide and relatively unpredictable net of possibilities and contacts, human loss, and tragedy, yet in all dealings she acted with both professionalism and an easy, even merry, manner. Extremely humble, older than the others, and the only female staff member marked by her minimal use of makeup or revelatory clothing, she was treated in a friendly way by my two colleagues but was not close to them. Pati's daily work illustrated the multiple inscriptions of migration on the bodies of Mexican citizens. Her gentle but matter-of-fact manner of enacting the department's incredibly broad policy mandate suggests the importance of policy which is based on an open-ended approach to the definition of problems to be addressed by citizen appeal to the state, and a bureaucratic style which includes a consistent acknowledgment of the human dimensions of large-scale phenomena.

MIGRATION AS FLOOD

Migration between Mexico and the United States is heavily researched; its impacts on people are explored in many domains. Despite or perhaps because of this, it has been relatively unexplored as *itself* a transnational symbolic construct, one that is deployed within a specific and current, historically and politically determined economic context. Its very construction as a social and political "problem" is and has long been dependent upon the needs of powerful elites on both sides of the border, which marks debates over it indelibly with hypocrisy. Where for many in the United States migration is understood as a threatening tide of human beings, linked to crime, hyper-fertility, and drugs, the overriding meanings invoked in many Mexican contexts are those of loss and sorrow over these absent, vulnerable citizens and family members and their diverted potential. From both directions, then, there is a sense of a mass-scale phenomenon that has become naturalized and mythologized.

Besides finding work for themselves, migrants have also contributed to the careers of decades of scholars who theorize "strategies" and analyze statistical data about the rather obvious fact of a wage differential between the two countries. Organic conceptions of society have fostered the development of simplistic theories about the "push-pull factors" of migration or its function as a "safety valve" for the Mexican government, which reinforces images of the Mexican government's weakness. Notions of geographic isolation in rural Mexico, and their concomitant translation into racist imputations of a stagnant mental or intellectual quality among rural persons, are at least being challenged by migration realities and new scholarly theories. Beyond being "closed" or functioning in a push-pull migration mechanism, village life in Mexico is now acknowledged to include binational and multiply-territorialized identities, networks, and socioeconomically integrated transborder locations (Dresser 1993; Palerm and Urquiola 1993; Pries 2001; Rouse 1992). Judith Boruchoff (1998) notes the imagining of identity across transnational territory, as well as the irony that migrants' exit from their country brings them more attention from the government than they would have otherwise had. Concepts of space and time are now affected by agribusiness and "the hyperspaces of production," perhaps more so than by local geography, as in a migrant worker's reference to "when we were in tomatoes" (Kearney 1996, 118).

These new ideas are replacing more simplistic emphases, but their lack of linkage to more detailed political and theoretical analyses often leaves them oddly arid and rarefied. But at least the overwhelming evidence of labor mobility may challenge economic theory and thus the very construction and imputation of the relative weakness of laborers, as opposed to the image of dynamic, flowing capital.

The statistical tracking of migrants and their money by journalists, public policy officials, and scholars takes place within contexts of varying efforts not only to understand but to control migration. Statistics are symbolic in themselves, used to mediate the terms of the debate over the issue. For although data are faithfully reproduced about migration—noting, for example, that 340,000 people migrate each year, illegally and legally (Thompson 2000a), that between 2.5 and 7.5 million Mexican voters live in the United States (Quiñones 1998), or that 7 million Mexican-born legal and illegal immigrants live there (Falk 2001)—scholars are often obliged to admit that the nature of migration, with multiple crossings and recrossings and the need to escape official scrutiny, makes estimates unreliable. Moreover, the fact that the PRI-state would have an interest in downplaying migration statistics is left unexplored in citing official statistics. Unreliable statistics are carefully reproduced, maintaining the debate about migration at the level of a crisis of population movement and deferring or precluding analysis of the other issues behind the data. Rather than leading to a wider critique or to less-confident usage, the unreliability of the data itself becomes natural *to the migrants;* its quality as unreliable is implicitly due more to their existence as somewhat outside of the law rather than to any problems in the construction and gathering of the data. This may be similar to the way in which the "informal economy" has itself become a politically useful concept for the PRI, because it masks the causes of poverty (Connolly 1985).

The reasons for the need to escape scrutiny, and indeed the political and economic reasons which often lie behind the imperatives to leave Mexico, are ignored in the move instead to reproduce an image of the elusive migrant worker: this new, strategizing, rather cagey version of "the peasant." Deeper structural analysis of, for example, the connections between federal funding of education and federal subsidies for corporations in the United States is diverted instead to discussion of Mexicans "using up" the "limited" social services in a country of billionaires. An official, biologistic discourse in the U.S. Congress over migrants as a "flood" and a "population," which invokes fears of "species differences" (Chock 1998), and with implications of damage and cost to taxpayers, is deployed within the context of massive and highly militarized government power in the United States—power that is personally and intimately connected with enormous financial influence.

Stuart Gilman of the U.S. Office of Government Ethics described to me a plan his office was preparing for President Fox that linked migration to internal corruption in Mexico. He believes that if Fox can promise to account for some of the floods of money which enter Mexico from the World Bank and "disappear," then the United States may be able to move ahead on demilitarizing the border regions or opening them up further. Gilman's key assumption was that simply accounting for this lost money would lead to it actually being invested in the well digging and other rural projects for which it was intended, thus reducing migration. This series of almost magical linkages suggests the lengths officials are willing to go, on both sides of the border, to imagine that they are seriously addressing "the problem of migration."

The sense of migration as a threat to the United States is countered in Mexico by widespread popular and official assertions which point out the fundamental necessity of this labor to the U.S. economy. Many note the dangers for Mexican migrants in the United States and the hypocrisy of hostile U.S. officials, executives, and citizens, who mask both the exploitation of Mexican laborers and the appalling social inequalities within their rich political economy. The issue is also intrinsically connected to the U.S. war against Mexico. The 1846–1848 war was provoked intentionally by President James Polk in order to obtain California and New Mexico. The Republic of Mexico, two decades after winning its independence from Spain and ending centuries of colonial rule, was stripped of half of its territory by its northern neighbor in a war described as "unjust" on page two of second grade textbooks in Mexico (but not covered in the United States until seventh grade, and always referred to as "the Mexican War"). From the point of view of many Mexicans, the hypocrisy toward Mexican migrants has very deep roots.

After U.S. expropriation of Mexican land in 1848 made Mexicans "foreigners in their own land," the movement of people between the two territories was free; the borders were "scarcely enforced," and Mexican labor was heavily recruited by employers in the United States (Portes 1990, 162). The loss of Mexican lands and the fetishization of Mexican labor during the period of capitalist growth along the border from 1860 to 1880 were concomitant processes (Vélez-Ibáñez 1996). From 1880 to 1930, California landowners used Chinese, Japanese, and Mexican agricultural laborers, but by the 1920s Mexicans were the preferred group, in part because they were seen as more docile and were not seen as integrated into life in the United States (Guerin-Gonzáles 1993). The sense of loss over these citizens was evident in the activities of Mexican consuls in Los Angeles during the 1920s, which reflected their government's efforts "to maintain the allegiance of its sons and daughters . . . Mexico's most vital and strongest people, its most valuable natural resource . . . workers in their physical prime" (Monroy 1999, 63). Legislation to control the U.S. border, which dates from 1921 and 1924, introduced the term "illegal" immigrant amid news reports about the "excessive fecundity" of the Mexican "peons" (Reisler 1996, 30).

The numbers of people leaving Mexico increased after the 1910 Revolution and continued to be high during the subsequent years of civil violence and rural destruction from 1913 to 1929. Public rhetoric at the time by U.S. officials like Harry Laughlin, a "eugenics agent," focused on Mexican "unclean" practices, the threat to "moral fiber" and democracy, the risk that "Indian blood" would "pollute the nation's genetic purity," and the "economic menace" of cheap labor (Reisler 1996, 32–38). It was not until the post-Depression and post-World War II eras that the "traditional inflow" of Mexicans was criminalized (Portes 1990). The United States and Mexican governments arranged for legislation (the Bracero Act, in force from 1942 to 1964) to channel Mexican labor into the United States. The policy was designed to calm business fears over labor shortages during World War II and the Korean War and to facilitate the PRI's removal, or "selective exodus," of restive *campesinos* from the North Central region, which includes Guanajuato. The Sinarquistas had formed a political party in León, Guanajuato in 1937. This militant pro-Christian group (a forerunner to the PAN) was made up mostly of "peasants" and was later outlawed by the PRI (Cross and Sandos 1981; Kirk 1942; Meyer 1976). The corruption and other problems that existed within the program made illegal crossing a corollary of the Bracero program. As in earlier and later rhetoric, Mexican "wetbacks" were blamed for a variety of ills: "disease, labor strikes in agriculture, subversive and communist infiltration, border crimes, low retail sales in south Texas, and adverse effects on domestic labor" (García y Griego 1996, 58), at the same time as U.S. employers violated Mexican citizens' rights (ibid., 69; Cross and Sandos 1981, 46). The Mexican government thus "accepted conditions that turned its peasants into 'exportable merchandise'" (González 1972, 218). Although it was unilaterally ended by the United States in 1964 in response to racist fears, the Bracero program "institutionalized" migration as a way of rural life, and indeed, "laid the foundation of illegal Mexican migration to the U.S." (Cross and Sandos 1981, 35, 58).

While practices in the United States illustrate the economic and political construction of "the illegal immigrant" over time, migration must also be seen within the context of politics in Mexico. For these choices by citizens to leave have also constituted a rejection by Mexicans of the national government and even explicitly the PRI-state and its policies and practices. A scholar of migration who works in Guanajuato noted to me in early 2000 that the ruling party government was embarrassed and ashamed that they could not maintain the national employment needed by the population, so their official position had been to downplay or deny the high levels of migration. Migrants who responded to one survey expressed their love for Mexico and their desire to improve social services, education, and health there. They also wished for a change "with the overthrow of the party which is in power (PRI)" (INEGI 1992, 17).

Policies of agricultural reform dating from the 1930s have contributed to both internal and international migration, as land settlement patterns were altered in national modernization efforts which were undertaken without redress of existing social inequalities (Cross and Sandos 1981). The percentage of the Mexican population living in urban areas rose from 28 percent to 63 percent from 1910 to 1990 (Guerrero Reséndiz 1999). Perhaps as many as 10–30 percent of Mexicans living in the United States are "political" migrants: the middle class and university trained in whom Mexico has invested. These are people who "represent the contemporary failures of the Mexican state" (de la Garza and Szekely 1997).

The federal government has been obliged to recognize and acknowledge the large numbers of citizens who leave, while also facilitating the flow of money that these citizens wish to send home. One federal publication refers to lists of persons "authorized to receive donations," which include food, medicine, clothes, school buses, medical services, used clothes, computers, and automobiles. The thick document establishes legal controls over the giving and receipt of all forms of aid, further acknowledging its importance. Like the act of migration, *las remesas* (the remittances sent back home by migrants) that are applied by citizens in collective projects can be read as an indictment of government inability or unwillingness to address such serious local needs as potable water and paved roads. This money has caught the attention of the powerful and has contributed in part to a recasting of migration within political debates.

WEALTH AND SORROW

The U.S. focus on migration as a "border problem" was redirected by candidate Vicente Fox to the theme of migration as an enormous loss of potential for Mexico. In this rhetorical move, Fox again reappropriated the future from the PRI. He recast the future as emphatically Mexican, as a place for possibility that was in fact being undermined by the PRI. Fox's presidential campaign speeches, begun while still governor, specifically noted his plans to create more work in Mexico so that "our future children won't have to take that difficult trek north" (Corchado 1995). The sense of helping people so that future generations will not *have to* migrate deserves emphasis, as this meaning of migration, nearly a forced act and one that is part of an ongoing loss, challenges the commonsense views of Mexicans as clamoring to live in the United States. In playing upon a concept of human resources which would be respected within the international and domestic business community, he also invoked wider themes within Mexico of wealth, loss, sorrow, guilt, and responsibility.

Migration cast as a sorrowful loss in both the present and the future is resonant with the experiences of physical and everyday closeness in Mexican families and with the roughly 90 percent of the population in Mexico who are Catholics, whose Holy Week rituals elaborate the loss, suffering, and *misericordia* (compassion and mercy) of Good Friday much more intensively than the Easter Sunday meanings of joy and spiritual rebirth.

A common message from the state of Guanajuato to its migrant citizens is sadness over the loss of people as a collective resource. While the absence of those who have left Mexico is very openly mourned in personal expressions by citizens, it is also explicitly a focus of concerned messages emanating from the state government through such programs and services as Mi Comunidad, the periodical *Pa'l Norte*, and the thirty-two Casas Guanajuato in the United States. There is a tone of official solicitude regarding citizen experiences in crossing the border and living in the United States, expressed in texts and pamphlets. One brochure entitled "Don't lose your Mexican nationality" is published by the Foreign Relations Department, reflecting these concerns at the national level. It explains how to maintain Mexican nationality abroad, while another from the Mexican Government Program for the Prevention of Migration uses the intimate *tú* form for "you" and asserts, "your work and talent are needed here." Nevertheless, it acknowledges, if you are going, then here are migration tips, followed by useful telephone numbers, visa information, advice on not breaking laws, hints on whom to trust and on certain rights that apply. There are also invocations of guilt for those who stay away for a long time and pamphlets welcoming them home. The latter provide reentry information (bringing in a car to Mexico, understanding road signs and education laws, etc.) that they may not know about in terms of citizen rights and obligations.

More recent policies seek to address health problems of migrants, reflecting official awareness of the patterns of migration which include continuous crossing and recrossing of the border. For example, in 2002 the new DACGE director described state government efforts to prevent and treat illnesses among migrants while they are living in the United States, in part so that upon return to their families and homes, they do not infect relatives living in Guanajuato. A policy on identification cards, which can be used in both Mexico and the United States to facilitate the education of children, also reflected this pattern of ongoing, binational exchange.

Governor Juan Carlos Romero Hicks, in a speech at the Casa Guanajuato in Dallas, stressed both the importance of offering work in Guanajuato and the difficulties for migrants, including the sufferings of those who must negate their national origins. Invoking the pride of Guanajuatenses, he said that this loss was especially problematic, because "our state is the Cradle of Independence and one cannot understand modern Mexico without understanding what has occurred in the past century" (RedNet News 2000).

State discourse toward migrants continues to change. The new DACGE director noted to me that her message to migrants is that they should not fear losing their culture and their identity, but indeed that they should take up the challenge of integrating themselves more into the culture of the United States, recognizing its diversity as a source of positive strength in which they can share.

The sense of concern for the distant migrants, and of migration as a loss, were at the base of the Mi Comunidad program. The emotional foundation for the program was the guilt of those who had migrated, enacted as responsibility and capital invested back home. Essays written by Pati in several different editions of *Pa'l Norte* evoke the sad ones left behind and the poverty of the wife and the children, symbolized in repeated references to a meager diet of just coffee and beans. One edition of this publication carried a front cover photograph showing a young teenage boy near a humble dwelling; in the background is an older woman who could be his mother or grandmother, wearing a sling on her arm. In another, a man hands several fanned out, clearly visible dollar bills to a woman seated on a step outside of her Mexican home, depicted as such by its walls and grounds.

It has been primarily *males* who leave: for example 82.35 percent of migrants from the municipio of Yuriria in Guanajuato were male (*Primera Encuesta* 1996). This continues to be the case as of 2002, although some officials note verbally that more women and families may be accompanying these male migrants. Since most of those who leave are also *young* males, it is specifically their youthful male strength and potential which is being sapped away into the United States, there to be violently attacked or exploited by *gringos* or undermined by the luxuries that will tempt men to stay. The physical dangers they face, the marking of their bodies by injury, illness, and death, are the terrible symbols of the risk of leaving the family. Sorrow over migration loss also includes the fact that many of those who have left Mexico to work in the United States are *not* doing so well. This is one of the other messages that the state government paradoxically communicated, at the same time as it sought investment dollars from migrants. A poster on the office wall and many *Pa'l Norte* essays, which were accompanied by photographs showing barbed wire fences, dramatized the grave physical risks in crossing over (risks which one maquila investor told me were too great for women to bear), as well as the problems attendant on life in the United States.

Unfortunately, the vigilantism cases in the United States that occurred during the Mexican political campaign of 2000 are not unusual, and the dangers warned of are not exaggerated, neither are the discriminatory practices toward those who do survive the crossing. Migrants are also understood as vulnerable simply because the United States is considered to be such a violent place. Racism, widespread gun ownership, the death penalty, low spiritual values, fractured families, hours of television watching—these are qualities synonymous with U.S. culture for many people I met. All of these experiences and dangers may well add to migrants' glamour when they return to villages in November and December for holidays, weddings, and baptisms. In contrast, the superior culture and way of life in Mexico, and especially *la gente* (the people) and *tranquilidad* (the calm) in Guanajuato, are everywhere asserted.

Related to the general loss of the young male migrants is another sorrowful social fact: the women who remain (*las que se quedan*). State officials and documents refer to this population explicitly in trying to make men honor family commitments. The emotional appeals were framed in terms of guilt and responsibility regarding family members, but they were also overlain with tones of betrayal to village, Church, and nation. A radio program taped in Silao, Guanajuato, and broadcast in Texas and Illinois uses sounds of village life and the halting, poignant words taken from interviews with those who remain there, sometimes seeking information about relatives, as a part of regular transmissions which pitch the Mi Comunidad and other programs of DACGE. A sense of support for the abandoned wives, children, cousins, grandparents, in-laws, and siblings was explicitly invoked in appeals for funding for the maquilas, through the documentation itself and in meetings, verbal descriptions, and official letters. One investor's letter in the files reflected this sense of the state's discourse, stating that the investor's "only interest is in providing economic support to the poor families of this township." The program conferred another meaning to the investors' money, for Soco and Rosi's work was to safeguard that money, that symbol of responsibility. In a sense, the success of a maquila helped to ensure that the meaning of the investment as *atonement* was fulfilled.

DEFERRED POTENTIAL

The sorrowful loss from migration is resonant with powerful themes regarding fantastic wealth, diverted potential, and stolen or lost wealth. Many people I knew in Guanajuato noted the large amounts of money existing *outside* of Mexico but derived in various ways *from* Mexico and especially from the labor of its people. Expressing a common view was this quote from one man interviewed about violence against migrants: "The United States has a great economy built on the backs of Mexican workers" (Shaffer and Kammer 2000). Studying public policy in rural Mexico, Monique Nuijten (1995) noticed a belief among *ejidatarios* in Jalisco in regard to their own "lost land" and its validating, official corollary, a map said to prove the original ownership of this land. This "definitive *ejido* map" has been sought for years, at great expense, in government offices in Guadalajara and Mexico City, through bribes and other payments, and continues to form a central theme in all dealings with the federal agents who visit the area, but it may never have existed. There is a theme in Huasteca Potosina of "secret, regional wealth," in part to do with the value of the area itself as a "frontier" but also associated with "secret treasures" (Lomnitz-Adler 1992, 52). George Foster (1948) wrote about Mexican villagers who expressed beliefs about the "impossibility" of wealth; his 1965

notion of the "image of the limited good" must be read as an indictment
of corrupt or inept local officials.

As in the lung disease case, there is a sense of money that is wrongly
extracted and *kept*, money that has been earned and given by Mexicans,
but perhaps cannot be regained. One of the many legends of the city of
Guanajuato, "In the Days When Our Miners Earned a Lot of Money,"
lingers on the costly details of the clothes of miners and their girlfriends,
describing their strolls on Sunday and their shopping sprees, and the
boom of silver from the Valenciana mine, thought to extend two-thirds of
the way around the world (*Leyendas* n.d., 48).

Lost, legendary, or stolen wealth is linked with the loss of male virility
in the fact of migration, in that the real potential within Mexico has been
diverted, stolen, or otherwise deferred. The externality of wealth, the absence of the young men who have migrated, and the enrichment of others
at the expense of Mexicans are embraced in a still wider theme. The great
wealth of Mexico is seen by many citizens as robbed or sapped by the government, specifically the PRI, or as stolen by outsiders, as in the U.S. appropriation of Mexican territory. In a kind of postcolonial twist on the
notion of Utopia in the New World, fabulous wealth is understood to have
been spirited away to *el extranjero* (abroad), usually to Switzerland. In particular, petroleum wealth is thought to have been stolen by the wealthy or
by the ruling party. The disputes over Mexican oil between bankers, U.S.
senators, and the Mexican government from 1917 to 1922 made oil "the
emblem of Mexican economic nationalism" (Hall 1995, 180). Petroleum remains an important symbol, underlined by the rapidity with which Fox
abandoned his unpopular plan to privatize the oil industry. In other examples, a friend told me: "In Mexico, we have so many riches that we
don't always even bother to take care of them," describing a rare books
collection that has only recently begun to be catalogued. These are not just
quaint beliefs; they mark many discussions. For example, a U.S. geologist
once noted to me that Mexico was sitting on "oceans" of oil but didn't
know how to take advantage of it, and Robert, the garment industry dealer
mentioned in chapter 2, dreamed of the money to be made from the wealth
of piles of textiles and "off-price garments sitting on the floors of ware-
houses all over Mexico." Even financial documents capture this wild sense
when they note the "economic hemorrhaging" of countries like Mexico
that have a strong state role in the economy (Rose 2000).[1]

In the absence of this lost or stolen wealth, the resulting poverty, in-
equity, and continuing grave problems with water, education, and so forth
are there for all to plainly see; time will tell the details of how the thefts occurred. This theme may be related to the contexts of seemingly arbitrary
and often whimsically personal government and PRI-state practices within

Mexico. Of post-Soviet Russia, Nancy Ries writes that "in the absence of reliable, coherent and accessible state arbitration in business matters, the mafia are also, of course, the primary suppliers of the key 'services' of mediation, compensation and conflict resolution" (2002, 290). In such a setting, "money is the fetishized agent of social decay," and myths about its magical properties flourish in narratives about overnight wealth, swindles, morality, and redemption. She theorizes that "people's yearning for a distinct, strong and rationalized state apparatus" in part drives these narratives. In Mexico, perhaps the arbitrary and corrupt practices of government are expressed and understood through practices and beliefs which have eluded outside analysis. But ideas about fabulous wealth also constitute a relatively accurate guess about the manipulations of elites both within and outside of Mexico. For example, *ejidatarios* who met with federal agricultural agency officials listened to the new policies being described, but also repeatedly brought up their own personal loans from banks (Nuijten 1995). Although Nuijten does not analyze this, it is clear that the different levels of authority in these citizens' lives are not just being confused: they *are in fact* conflated. From their point of view, the government *truly is* all-pervasive, and the agricultural official may well know about the status of a given bank loan. In fact, a water pump did miraculously appear at the door of one man who had written directly to the President of the Republic asking for help after he had waited months and appealed to many lower level officials at various agencies and banks for "justice" in his application for a loan (Arce 1989).[2]

RECASTING LOSS

The absence of wealth and of male sexual potency, the loss and redirecting of these resources to the gain of others—gain which rightfully belongs to the nation of Mexico, to its women, and to parents who are longing for grandchildren—all of these powerful meanings are fused in migration. This delicate issue was shrewdly incorporated into a jobs policy like Fox's Mi Comunidad program. As noted, migration from Guanajuato is among the highest of all the states of Mexico. Migrants from Guanajuato have made up about 16.2 percent of the national total (INEGI 1992). Documents from a 1999 seminar noted that about two million Guanajuatenses are in the United States. The Mi Comunidad policy moved the debate beyond the mere fact and data of migration and sought to demonstrate a pragmatic government response to the many causes and effects associated with it, at the same time allowing pointed political critiques of the PRI.

The dire poverty, lack of job opportunities, and low wages persisting in the rural areas of Mexico are assumed to be the primary reasons behind the high numbers of migration; these conditions were blamed on the PRI time and time again by candidate Fox, who brought up the irrefutable point that in seventy years, little had improved or changed on this score, thus, change was necessary. As president, Fox moved on to create still another meaning of migration: "No more talking about migration as a problem. From now on, we will make migration an opportunity for the future. We are going to make sure that migration is an asset for both our countries" (Thompson 2001). This quote is from a speech in which Fox promised to "open Mexico to greater flows of investment," drawing cheers from his corporate audience.

The Mi Comunidad program would not have existed without the geographic and economic fact of the behemoth to the north, with its beckoning jobs and dollars and its intimidating but not impenetrable borders. It was based upon a belief that those who have left to make a better life for themselves by crossing into the United States have an obligation to send something back not just to their own families, but to their countrymen, their *paisanos:* in this case, to try and create work and a better life in Mexico so that others will not have to leave, as they did. A belief in the connection between wealth and concurrent responsibility was manifest in many ways. One day we met with a group of artisans in the town of Celaya that expected direct support from migrants in the form of funding for their activities, and as contacts to help sell their ceramics, embroidery, and other goods in the United States. Many of the citizens who came to see Pati also expressed hope in making direct appeals to unknown Guanajuatenses abroad for money for schooling and other necessities. Fueling the belief in migrant responsibility are data about the money which they send home, fantastic amounts now being tracked by governments, scholars, and journalists. Remittances to Mexico are said to total about U.S.$8 billion per year (Weiner 2001); it is estimated that U.S.$1 billion enters Guanajuato each year (*Migration News* 2000). Total migrant remittances are often cited as third, after oil and tourism, in the national sources of income (Weiner 2001), although maquila revenues are also listed as third (Kopinak 1996) and are given as U.S.$10 billion per year (Lindquist 2001).

Remittances have long been used by Mexicans to improve their own housing and to buy land, livestock, or consumer goods (Reichert 1981).[3] More recently, they are a major component of Mexican rural village economies—being used for roads, schools, and other infrastructure projects—signalling possibilities for empowerment among citizens and offsetting dissatisfaction with federal government inaction. There are other examples of state-citizen partnerships like the Mi Comunidad program, for example, Tres Por Uno (three for one), a state program in Zacatecas which matches remittances with government grants, and projects in Guerrero initiated by migrants who later approached the government for assistance (Boruchoff 1998). In Guanajuato, such investments in infrastructure were growing more common by 2002.

Soliciting support for the Mi Comunidad program through radio and print media, the state government demanded that its migrants acknowledge their multiple responsibilities, which they have left behind, by sharing their wealth. There was also a pragmatic appeal to the program: in March 1996 Fox, a former Coca-Cola executive, told an audience in Dallas that a binational foundation to create jobs in Mexico would be important: "Because the money you invest today, you're going to be saving tomorrow" (Trejo 1996). This reference could be to the cost to U.S. taxpayers of social services used by immigrants—which many U.S. citizens resent—or to the money which migrants send home to support family members. Either meaning would make sense, given the likely diversity of Fox's audience.

Another common reference was to the "dream" (sueño) of creating the businesses. Since references in Pa'l Norte referred to the migrants as pursuing "the American dream," this usage may have been an intentional recasting of this notion of a dream, only in the reverse direction. A 1999 internal office document entitled "Primer Seminario" notes that "The DACGE office promotes through radio, TV, and information bulletins the reality, life, and dreams of our countrymen who are participating in the development of Guanajuato." In the government movie about the program, investors and managers also refer to the maquilas in terms of realizing a dream. According to one study of migrants, there is a common wish to return to Mexico, where it is "still" seen as possible to run one's own business (Rouse 1992).

Through the program, the abandonment of family, state, and country was understood and indeed forgiven. There was a dual recognition: that the act of leaving has been painful for the migrants and that it was in fact an act of entrepreneurship which could now be safely redirected back home. During the presidential campaign, these phrases also constituted a way of reaching out to key voters. Not only do the migrants return home to vote in great numbers, they also influence family members' votes, one businessman told me. As election day drew nearer, there was great anxiety, fanned by news coverage, about the possibility that the PRI had intentionally limited the number of voting booths installed at border locations for migrants in order to make it more difficult for Fox supporters to vote.

This recasting of the sorrowful and even shameful phenomenon of migration as instead a sign of latent entrepreneurship was an important aspect of the Mi Comunidad program. In redirecting the dreams away from the United States and back to Mexico, the program communicated to migrants that they were still valued at home, that they were still responsible men, and that Mexico was changing into the kind of country that would appreciate them and all their hard work. There was an implication that this had not occurred under a PRI-controlled government and does not occur in the United States. In fact, President Fox has referred to the Mexicans working in the United States and sending money home to Mexico as "heroes" (Weiner 2001).

"Bureaucratic discourse" produces *clients;* that is, it produces "individuals whose subjectivity is molded and shaped by the parameters of the discourse" (Ferguson 1984, 136). At the managerial level of the program, the state government's "clients" were produced as investors and incipient entrepreneurs, as people with a future. One *Pa'l Norte* editorial proclaimed the attractiveness of Guanajuato as a site for investment "for those who dream of being reintegrated into the social and economic life of their country, participating as true businessmen." The references to "investment" in Mexico, and to the investors as "entrepreneurs," projected a hopeful future as against the sorrowful losses due to migration. This business finance terminology also drew attention to the role of the men in the program as valuable, financial, and foundational. As a businessman himself, el Licenciado played a highly visible and significant role in the initial stages of developing each maquila—visiting the Casas Guanajuato or other social gathering sites for migrants in the United States to describe the program and develop investment interest. Copies of *Pa'l Norte* were also distributed to these locations, and every issue mentioned maquilas, remittances, and home communities. El Licenciado's presence as a successful man and government official was symbolic of the promise of the program during these early stages of attracting investment.[4]

As a public action—turning the laments for the lost into a part of a success story in Mexico, a dream come true—the policy has been a very powerful gesture by Fox and the PAN. A policy designed to help the women left behind or to prevent new migrations, through the provision of work financed by those who have already left and who feel great sadness and guilt over their choices, is on paper a wonderfully symmetric and highly symbolic creation.

FROM PAPER TO PRACTICE

Rosi pointed a thumb toward el Licenciado's office and shrugged with a certain resignation when I asked her who it had been, Vicente Fox or el Licenciado, who had taken the original notion of job creation in the program and specifically formed it into one of maquila jobs in particular. "I think it was . . . him," she said somewhat accusingly. By this time in our relationship, she knew of my doubts about the way in which the women workers had been incorporated into the program, which might explain her accusatory tone toward the boss. Her evasive replies on this and other occasions never really addressed the details regarding gender and migration within the program. For example, in the planning stages, were other kinds of jobs considered?

The work provided by the program was said to be originally aimed at reducing migration: preventing the dreaded loss of young males: a shame for the nation. But the jobs created have been in textile maquilas, a form of industry which tends to provide exploitative and insecure work. Given the wide discussion and assumptions about vast amounts of money to be made in the United States, these low-paying, low-skill, low-autonomy, structurally "female" jobs (Gherardi 1995) do not make the maquilas a sufficiently attractive alternative to migration, although more men are now working in the maquilas along the U.S.–Mexico border (these factories are discussed in chapter 6). All of the young men will still leave rural areas by the age of seventeen or eighteen, as one investor told me, himself noting that the maquilas do not pay well.

Rosi affirmed that no one had ever done a study or survey to see if the program actually was having an impact on migration, then added that nothing could affect that anyway as it was an unchanging part of the culture. She then added in an offhanded manner that this was just a "secondary goal" of the program anyway, but other documents had clearly placed it at the forefront as a goal. As with many other practices, asides, deferrals and evasions, I wondered how to reconcile what seemed to me to be clearly contradictory program goals. Had the goal of "preventing migration" become narrowed in practice to a small pool: the young, usually male relatives of the maquila investors and jefes who had the jobs of supervising the female workers?

The provision of work was increasingly being described as targeted at the women left behind, a subtle shift in phraseology that showed an awareness that migration of young men was continuing regardless of the program. Rather than an act of prevention and assistance by the older men who long ago left for the United States, investment in the program was being solicited more broadly, and expected as a responsibility of the young men who have left behind young wives and children. However, investment was still elicited as "entrepreneurship." What these forms of program rationale had in common was that they specifically valorized men, no matter what the men did. Males leave: that should be prevented by creating jobs. Males continue to leave: that must be admitted, but also lauded as a positive virtue, presented as a sign of good business sense, and ma-

nipulated to solicit funds for the program. The flattering of men as potential investors was of a piece with the other ways in which male contributions to the Mi Comunidad program were positively valued, appreciated,
nurtured. As program policy shifted from seeking to prevent migration,
no doubt a politically phrased goal to begin with, to "attracting investment," it quietly acknowledged that migration was ongoing. Migration
had moved into an area beyond direct resolution by any one policy, and
other endemic problems in Guanajuato and Mexico rushed in to fill the
void.

Perhaps inevitably, the Mi Comunidad program bore the birthmarks of
its complex contexts. As part of Fox's presidential campaign, said to have
begun as soon as he was elected governor of Guanajuato, the program enabled an attack on the PRI and an advance of "Guanajuato." It claimed to
be about jobs, migration, the need for entrepreneurs, and abandoned families: addressing a myriad of overwhelming, and often politically charged,
social and economic needs which are interwoven in ways that may preclude resolution through any one plan.

Migration scholar Jorge Isauro Rionda told me in an interview that migration from Guanajuato had become less permanent; he also noted that
remittances were lower because entire families were actually going along.
He argues that migration is not a question of *labor* but of *culture*—the latter word used in a kind of short-term, instrumental or contingent sense
which he illustrated with the example of people leaving for short periods
in order to get money to start a business or to enable them to get married.
Rosi asserted that migration is "something of our culture that we cannot
change," suggesting a meaning of culture as something inevitable, inherent, and outside of time. She has also described it as a "tradition" among
many people. These comments illustrate some of the perspectives on the
reasons for migration and its situatedness within rural communities that
continue to resist outside analysis. Reflecting the entrenched nature of
these issues and in an odd kind of exculpation of Oscar Lewis, migration
was assumed at a conference we attended on gender and rural poverty to
be a natural part of the life cycle for both men and women. The coordinator of the workshop wrote on a chalkboard simply *migra* (in this case, "he
migrates") under the column titled "Juan" in her comparative example of
the gender differences in the countryside. One participant noted that migration was a "traditional cycle." Thus it is that politically and economi-
cally influenced choices and facts come to be seen as natural.

SUMMARY

Sorrow and loss over the spirited-away wealth and virility of Mexico were
powerful undercurrents in the discourse of the Mi Comunidad program,

as were the legendary ability of Mexicans to work hard, combined with visions of the mythic proportions of money thought to be available in the United States. These meanings of migration provided important symbolic and emotional bases for the program: of sorrow, loss, guilt, and responsibility, coupled with possibility, bright futures, entrepreneurial potential, and intense hope. They were an important source for the program directors and el Licenciado to draw upon in describing the program and their own role in it to outsiders and to potential investors. Emotions were fused with the power of state discourse. Program meanings were permeated by family imagery: the women and children abandoned by migrants, and the family of fellow citizens of Guanajuato and *paisanos* who, though far apart geographically, can be reconnected through the program. Indeed, as noted, the program was originally called Mi Familia.

Using this evocative imagery and other practices, the state government intervened in the local community and in the family lives of its participants as if it were another family member. Program representatives recast the meanings of the program in accord with the changing situations in which they found themselves. The family rhetoric softened government entry into the private lives of citizens caught up in the painful and even tragic processes surrounding the phenomenon of migration. In the form taken by Pati's job, shaped by the context of social welfare, the entry was welcome and requested by the citizens, who were often frightened and worried about confusing official forms and long-absent family members. In the case of the Mi Comunidad program, the entry had multiple effects, shaped by the nature of work in the international global assembly industry, in this case in textile maquilas.

CHAPTER 6

Work in Textile Maquilas

In the first month of my work in the office, a report about the maquilas of the Mi Comunidad program arrived. It summarized the research of a group affiliated with a Monterrey-based institute. Soco was excited about it; in her usual optimistic way, she smiled and winked confidentially, assuring me that they would seek a grant very soon, maybe from the Ford Foundation, in order to pay for a program proposed by the research team. Neither of the directors had time to read the report, but it was photocopied and passed out; an intern and I read it, and later discussed it with Soco and Rosi.

The research group proposed to address issues of quality in a 98,000 peso per month (about U.S.$9,600), eighteen-month project which was otherwise unspecified and unelaborated. It cited problems such as lack of work, unmotivated workers, and low quality of finished products in six of the ten maquilas visited. The written text and photographs noted conditions such as dangerous and illegal lighting and electricity, bad smells, poor or improvised bathrooms, with some lacking water, and so forth. Organizing the program files, I had already noticed numerous quality reports and evaluations of the program conducted over the years that uncovered many different kinds of serious problems. A 1999 study of six maquilas cited problems with poor lighting and ventilation, poor order and cleanliness, slow line movement, and poor use of music. Four lacked a "quality system." In one report, even the higher levels of authority were criticized: only one maquila was said to have a supervisor in the areas of production and/or quality who was deemed "very good," the others "lacked ability," and one was judged "inadequate."

The newest report did not present new or unusual data. Yet Soco did not seem at all worried: indeed she was pleased. Official data about the program and a discourse on "quality" were just two aspects of everyday practice which were marked with such complexity and ambivalence. Before reviewing these practices, some context on the wider maquila industry is needed.

TEXTILE MAQUILAS

The Mi Comunidad program bore the problems, risks, and contradictions which mark wider policies in the state of Guanajuato that are designed, as in the rest of Mexico and throughout the world, to attract foreign investment and spur jobs in the assembly industry. These policies are attended by debates about the multiple effects of globalization, raising issues which have no easy or straightforward answer, and reflecting widely differing scholarly positions and macro/micro levels of analysis. A brief review of maquila history and the major issues regarding labor, gender, the environment, public policy, and capitalist growth is useful in contextualizing the Mi Comunidad program, which is engaged in a relatively small-scale version of this industry type but which is marked by several crucial differences. The program's maquilas are Mexican-owned, state-subsidized, and located in the interior of the country; and they are run on a far smaller and far less organized scale than those along the border. While all of the program's factories produce textiles only, those of the border areas are more diversified.

Mexico has over 3,600 maquilas, which, as noted in chapter 5, generate U.S.$10 billion in revenue and employ 1.3 million workers. This industry sector accounts for 45–50 percent of Mexico's total exports (Lindquist 2001; *Wall Street Journal*, 6 November 2000). More than 50 percent of all maquila plants are located in six border cities (Ramirez 2000). Although only about 20 percent of all maquilas are in the interior of the country, they are spread widely throughout it. Of Mexico's thirty-one states (plus the Distrito Federal of Mexico City), maquilas are located in twenty-six (Kamel and Hoffman 1999; Wilson 1992).

The concentration along the border is due to patterns in legislation. Mexico's 1965 Border Industrialization Program (BIP) was initiated to create work for newly disenfranchised men in the border region when the United States unilaterally ended its Bracero, or "day labor," law. BIP provisions were expanded to the nonborder regions of Mexico by 1971, but maquila development in the interior has not been widely considered a success; transportation, repair, and personnel problems are reported, and most of the work is in subcontracting (Sklair 1993, 146). By 1994, there were 2,065 factories in Mexico employing 579,519 workers (Kopinak 1996); between 1993 and 1999, the number of factories grew from 2,405 to 4,235 (*Mexico Business Monthly* 1999). Many non-maquilas have converted to this status, suggesting that *maquilization* may be about a *social* type of industry in terms of production and labor organization rather than a set of customs rules (Kopinak 1996).

The laws governing maquilas changed in January 2001 under provisions of the North America Free Trade Agreement (NAFTA). The duty free importation will now apply only to NAFTA countries; otherwise, a 25 percent tariff will apply. Corporate income taxes are being implemented, to the alarm of business executives (Lindquist 2001; *Wall Street Journal*, 6 November 2000). Foreign ownership (estimated at about 55–60 percent of the total) of maquilas is dominated by U.S. transnational corporations (TNCs), which have "traditionally accounted for 90% of maquila investment" (Sklair 1993, 75).

The sectoral composition of the industry in 1998 was divided among garment assembly (28 percent), transportation equipment (7 percent), and electric and electronic equipment and materials (20 percent), with the remainder including general manufacturing, assembly of furniture and toys, chemical products manufacture, and others (Kamel and Hoffman 1999, 19). The number of plants in the apparel sector declined by 10 percent between 1979 and 1985, while transport equipment and electronics grew rapidly (Sklair 1993, 70), which some analysts see as a relatively hopeful change if it indicates a transition to higher skilled work.

Economic analysis of maquilas often reflects positions on the virtues of the free market. For many economists at the macro levels of analysis (nation-state, regional, or global), attracting investment and spurring job growth is an unalloyed good, even with "the high, albeit necessary, price" of economic "transition" (Cárdenas Sánchez 1998). Business and industry publications assert that the maquila industry is shifting from a dependence on cheap labor to an emphasis on skills and "second-generation manufacturing with all the technical attributes of modern industry, including research and design capability" (Linquist 2001, 26). In describing the use of assembly factories to guide the "Asian Tiger economies" to relative strength in the world economy, Wilson notes that the Mexican political economy does have some factors that would allow it to benefit from directing this form of industry as a "stepping stone" toward full, export-led industrialization. She writes that maquilas should be seen as "a transitory measure—by choice and necessity—in an export-led strategy that can lead to a comparative advantage beyond that of cheap labor" (1992, 35) and notes how successfully Mexicans have adapted to new ideas of "flexibility" in manufacturing. She stresses the importance of local controls and networks, and the role of policy to encourage the use of domestic inputs, but in Mexico the usage is still lower than planners had hoped, estimated at about 3.2 percent (Lindquist 2001, 24).

Negative effects of TNC assembly work are also evident at the macro level, especially for women. This work, particularly in labor-intensive textile plants, tends to be both exploitative of the particular and cross-cultural forms of female social vulnerability (Fernández Kelly 1983; Pearson 1986) and associated with "clandestinity" or nonregulation (Wilson 1991). Contrary to the policy intent of BIP, in the early decades the border maquilas provided work mostly for young single women, a particularly vulnerable group, and, far from offering autonomy, offered "wages and benefits that keep women only a step removed from the circumstances that can lead to prostitution" (Fernández Kelly 1983, 143). The total maquila workforce is now comprised of about 60 percent females and 40 percent males (Ramirez 2000). Debates are ongoing, especially among feminist scholars and economists, about maquila work, wages, and gender; these are carefully reviewed by Leslie Sklair (1993). Some suggest that such work may contribute positively to the entry of rural Mexican females into the formerly male world of "the proletariat" (Wilson 1992). However, the powerful, virtually all-female telephone operators union has long been a force in Mexican labor, and women already have formed a part of labor movements in the education sector (Cook 1996; Cortina 1989; Dubbs 1996; Vaughan 1990).

If Mexico is indeed seeing trends toward more highly skilled work in maquilas, it remains important to track the relative presence of females in these better jobs. It is also important to ensure that theoretical assumptions about the value and definition of "female autonomy" are made explicit within a broad context which takes account of other possible meanings and values.

At the macro level, evidence also exists of the high infrastructural demands and massive environmental damage caused by the border maquilas (Peña 1997). The future potential and local commitments of such plants is also an issue: they have been called "runaway shops" (Fernández Kelly 1983) because of their cheap, temporary construction, and as new regulations and responsibilities loom in Mexico, the specter of "maquila flight" is invoked. Regarding the future, an industry executive warns grimly: "Delphi, as new investment is considered, will look at whatever location best suits our business. Whether that will be Mexico or not will depend on the Fox administration's approach" (Lindquist 2001, 26). Leslie Sklair, in one of the most thorough and careful reviews of the industry and literature, concludes that the promise of maquila growth has not worked out as hoped, and that "Mexico is better off without it" (1993, 238).

For those at the micro levels of analysis, such as sociologists, activists, and journalists, specific cases reveal a variety of contradictory, but mostly negative, impacts on workers within the maquilas. Research has focused on the border plants, drawing attention to unsafe, toxic, and illegal work conditions, exploitative wages, pregnancy tests of workers, and widespread environmental destruction, but also noting some resistance and empowerment among workers (Kopinak 1996; Peña 1997; Tiano 1994; Tiano and Fiala 1991). The prolonged series of incidents of brutal and sexualized violence against female workers in Ciudad Juárez, and the poor living conditions and water scarcity among those who live near the maquilas of the border, are also deplored in the press and by religious groups, unions, and activists (Kamel and Hoffman 1999). Attention is being drawn to the huge profits of foreign corporations and executives, including former U.S. Secretary of the Treasury Paul O'Neill, who in 1999 exercised U.S.$33 million in stock options besides his $3 million salary at Alcoa, which runs a plant in Acuña at which workers were being limited to three sheets of toilet paper on trips to the bathroom (Dillon 2001).

Modern-day conditions evoke comparison with nineteenth century industrialization. There were 853 cotton textile shops in Guanajuato in 1876; by 1910, most urban and rural weavers were replaced by cotton mills that exhibited the harsh conditions associated with early capitalism in Europe and the United States (Anderson 1976). Cotton and textile industry protections of the mid-nineteenth century were dropped in the shift toward free market ideas; the new mills were run like colonial haciendas and included moral supervision, paternalism, and near servitude, as well as chapels and schools (Keremetsis 1973, 15, 197–98). Employees protested deductions from pay for equipment breakage and debts at the company stores, and resented their wages, work schedules, and the ideology of the period which stressed their "vices" of violence, laziness, and heavy drinking (Anderson 1976; French 1996). The Porfiriato, or era of President Porfirio Díaz (1876–1910), was characterized by massive industrialization and forced removal of peasants from their land. It was also marked by harsh measures against labor and an emphasis on moral virtues, especially for women. Like the mining strikes from 1873 to 1877 and incidents of railroad employee activism, protests by textile workers in Mexico formed a part of the series of crises and armed repression which culminated in the 1910 Revolution.

Many of the problems noted in quality reports about the Mi Comunidad program's maquilas and found in the border maquilas evoke these earlier, repressive times. Indeed, activist-scholar Devon Peña (1997) asserts that if Henry Ford were alive today, he would be running a maquila, but Mexican historian Javier Villareal Lozano avers: "A hundred years ago, U.S. employers would have been ashamed of these conditions. Henry Ford's workers living in cardboard boxes? He'd never have tolerated it" (quoted in Dillon 2001, A3). In the midst of globalization, the relative position and strength of unskilled or semiskilled laborers in Mexico, as in the rest of the world, is far from clear. Active cross-border organizing and protests among workers continue (Dubbs 1996; Kamel and Hoffman 1999;

Peña 1997; Sklair 1993), but the historically close relations between the PRI-state and organized labor in Mexico, the complexities of labor regulations and local enforcement, and the power of entrenched domestic and foreign capital combine to hinder domestic labor reforms and their enforcement in Mexico. Workers in the Alcoa plant noted above have no chance of forming a union because the local mayor gave "a stake" in the industrial parks to a top labor official (Dillon 2001). In 1989, only 1 percent and in 1992 only 30 percent of inspected maquilas were complying with Mexican regulations regarding occupational hazards, sexual harassment, wages, and other worker protections (Peña 1997, 301). Even if this increase is based on real improvements rather than changes in statistics-keeping, the low level of compliance is striking.

In one sense, the Mi Comunidad program was in accord with the policy prescriptions offered by development planners and those who stress the potential benefits of such work for the country as a whole. Rural areas in many developing economies have been targeted for local initiatives that will create work and thus reduce the loss of temporary labor migrants (Grindle 1988). These losses in Mexico have created isolated villages with "frozen" economies that function primarily as rest, recreation, retirement, and reproduction centers for future migrants (Mines 1981; Reichert 1981). The increasing dependence of rural areas on migrant income or on opportunities outside of the local area has been seen as a problem which can be solved by—among many other, preferable plans—the use of maquila programs as part of a strategy of industrial decentralization (Grindle 1988, 71–75). However, according to Merilee Grindle and others, the costs of the particular choice of maquilas may outweigh the benefits, thus planners must be careful when using such a strategy. She identifies flexibility, responsiveness, and participation as key advantages of local initiatives, which are offset by the fragility of these local forms of business. She argues that such projects should entail very low risk for the people involved locally (ibid., 135).

Any social goal of job growth is clearly complicated by the types of jobs created, the scale of the businesses fostered, the industry structure in which they exist, and the multiple and often unpredictable impacts for both the short and long term at local, national, and regional levels. The Mi Comunidad program illustrates these many levels of complexity, reflecting the wider ambivalence of the maquila industry.

SUMMARY

Problems within the Mi Comunidad program suggest that the issue of scale will be only one of many that are important for the survival of such factories. In a market dominated by huge, highly sophisticated transnational corporations, small factories like those of the program may remain permanently involved in subcontracting work. But if they survive and co-operate with each other, it is possible that the managers of these kinds of factories may at least be more responsive to worker complaints than the border plants have been, if their small size and vulnerability translates into a sense of mutual need between labor and management. Clearly the issues are complex, and perspectives vary widely. The director at a state government science and technology agency in Guanajuato quietly and matter-of-factly dismissed the Mi Comunidad program as not creating good, long-term, high-skilled jobs in comparison to his agency, which was seeking to develop local, higher-skilled jobs in the computer industry. So-cial workers from the rural areas of Northeast Guanajuato also dismissed maquila work of any kind, saying it was always exploitative. The impli-cations reach far beyond the state of Guanajuato. A "senior official" has stated of Mexico: "We don't really have an industrial policy apart from promoting *maquiladoras*" (*Economist* 2000).

Obviously in this case, I cannot offer a resolution of these issues even from my attempted stance between micro and macro levels. The strength of small and medium-sized businesses, and the fostering of entrepre-neurship, *are* important projects within the context of the Mexican politi-cal economy, given the patterns of federal control of large-scale businesses, even though the latter have not been formally co-opted into the PRI as part of the party's official "sectors" of society. Where the "neocorporatist" rul-ing party has permeated so many domains of social life, the business sec-tor has the potential to challenge established power. If the maquilas such as those of the Mi Comunidad program were to remain on a small, labor-intensive scale in the textile industry, retain local managers and owners, and avoid the most serious violations of the border regions, they may well create some long-term value for local communities as a transitional job. The government maquilas of Guanajuato enabled workers to learn some skills, earn some money, and perhaps gain more self-esteem than has been possible within other constraints on their lives, but based on my own lim-ited observations, the low skill, low pay, and dead-end aspects of these jobs are not very promising for individuals hoping to gain additional skills and responsibilities.

Whether programs like Mi Comunidad end up functioning as a kind of in-country vocational training for women who are destined anyway for the U.S. labor market (or for the border maquilas) remains to be seen. These wider issues will have to be explored through further research into the specific, local contexts and impacts on women of the interior maquilas; I can only indicate the complexities of this one case and the way in which these wider issues have an impact on the very practices within this rela-tively small-scale job creation project.

The program directors were not purveyors of Taylorist efficiency in their own daily practices and use of statistics, but they did rely on problematic, traditional labor-management models, and they facilitated entry into an exploitative industry sector: the international assembly industry in textiles. But beyond the ambivalence of maquilas and migration, beyond party politics, deeper than the need for hope and personal mobility, there was a space inside the family of the program where shame and contradiction could not be resolved. As a category, the female workers in the maquilas were dismissed in many ways, which are important to review.

PART III

Deferrals and Asides

CHAPTER 7

Las Muchachas

In the "substitution project" of Mexican national policy, the future is "the place of progress," wrote Bonfil Batalla (1996). In the case of the Mi Comunidad program, the state government was the intended substitute *both* for absent family members and for the "free market." A wide wake of problems attributable to migration has been identified in Guanajuato; they have become the province of government action and planning at many levels. The sweeping mission of the Office of Support to Guanajuatense Communities Abroad (DACGE) has translated into the provision of bureaucratic, medical, legal, health, educational, economic, and social services to address the complex and often self-contradictory needs faced by migrants and their families. Issues once handled from within a family become subject to state policy and intervention, while the operations of business and government have become permeated with family images, metaphors, and practices. Individual dreams become linked with government power and class mobility, investment becomes emotional. Distinctions between different domains of social life grow problematic in such a case. Authors have described the murkiness and "magic" of the state (Coronil 1997; Nelson 1999; Taussig 1997); this case seems to suggest a metaphor of reciprocity regarding these complex relations.[1]

As sites for this crucial intersection, the workplaces of the program attested to the intertwined nature of family, government, home, and work. Numerous theoretical perspectives could be marshaled to analyze these intersections. Most of these perspectives presume important, but often reified, abstractions such as the state, capital, and patriarchy. I have used the Mi Comunidad case to suggest the importance of also analyzing these abstractions as enacted by living persons who are engaged in complex, multiple roles and identities. But my own emphasis on embodied knowledge and everyday practice as keys to understanding the state cannot be applied in a close examination of one crucial group—the working women, or las muchachas, of the program.

The dismissiveness toward these women, through program discourse and practice, was linked to the precise reified category which I risk reproducing here: "las muchachas" (the girls). Their lives, the impacts of work in the maquilas upon them, and other details were not my research focus. Moreover, although I was able to speak with a few of these women, our conversations were always limited in time and by the conditions of vigilance under which they worked, as well as by my evident connection to the state government. Many excellent works provide insights from the inside of maquilas and factories (Fernández Kelly 1983; Ong 1987; and Peña 1997 among them). I look forward to more research on women impacted by the movement of maquilas more deeply into Mexico's interior.

The lived experiences of rural, low-income women within families, villages, workplaces, and the global economy are almost always presumed to tend toward "marginality." But in Mexico, many rural women participate in fluctuating, transnational relationships and identities, primarily through their linkages to male migrants and to the extent that they themselves are also becoming binational citizens. As the presumed boundaries are dissolved between dichotomies like urban/rural, core/periphery, and public/private, the very idea of marginality may demand rethinking, of course along lines which retain the force of responsible social critique.

For this case, I can only sketch out the rudiments of the practices and work conditions which I observed, and the ways in which they differed from the warm sociality at the managerial level. It bears repeating that these maquila jobs differed enormously from those at the border, and that the small factories of the Mi Comunidad program have provided a clean, stable, and sociable paid labor environment that presumably is of some value to many of the workers. Whether and how each woman balances this value against other conditions of the workplace remains an important question.

NAMING

Las muchachas was the only word used within the program to refer to those who did the work of sewing, 80–90 percent of whom were female. A long-time scholar and activist in maquila settings, Devon Peña, has also noted (1997) the frequent use of this word by maquila managers along the border to describe the women who work for them. The word may not have quite the negative connotations it does in English, and may even be at times a courtly, flattering reference, yet its unvarying use is notable. A frequently stated program rationale, "to create jobs in the poorest regions of the state," was coupled with the constant use of "las muchachas" in program discourse. Both concepts invoked a series of meanings related to the sorrow and abandonment surrounding migration, but within the waged labor situation of the maquilas, they also reflected key assumptions about the intrinsic value and human potential of workers.

As a static, discursive category in the program, las muchachas symbolized the problems left behind by the migrants, and in fact represented the failure of the program in one of its original intents. For not only was the goal of reducing migration not being met, but state intervention in the local economies and abandoned households was needed *because* the migration rates remain so high. Many rural women of Guanajuato are becoming the sole financial support for their children and their extended families of parents and siblings. Documents reflected this new rationale, like the job application forms administered during the hiring process which explicitly asked about the number of other people for whom the job applicant was responsible. At meetings and conferences, the phrase "las que se quedan" (the women who remain behind) also captured this meaning. Such bureaucratic phrases were paralleled in practice.

Although both Soco and Rosi had degrees and work experience in business and marketing, they had tended to stress the meaning of their work as one of *social services* rather than economics or business; they always noted the fact that their program existed to create jobs in poor communities. But even within the first month of work, I saw that any linkage of social services to the poor women was not actually a part of everyday practice, and that in fact both the sociality and the service aspects of the program were directed at the management, as noted in earlier chapters. The service that was being provided to the female workers was limited to the provision of a job. But everyday practice, more than numeric data, reveals *what kind* of future is being imagined, who is being included or excluded in it, and how this exclusion is taking place. The dismissiveness toward the female laborers was noticeable on my very first visit with the directors.

On our way to this maquila, the program directors asked my opinion of the Monterrey quality report, which I gave honestly, and we continued discussing it during the long car ride. I was surprised to hear Beatriz, another staff member who was with us that day, agreeing openly with me that the report was marred by its pro-management tone. (See chapter 8 for further discussion.) The directors shared some of my misgivings about the report. In fact, Soco later asked me to help draft a response to the authors of the Monterrey report, which I was honored to do, seeing it as a sign of trust, but the request may have simply indicated their own disinterest in paperwork.

Beyond our discussion of the report, however, Soco and Rosi made a point of telling me that it truly is a problem in Mexico to get certain kinds of people to work hard and well. One had worked in a parts factory, in which she had seen workers sabotage the equipment rather than work. On many other occasions, I was told that the female workers lacked "a work ethic" (*una cultura de trabajo*).

Later, as we were leaving the maquila after relatively informal discussions with the management staff, Beatriz and I were approached in the courtyard by two young women on their lunch break. They rather bitterly and angrily denounced the management for broken promises over salaries and Saturday overtime pay. "Did you ask them how much we make?" one asked, her arms akimbo; they looked discouraged when we said "no." They sarcastically mimicked their bosses' falsely friendly manner of prefacing their requests for extra work, and their vows to compensate them for this work, which were never fulfilled. Beatriz told me they make about 350 pesos (U.S.$35.00) per week for working Monday through Friday, 7:00 A.M. to 5 or 6:00 P.M., with a half-hour lunch break ("that's illegal," she added in a low voice, referring to the short lunch hour). I did not know at the time that their salaries for that period were being paid by the government through training scholarships: nevertheless, the remarks were troubling. Beatriz noted that jobs working in the fields might pay 50 pesos (about U.S.$5.00) per day for a 7:00 A.M. to 2:00 P.M. workday with a one hour break for the big meal of the day. The state minimum wage at the time was 36 pesos per day.

Neither Soco nor Rosi were interested in listening to these complaints and dismissed them later when we returned to the office as fairly routine: "We hear that kind of thing all the time." Again I noted the fact that, regarding managerial policies and actions undertaken within the context of their own program, Rosi and Soco, even as state government representatives, did not see themselves as being in a position to enforce labor laws. Yet the concerns struck me as quite serious. For even if the workers were approaching Beatriz and me in part because they saw me as either a gullible or powerful American, that did not explain entirely why they would take such a risk in speaking to me, or why they would also speak with Beatriz, my Mexican colleague. The latter was as dismayed as I was by the possibility that the women of the program were being exploited at this and other maquilas, in this case, as she said, "by their own countrymen," but nothing was going to be done or said about this particular situation; it was utterly dismissed.

PROGRAM DIALOGUES

The strong words of Beatriz, and her vocal skepticism about the program on numerous occasions, revealed that critique of the program was indeed coming from *within* the office. In those early days, I was interested to note this conflict, as I thought it might lead to other developments for the program and for my own understanding of it. But with time, I saw that as friendly and close as the directors were to this woman in many ways (through many social outings, meals, and events), they also dismissed her as a malcontent, always critical and often wrong about things. They were

thus able to overlook her criticisms of the maquila work and of the treatment of the workers. Her own origins in the country may also have been
a part of this dismissal.

As limited as my own perspective is, as a former blue-collar girl from
the United States who loved work in an Ohio steel mill, I believe that our
many conversations generated some value for all three of us during our
travels through the state or as we sat talking in offices, restaurants, and
elsewhere. They told me one day that I contributed a good kind of "chem-
istry" to their work. Of course, I began as a complete novice to the program, asking about the obvious, which in anthropology can be a way to
understand culture and even to critique certain ideologies. But soon we
began to debate issues directly. They knew I was beginning to form an analytical view of the program, and we all knew that it was their own patience and generosity which had taught me so much, although of course
still far from everything they knew. They recognized that I was using other
pieces of knowledge to make sense of what I learned, and they wanted to
learn about and debate those pieces too. In a memorandum (Appendix A)
which I wrote to the administrators shortly before leaving, I summarized
what I saw as key issues in the program, hoping to leave a text-based
record which would reinforce other, more informal conversations we had
had about labor-management relations, gender, and workplace motivation. I also wrote a document for Soco summarizing a "human development project" for which she was hoping to seek funding (also included in
Appendix A).

I was described at one meeting as an altruistic volunteer who was interested in the situation of the female workers; this was met with a welcoming, polite response by the most-respected jefe at the meeting. In these
and other cases, my mere presence was used by Soco to quietly introduce
the existence of outside perspectives and possibilities. At a smaller meeting in the office, I mentioned using the factories as a place to post information on issues of urgency or importance for the women. A questionnaire
(Appendix B) which we designed for use in surveying the needs of the
women of the maquilas became in itself an educational tool, as we discussed how to structure it, how to elicit expressions of need, and so forth.
In this work we drew upon ideas from a gender workshop which we attended together as a result of a meeting at the Institute of Women, but Soco
also added questions which made it more of a bureaucratic tool. Our participation in both of these formal settings resulted, I believe, from Soco's
decision to respond seriously to my persistent inquiries about the women
of the maquilas. We also discussed offering courses on Saturday morning
for the workers, possibly on the general topic of self-esteem, although both
Soco and Rosi did express concerns that this might lead to "problems"
with the women at work. Beatriz asked sarcastically if the course would

be directed at making the women satisfied with the conditions of their work, in effect a brain-washing course, which led to a lively debate about what we each hoped from it.

A summary of my research (Appendix C), generated a warm reply from Rosi (we correspond via email regularly, but Soco prefers to communicate through occasional, surprise telephone calls or in person), who was pleased with the depiction of the program as "appropriate and truthful," but especially expressed her joy on my behalf in making so much progress in my work. Her personal fondness is always expressed, a priority over more lengthy discussion or implementation of my ideas, in part because the program directors already felt a multitude of overwhelming tasks were involved in merely keeping the program going.

The program directors could not dismiss my comments quite as readily as they had those of our other colleague in the office because of the value they placed on my status as an outsider, a researcher from the United States, and an older, educated woman. But this foreignness was perhaps enough to allow my ideas to be dismissed when they were too confusing or challenging, since perhaps in their eyes I could not be expected to understand all the reasons why the program had to be run the way it was. For example, I suggested once that it made good "business sense" to involve the female laborers more directly in a cooperative plan addressing quality issues. This was, in retrospect, too unclear and did not generate discussion.

Within a few weeks of our discussion with the workers about broken promises, one of the two workers in the maquila who had spoken to us had already quit and, on later visits I conversed several times with the other woman. By my last visit she was in a group, laughing with friends, saying that things were "more or less" improved, and even appearing to be in a comfortably senior position.

These early incidents suggested the commonsense beliefs and practices within the program regarding labor issues and the female workers. It led me to notice some of the ambivalence in program discourse and practices specifically regarding the value of these women in three senses: (1) their contribution to the program; (2) their salaries; and (3) their relationship to the issue of quality. This ambivalence regarding the female workers parallels that of two other, key shaping factors in the case which I have already noted—migration and the maquila industry—and is worth describing in some detail.

RESPECT

In late February, Soco and Rosi had interviewed Ana, a woman whom they hoped to hire as a quality overseer for all of the maquilas, or at least for those of the Textile Association of Guanajuato. During the interview, she struck all of us as very experienced, poised, and articulate. We three had recently discussed a proposed course to foster self-esteem and teamwork through an expensive workshop which was expected to last several months. Soco was thinking about other ways to address the linkage of quality and motivation, and in the interview she raised these issues. Ana expressed interest in the job, but asked to see some of the maquilas. Thus it was that one day the four of us visited two maquilas that each presented its own set of problems for Ana to assess, one in a crowded street of a bustling small city, one in a remote rural area.

The visits on this day differed sharply from all other visits in which I participated, because for once we were focused on the female workers and their jobs. Normally we arrived at the maquilas for meetings with the je-fes or for other business related to administration. It was extremely rare for us to interact in any way with the women at work sewing; this was sim-ply not a part of the visits. We always walked straight into the manager's offices. (Meetings convened quickly because we were generally so late in arriving that all others were already present.) Sometimes we strolled briefly through the workspace under the watch of one of the supervisors or jefes. If we lingered to chat in a group after the meetings, it was usually out of sight and earshot of the women. I had begun to understand just how unusual it was for the two female workers to speak to Beatriz and me about their wages.

In the first maquila which we visited with Ana, none of the women were in the work room when we arrived at about 11:00 A.M. All were across the narrow, busy street eating ice cream on their break. We walked around the cramped, disordered area. A few box fans on the floor blew hot air around the windowless, low-ceilinged room, in which sewing ma-chines, kitchen chairs, boxes, piles of gray and blue fabric, stacks of com-pleted sweatshirts and sweatpants, and electric wires running across the floor or hanging draped low from the ceiling suggested carelessness and neglect. Some hand-lettered papers were taped on the wall, admonishing workers not to run or eat in the worksite. Soon the women came quietly back in, passing by the high desk of the manager, which was posted near the only entrance, and took up their tasks again. Unlike the women in other maquilas, they did not catch our eyes or smile at us as we walked around looking at the machines and fabrics.

The job candidate expertly examined material and strolled around among the machines, talking easily with the workers, while Soco and Rosi drifted to the front desk to chat with the male manager, who usually at-tended meetings with his son. I stepped out into the main entrance for a moment to read the "Mission and Vision" plaques near the front door; un-der the heading of Values was a statement: "Respeto: Darse su lugar."

Loosely translated, this means: "Give respect its place," or "Include respect here [on the job]." I noticed that a man, a young woman carrying a baby, and an old woman had gathered in this small lobby and were peering in the crack of the door at the women who were working, one of whom made a slight gesture signaling to one person to return later. Then, as we left, some of the women came out to speak to these waiting relatives or friends.

The palpably low morale and low quality of work was affirmed in some of Ana's comments made as we left (after stopping so that Soco and Rosi could buy frozen yogurt). She remarked on the poor work flow and organization and the inefficient production line. When Rosi apologetically said it was "small," Ana answered at once, "I've seen smaller." Ana also noted as we drove away that the quality of the management is very important for the conditions of a maquila, and that it is very difficult to change poor patterns, or improve conditions, once certain habits are set in place. This alone was quite an unusual statement, in contrast to the typical discussions of quality in relation to the workers.

The low morale and neglected work conditions were clear, as they had been in some of the other maquilas. But the slight degree of physical freedom being exercised by the female workers was relatively unusual. As poor in physical conditions as this factory looked in comparison to others, the women nonetheless seemed to feel free to move about during the work day and to greet waiting relatives in the small outside lobby.

It took us over an hour to locate the second factory, which was on a dirt road in the middle of a field; no other buildings were visible nearby, and in every direction were clumps of trees and wide expanses of farmland, some smoldering as grass was being burned off. A huge banner hung across the front of the building over the doors advertising the need for female workers. There was a bus parked in the driveway which was used to transport the workers to and from the job. A small sign noted the name of the business. Soco and Rosi had doubts about its potential, because they felt the area had not been researched sufficiently. Inside the cavernous building, the women were again seated and a mechanic was on foot, moving around and assisting them. Two other young men were on their feet sorting fabric behind a table. The mechanic, it was whispered to me, was a real boon for this maquila because of his expertise. Several expensive machines, not being used, were nearby under sheets, and it was said that he knew how to operate them.

In this huge, white-washed building, the quality of electrical wiring, light, and air was higher than in the other. The electric wires were methodically arranged to reach every machine from above rather than snaking across the floor in thick wires that could be tripped over, as in the previous maquila. The tiny plastic Virgen leaned back slightly in the corner of the wall, resting on an exposed pipe; she was not one of the most tended ones. A cluster of plastic flowers was attached at her feet. The pieces of bright floral fabric that the women had used to practice on during their training were draped over the unused machines throughout the area, lending a gay atmosphere to the work space, and some simple, collared, short-sleeved shirts with buttons down the front in this same "tropical" pattern were folded on a nearby table for shipping. Rosi asked me how much such a shirt would sell for in the United States, and I said that, depending on the store, they would cost between U.S.$9.00 and U.S.$16.00. We turned to other topics, as she was distracted that day by some bad news, so I was listening to her in an unused front area of the maquila, while Soco chatted with the supervisor and Ana wandered around.

I saw Ana gently move a strand of long hair back from one young woman's face, out of danger of being caught in the sewing machine. This worker seemed to be watching the mechanic intently, and he lingered near her chair, ignoring other workers. Ana ordered him to fetch a certain tool from a nearby work area, and herself used it to adjust a foot pedal on a machine for a young woman who had complained of it. After we left, she offered her view that "Yes, he knows how the machines work, but he does not know how to explain how to use them." This man, seen as so knowledgeable by others, had not impressed her at all. We all began to hope that Ana would join the staff and bring her sense of quiet professionalism to the diverse situations within the program.

THE CONDITIONS OF SPEECH

On this day, in which we had not been in any meetings and had simply gone to the maquilas, waiting as Ana examined the conditions, eating seafood between visits, I saw most clearly that engagement with the working women was simply not a practice in the program. Even when we were visiting the maquilas for reasons other than management meetings, with plenty of time available for other purposes, we passed through the worksites without a single incidence of the program directors communicating with the women working at the machines. On the day that we visited the maquilas with Ana, they left this role entirely to her, and on other days, they simply did not look at or speak to the women at all. In addition to the work discipline of expected quiet, respect, tidiness, and concentration, the women were categorized as those to whom official speech is not directed. When some of us from the office did speak to them on a few occasions, it was highly unusual, almost quirky. My gregarious comadres never spoke to the women at all, and seemed uninterested in my occasional efforts to do so ("Speak to them if you like!" they shrugged, when I pressed them on the topic).

In all of the maquilas we visited, I was not free to converse for long with any of the workers, but one day I had a chance to speak with one of the women who had complained to us about broken management promises. As we chatted, she told me that I reminded her of her aunt. When I told Rosi this later, she shook her head over such insincere flattery and warned me with a sad but fervent kind of self-awareness: "Don't believe us!" She went on to say that in general, Mexicans make a lot of false promises and do not want to offend; they want everyone to like them, so they often say things that are untrue. She openly doubted that the woman even had an aunt. This distrustful response was similar to some others which she made in response to my efforts to speak with the women workers, but differed in an interesting way in that she included herself, and indeed all Mexicans, in her skepticism.

The women workers were not involved in the financial and other kinds of planning stages of the maquilas, nor in the program design or adaptation to their own communities. They did not participate in decision-making, even on shopfloor issues about which they would have firsthand knowledge. They did not have a representative to articulate their concerns to the boss or to the government. I was not able to see if they had conversations with their bosses of any length or substance. The program files showed clearly that they had been interviewed by various consulting agencies, but the results of those surveys were not made available to us; they were withheld as a part of the various expensive project proposals made by these consultants. Even the idea of designing a questionnaire to solicit the women's ideas about their own needs was unusual in this context, for it involved the notion of creating an opportunity for them to express themselves in words and of giving a voice to them within the language that bureaucracies hear.[2] We designed such a questionnaire nonetheless, but even my brief attempts to explain it and discuss it with some of the workers and a staff member one day led to mutual confusion. Primarily this was because the idea of it was so foreign to them, although we explained repeatedly the idea of the form as a way to hear their opinions.

Yet, they were not completely silenced. Amongst themselves, the female workers would whisper and giggle while glancing over at visitors. Clearly, they were aware of us: as we walked past their sewing machines some of them smiled shyly at us. I always wondered how we appeared to them: keys to an outside world that could help them, or an amusing sight with our motley assortment of heights, clothing styles, and skin colors, especially as we were usually disheveled from traveling in the hot, windy car for several hours. Female personal appearance in even the remote maquilas was highly tended to, and took similar forms to those in the city. Especially among the younger women, the use of eye pencil and mascara, lip liner and thick application of lipstick, hair pulled tightly back and held in place with shining mousse, and tight clothing (usually jeans and simple shirts) were the most common ways to display female beauty. Footwear tended to be sneakers or flat shoes; high heels were for special ceremonies. I was not able to learn how they made sense of us or of the government photographers, documentary filmmakers, journalists, and other visitors that were regularly brought through their workplaces. But clearly they noticed us, even if some among our group did not notice them. We three were the ones who came and went, existing far outside of their most important relationships.

In this relatively disciplined work culture, the women expressed themselves in shared private humor and in their choices to be physically absent from the workplace, or to leave it entirely. Skipped days or weeks of work are reasonable given their work loads at home. Director Laura Lozano of the Institute of Women noted to us in a meeting that, far from lacking a work ethic, what the women lacked was enough time and support to complete all of their many, physically onerous tasks. At a workshop on poverty, social workers from the northeast areas of Guanajuato noted the gendered division of labor in the country: in a typical day, "Juana" wakes at 4:00 or 5:00 A.M. to begin preparing food: she grinds corn, tends the animals, carries firewood, makes tortillas, prepares breakfast for the family, cleans the kitchen, washes clothing, prepares the large midday meal, and so on, with many other chores, ending at about 7:30 at night when she prepares the *nixtamal* (dough for tortillas), looks after the children and their homework, then does some sewing or embroidery, and cleans up from dinner. The group agreed that rural women's domestic work amounts to 17–18 hours per day.

The problems categorized as "labor" issues in the maquilas were not gravely serious; I did not hear of any violence, theft by the workers, or sabotage. The jefes worried over the women; a general letter to employees, stating that absenteeism was a very grave problem for the maquila, was taped on a wall outside one office. Bosses discussed problems with making the women work well or hard; with handling breaks, absenteeism, and turnover; with the women leaving their jobs after they received training for better wages elsewhere; and with the poor quality of materials produced.

There was potential for comfortable relations. Some instances even suggested warmth between the workers and bosses. Avila, an especially beaming owner-manager of one of the maquilas who was well regarded by the program directors, had come back to Mexico after many years of work in the United States. He told me on the inaugural day of his maquila that he returned because it was becoming too difficult for migrants to the United States to thrive there. One day about a year later, he was interviewed by the television documentary crew. They seated him at one of the sewing machines in his maquila. All of the women who were sitting and working at nearby machines watched the scene with smiles and grins, catching each others' eyes and winking, or giggling and laughing openly at the sight. The tall, portly man who was interviewing Avila was uncomfortably perched on one of the women's chairs, which was adorned with a Mickey Mouse pillow on the seat. His ample behind seemed to smother the Mickey Mouse pillow and overwhelm the metal folding chair. This was a source of so much laughter that one of the men from the technical crew had to ask the women to quiet down for the filming to take place. Avila also exchanged a smile with them over the incident. The ease of manner between this owner and his workers—the joking, laughter, and curious glances—was notable on several occasions and seemed to be genuinely shared.

PHYSICAL CONTROLS

Quality consultants studying the program's maquilas did not undertake a very deep analysis of labor issues in their investigations, but they did point out the poor working conditions in many of the maquilas which they had visited, noting unsatisfactory environmental factors such as poor lighting, air circulation, and electricity, bad odors, untidy floors, and overly loud music. From my own observations, the work conditions seemed to vary widely, but one pattern was common. In most of the maquilas, physical freedom belonged more to men: the jefes, supervisors, and mechanics, and male assistants who moved about from one sewing machine to another. Men helped the seated women by carrying away the completed products from the machines or by bringing the piles of pieces to be sewn. They also often fixed and adjusted the machines, although at the opening of one maquila, the women had demonstrated how they made minor repairs to the machines.

Men also tended to be involved more often in the work at the interface with the outside world: the final inspections, the folding and wrapping in plastic, piling in boxes, and loading and unloading delivery trucks. The relief to be provided by standing up to carry one's own work over to the folding tables or going to get new bundles of fabric was thus largely precluded for the women, whose work on the machines seemed quite constrained. During one meeting, I saw women walking slowly past the office window at noon to buy cans of soda from a machine, then returning to their sewing machines, apparently without a longer lunch break than that. In another maquila, they did gather in their lunch area for a half hour. In a third, women did some of the inspection and packing; once I saw them comfortably sitting on the big folding tables and chatting amongst themselves as they inspected little girls' short sets—as well as any visitors. Another time at this same maquila, several women were standing and ironing shirts, while others inspected them and hung them under plastic bags. But the norm was that women were seated, while men moved about providing advice, materials, and so forth. During another meeting, a working woman raised her hand to summon Gerardo when she had a question: he saw this from the office window and left our meeting to go and help her.

Across cultures, class and gender ideologies intersect to keep women in their place. Physical freedom, in which the body moves freely in space and is seen as normal or even powerful rather than as solely an object of desire, remains a prerogative of privileged males in much of the world. Men at home in Mexico are free to move within public and between public and private realms, to "regulate" movement across the boundaries of their property and to mediate relationships (Rouse 1992). Fiona Wilson (1991), who uses a "household model" to analyze workshops in the Bajío region of Guanajuato, argues that conditions within the home, such as the seclusion of women, can explain gendered space and production in textile workshops.

The Mi Comunidad maquilas differed in important respects from the ones that Wilson studied, but it is worth thinking through her model. The differences are, first, that the state partnered with private capital, thereby introducing an aspect of business cooperation. Wilson's case involved the state as an outside authority which taxes and pressures private capital through the exchange of favors and support. Second, the role of powerful females involved in the maquilas was explicitly *not* like the "owner's wife," who Wilson describes as nurturing and protecting the young females entrusted to her care in the workshops.

Nevertheless, this sense of regulated and unregulated movement was evident in the Mi Comunidad program in the very physical layout and structure of the maquilas and in the way the ability to move about was granted. The male investors who contributed to the program enjoyed the most freedom of movement in this case, for they were thought to have entered a world of money and power outside of Mexico. But personal mobility was not a simple issue of gender, for we three women from the state government were completely free. Enacting authority in this case meant constant travel. Ease of physical mobility was a privilege in the program that was actually more linked with relative power and class, not simply gender, adding additional complexity to this case beyond the small workshops which Wilson studied.

The pattern of physical control or constraint in the maquilas was supplemented by a constant sense of observation, a concept well developed in scholarship on power following Foucault's development of Bentham's panopticon. The managers' offices faced out through glass windows to the floor of workers seated at their machines, who could never feel unobserved. To walk across the floor toward the bathroom, the exit, or the soda machine entailed being observed by anyone who was in the office. Indeed, the physical comportment of many rural females in Guanajuato seemed to reflect regulation and a consciousness of being observed: walking slowly and steadily, keeping one's head down, with limbs moving in orderly succession, and minimal eye contact, extreme shyness, quiet voices and giggles, and modest clothing.

Even the relatively colorless, hard appearance of the interiors of the maquilas constituted a form of discipline in a country where brilliantly colored paint shines on houses, walls, doors, window frames, and alleyways. The buildings were constructed in a simple and inexpensive fashion; the floors and walls were of poured or plastered-over reinforced concrete, the roofs were made of corrugated metal with gaps between them and the tops of the walls that let in the summer's late afternoon heat and winter's morning chill. The gray walls were generally unpainted, bare, and rough textured and the chairs were of metal or plastic. Loud music was often being played over speakers; I saw audiotapes being changed by people in the managers' offices, suggesting that the workers themselves might have little influence over which kind of music they hear. Occasionally I saw workers with face masks on, whether against bad smells or some toxin was not clear.

For the hiring process, Soco and Rosi provided outlines of job application forms to the bosses. These forms solicited information about any relatives in the United States that the women have, asking if they have worked in or visited the United States and if they would ever want to work there. For most of the job applicants, the application form would be their first experience with filling out an official work-related document. This piece of paper with its odd personal questions was issued in a context already saturated with power differences. Clearly at some time in the program these facts must have been deemed to be of interest, although when I was organizing the files and asked Soco about the completed forms, she decided they could all be stored in the archives. I do not think they were ever read or tabulated in any way, but simply distributed and collected. When we designed a questionnaire in order to plan a self-esteem course for the women (Appendix B), Soco wanted me to add several other questions to it about whether the women had control over their earnings, how old they were, how many children they had and of what age, and so on. No doubt she was strategically planning the new statistics that could be generated to show the value and impact of the program, but, again, the documents seemed designed to probe for data which might never be used.

Although none of these practices and conditions alone were illegal or grossly exploitative, they did constitute a form of discipline for the workers which, combined with other attitudes, helped to maintain them in a category outside of the personal warmth of the program "family."

CLOSER TO NATURE

Rural Mexican females have long been invisible; they "melt into the family" in terms of land ownership, agrarian law, and labor statistics (Stephen 1996). "Family labor" in agricultural production "means the unpaid labor of women and children" (Robles, Aranda, and Botey 1993, cited in Stephen 1996). Much more generally, women's work has rarely been recognized, counted, or valued as *work* in international sources of economic data (Himmelweit 1995; Waring 1999). Rural women across many cultures do not see their own work within the home as work, moreover, it is seen as "natural" to them (Moser 1995), while outside of the home, women are seen as "volunteers." Gender differences are said to begin at birth in the Mexican countryside; we learned at a conference that the midwife may earn more for a boy, and the expression upon the joyful news is proclaimed: "It's a boy!" whereas for a girl, "Oh well, it was a girl," is the resigned sentence. The girl is often seen as a cost, and the boy as an investment; boys may even be fed more while growing up.

One afternoon as we chatted in the courtyard of the successful maquila noted in chapter 1, Rosi reaffirmed a point Soco had made earlier during a car ride discussion of the Monterrey quality report. She said that the people of the country do not always have appropriate work attitudes; they take a lot of breaks to go walking with their boyfriends or to eat, because that is what they are used to from their work in the fields. This judgment was quietly disputed later to me by Beatriz, the other woman from the office who was with us that day, who knows the region and who asserted that this work in the fields is actually subject to much observation and strict discipline. Nonetheless, even she said that the responsibility for maintaining the cleanliness of the bathrooms rested upon the workers, not the management. All three of them noted, with wrinkled noses and dismissive hand gestures, how filthy the bathrooms of the maquilas generally are.[3]

Another anecdote noted that the women workers of one maquila were so unused to being inside that in the first weeks of work they ate outside on their breaks. This was seen as indicating how little sense they had; it evokes the bestial sense of rural and female persons as "closer to nature" and thus, of course, farther from "culture" (Rosaldo 1974). The women of the maquilas were described as slow and lazy; like the linkage of poor quality between work and worker, these physical attributes in a sense passed into the progress of work within the factories, also said to be slow. F. W. Taylor's view that workers "naturally loaf" (Banta 1993, 96) is echoed in this description. Indeed, the frequent Taylorist implication of women's "inherent emotionality" (ibid., 161) seemed to correspond to the use of religious imagery to spur efficiency.

This sense of slowness applied to the women's intellect as well.[4] Seen as susceptible to such tactics of productivity-boosting as the strategic placement of flowers in front of a statue, they were assumed to be simple-minded, insensate to the conditions around them. They were also constructed as stationary beings, defined by what they are *not*: they are not migrants, not moving, dynamic, or active. There are posters which advertise money transfer services by depicting the United States and Mexico as one contiguous landmass all of one color; a male silhouetted figure (with cowboy hat) stands in the United States, and a large arrow with a dollar/peso sign in it points down from him toward a woman's figure, holding the hand of a child, standing in Mexico. The sense of dominance of the mobile male/north over the immobile female/south was striking in this image, as was the absence of any image of the border at all.

Although most of the female workers in the maquilas did not bear the obvious markers of indigenous categories, they did share the geographic fact of life in the countryside with indigenous people. Soco and Rosi were in turn sympathetic and judgmental about such persons. They would be the first to give out small coins for beggars along the highway or in the streets between cars at a stop light. They bought pens from disabled vendors in restaurants and at traffic lights, gave coins to charities, and bought sweets from the hunched old women who made their slow way up the stairs of el Palacio to sell homemade products in the state government offices. I think they looked to their own cherished parents and grandparents as indeed not so very far from these lifestyles themselves. Although their statements about the maquila women sometimes reflected wider stereotypes about rural and indigenous people as a "class-ethnic" group, and also specifically as women of this group, they did not set themselves up as necessarily superior to these women. Indeed, one of Rosi's favorite themes was that "we are all human beings," with every one of us flawed.

In discussions of candidate Fox's chances of winning the election, many people stated that he would win in the cities, but it was the countryside, historically the locus for suspicion about restiveness, that was in question. This was not only because of the PRI's power and trickery there, but also, it was said, because the people there were less "educated" and thus more susceptible to deceit and manipulation. Soco believed that a first-born girl in the countryside is always sent to the convent, another discursive variation on the gullibility of the *campesinos* as being heavily influenced by the Church and the PRI. The Catholic Church does play an important role among this population; as one social worker pointed out, what "the priest says is the only truth." But even among devout persons like Soco, skepticism about rural people seemed to lead to the judgment of their faith as somehow less rational than the faith of people in the cities.

Although they do not live in the countryside themselves, Soco and Rosi's lives and experiences are marked by painful problems and by awareness of prejudice. Their lifestyles and advanced degrees differentiate them from "las muchachas," yet in explaining these matters to me, they spoke of themselves, in shared terms, as Mexicans. My expressions of concern for the women generated responses intended to instruct me in how to deal with them, instructions framed in advice about Mexicans or the workers of the maquilas in general. But when the strutting camera crew of the documentary film ignored her throughout an entire day of travel around the state together, Rosi's laughter at a restaurant that night over their behavior was about *their* stupidity and snobbishness in dismissing her as an ignorant girl of the country or of the provinces. She did not take this perception personally, she merely viewed it as an example of the ignorance of people from Mexico City.

THE VALUE OF LAS MUCHACHAS

The low value accorded to the female laborers was expressed in many ways, from such small details as the cheap metal folding chairs to larger issues like the foreclosure of possibility for advancement within the maquilas. It was also expressed in a program discourse which obscured the relation between the women and money through assertions about the training period and provision of work as an investment sufficient in itself, contingent upon the worker's moral merit. The women's salaries were paid for by government grants during their six to eight week training in sewing, simple maintenance of the machines, and other work practices. I did not witness these training sessions, but according to Peña, training in the border maquilas amounts to little more than "a farcical imitation of apprenticeship," which "basically involves learning and accepting a regimented and hierarchical system of order giving and taking," or "apprenticeship in work discipline"(Peña 1997, citing Carrillo 1980). For the Mi Comunidad program bosses and heads, there were periodic meetings, training sessions, and workshops to review changes in relevant legislation, but I did not hear of additional opportunities for the female workers. This training was seen as a gift to the women, thus it was resented when they accepted it and then left for higher paid alternatives, as happened in the maquilas which are near larger, urban areas.

The existence of these women as a group comprised of differentiated individuals with varying skills and even potential for leadership was negated in the reluctance to promote women within the maquilas. This too is common in the border factories; managers cite the possible resentment among male workers, gender-specific stereotypes, and their preference to reward innovation instead with gifts ranging from pens and blazers to vacations (Peña 1997, 72–73). As in the early industrial United States, factory women are thereby denied "a sense of future time," with "no advancement in sight" (Banta 1993, 162–63).

Another form of dismissal came from a visitor to the office who knew Soco and Rosi from earlier involvement in the program. He responded negatively to Soco's excitement over plans regarding the women as "human resources." He said that in Mexico, the rural women "only" work to earn money, so no further investment is worth it for owners. Then, nodding to me (we had met already in the United States), he said that in the United States, people *would* work harder and thus any additional investment in morale or productivity would be rewarded. Analyzing similar stereotypes, Lomnitz-Adler argues that "Indian" labor is fetishized in the rural Mexico case of Huasteca Potosina. Mestizos see Indian products as a "natural" outcome of Indian labor and mystify drinking and fiesta rituals in an effort to import the unchanging Indian into the market, thereby keeping prices "traditional" in the markets and devaluing the labor of the indigenous (1992, 30–31).

One official pointed out to the three of us that if we were asked about our life plans or goals, we would be able to answer with various long and short-term plans, whereas the women of the country would either answer "I don't know!" or would say something about marriage and children.[5] Their life project or goal, she summarized, is "to have children, or to make the tortilla soup for today"—it is not something they think about or have even been taught *how* to think about. She told the program directors that the rural women were working for money alone, and if they work for one week and have enough for what they need, they rest. They may well quit or simply not come in to work the next week. "They are not lazy," she said carefully and clearly, "They are very hard-working. But, they are tired." It was mid-June, and it was the first time in six months that I had ever heard someone speak so sympathetically and knowledgeably about these rural women. Her straightforward manner affirmed the simplicity of the labor contract from the point of view of the women, as opposed to the complex of reciprocity and merit evinced in program discourse.

Like other mystifications of the women's value to the program, the issue of wages was a complex and relatively vague topic in meetings and in answers to questions from outsiders. During one meeting of several maquila directors, when Soco pointedly asked about the wage being paid, there was a kind of uncertain mumble by one jefe, but another stated the exact amount at once. The directors knew the maquilas should be paying minimum wage; it was not clear if they could detect deviances or even enforce changes if they had to; they were surprised one day to learn that one maquila was still paying everyone minimum wage after an entire year of work, ignoring different levels of skill. Small businesses (employing 1–5 people) may pay as little as *half* of the legal minimum wage to an uneducated worker in Mexico; the minimum wage is "not binding" in rural or urban areas (Dávila Capalleja 1997). Soco noted matter-of-factly at one meeting, in one of the few overt references to wages: "As we all know in the beginning, the wages are not very attractive." Low wages in the exploitative, clandestine subcontracting segment of the textile industry are known to be associated with women's labor (Wilson 1991). Even being a part of a government-sponsored program does not guarantee that labor laws will be followed. Indeed, if the work is in rural areas where there is more resistance to federal oversight, wages may reflect the fact that certain workers are affected by textile sector informalization in different ways. As Fiona Wilson found, some are considered "worthy for protection" through law, while others, notably rural females, are seen as "more amenable to private forms of protection and control" (ibid., 191).

Through everyday silences, mumbles, and the use of widely available stereotypes, the category of las muchachas was reproduced as an exploitable resource. This was especially evident in a new plan, the Northeast Project, that was being developed within the rubric of the Mi Comunidad program in mid-2000. The plan was included in program statistics, but it was to be run in a different manner. First, a specific region of the state was being targeted by DACGE officials for maquila development. This regional targeting had *preceded* the solicitation of investment, and in this case, it was not even the migrants from Guanajuato who were being solicited. Second, the dealer involved in the Wal-Mart contract was being recruited by el Licenciado to invest in this project and to become involved in finding buyers for its goods. This dealer told me he was not sure exactly what was expected of him, but that our boss had told him that the government would back up his investment and that the rest of the money would come from the boss himself.

Development in this area was being promoted by el Licenciado explicitly for its low labor costs: indeed Soco referred to the workers there as a "captive labor" pool, an advantage of the area, during a meeting with the jefes of the program. However, in other settings, the same region was also described by Soco and Rosi in sad tones as "extremely poor," and thus as requiring investment. The planned jobs, in leather and furniture factories, were explicitly planned to be constructed further away from the booming economy of León, where competition was making it too hard for the government maquilas to keep wages low. A member of the staff charged with writing up el Licenciado's ideas for this project was openly sarcastic about it, joking about how hard it was to think of a sufficiently good word to justify it and hinting darkly that it was being planned simply to benefit the boss. This area of the state is very remote and has poor roads and infrastructure, thus a major problem would be transportation, access, and trained engineers for machinery repairs, but it was apparently considered worthwhile, despite the evidence of similar problems adversely affecting Las Cruces, also an isolated maquila. In fact, the Northeast Project showed that one key goal in the program (providing work in remote villages) was clearly not being reconsidered in the wake of problems at Las Cruces. Shifting the blame to Gerardo and the workers perhaps precluded confrontation with this uncomfortable issue.

The Northeast Project was mysterious; as time went on, the person who had been so sarcastic about describing this project in official documents began to be increasingly discreet about it, and I realized that this staff member was becoming closer to the boss in terms of their mutual career planning. Trends toward "flexible production" and subcontracting in the Mexican garment industry, as work is "pushed out to poor urban peripheries and to towns and communities of the country's interior," has lead to what Fiona Wilson calls "clandestinity" (1991, 6). Production in these places is easier to hide and taxes and regulation are avoided, but this "concealment" is usually also related to women's employment, since "women cluster" in the most exploited forms of production (ibid., 11). But in the Northeast Project, it was not private capital, as in Wilson's model, but the state itself, embodied in el Licenciado and his partners, which was intervening through the structure and subsidies available in its own program in order to redirect investment to these areas, specifically to take advantage of the lower labor costs and fewer wage work alternatives for the workers.

One could argue that in cases of extreme and widespread rural poverty, *any* village is a good target for investment, thus the simple availability of investors would become determinative. Rural village economies absorb outside investment in different ways (Massey et al. 1987; Reichert 1981); this variation is acknowledged in documents which state that the first phase of Mi Comunidad is a "General Notice," which includes a business plan or study specifying the investment, work details, and the expected return on investment. I do not know if or how business studies were done in any of the specific cases; there was no documentation of any such notice or analysis in the program files, for example. This issue would require a more detailed economic analysis of specific villages.

DIAGNOSES OF NEED

The value of the women's labor was also obscured by bureaucratic phrases which invoked their "needs." Researchers who are familiar with projects targeted at women elsewhere in Latin American may recognize these discursive patterns.

Supplementing and justifying the phenomena of differentiated physical freedom, observation and scrutiny, exhortation and control, clandestine managerial practices, and aesthetically barren work environments were key bureaucratic discourses which produced clients. The women were first produced as needy clients: defined by their *lack*. But that which they lacked itself changed over time.

Nancy Ferguson argues that the discourse of personnel management turns problems of organizations into "primarily, even exclusively, problems stemming from the malfunctioning or misallocation of individuals within the organization and not from the structure of the organization itself" (1984, 66). This leads to what she calls a "medicalization" of the personnel problem. In this case, the women laborers who entered the program because of their multiple forms of "lack," were soon officially rediagnosed as lacking something else: a work ethic. This common characterization functioned to blame the women for the widely acknowledged problem of poor quality and redirected attention away from incompetent male management or other structural problems in the program. It also attributed an inherent characteristic to the women that, although not specified precisely, was something that could be targeted for change and improvement.[6] This physical quality passed onto the clothing which they touched and produced, as an object becomes imbued with the qualities of a person through contagious magic (Frazer 1965).

In other bureaucratic settings, allegations of a lack in work ethic are related to the receipt of certain benefits which bureaucrats themselves link with merit (Arce 1993; Leyton 1978). They worry that the receipt of the benefit over too long of a time will actually erode the work ethic, itself acknowledged as a limited good. Bureaucratic "reworkings of physical presence" (Greenhouse 1998) in this case were such that the female professional or middle-class bureaucrats created a necessary social distance between themselves and the rural females who were identified by the state government as existing in a specific state of need. The neediness of the rural women was constructed as differing qualitatively and morally from the needs of the state's entrepreneurial business partners. The male business partners to the state also exhibited varying and complex needs, but these evoked maternal expressions of care on the part of the program directors. Narratives and practices of the program privileged this specific form of *business* need. This neediness was not seen as inherent to the business partners, or as a permanent condition. Rather, their need was a transitional one: for assistance in entering the business world.

The status of las muchachas as recipients of government and private largesse affected the way they were seen, described, and treated, but in this case there is an additional complication. The lack of work ethic among the future employees of the maquilas was known and assumed before the work ever began. In fact, it was fundamental to the program, as shown in the Northeast Project, which *was founded* on the symbolic isolation and availability of labor, with its implication of docility (which is itself an interesting contradiction to the idea of rural "restiveness"). But the actual value of this cluster of features—docility/isolation/lack of work ethic—as central to the program was thoroughly downplayed relative to the other meanings of las muchachas. The discourse constructed this value as a problem, when in truth it was the source of any possible notion of profit. Rather than admit this, and risk admitting the absolute importance of labor in the scheme, the quality was described as something which needed to be changed.

Thus the planners and jefes of the maquilas both required and distrusted the quality of untutored innocence which is thought to be inherent to the women of the country. The phrase, "those women who remain behind in the poorest regions of the state," with its ring of social service and goodwill, captures this meaning, yet easily takes on a suggestion of potential financial gain in other settings. The Mi Comunidad policy, which based its projections and plans on the women's work, both misunderstood and exploited them at the same time.

Like "nimble fingers," docility is a quality classically associated with female labor and subject to much debate among theorists of gender and capitalism. Martha Banta asserts that docility was "the single virtue that helped to counter women's inherent emotionality and physical frailty" during early industrialization (1993, 161). And as Peña notes: "The reality of workers' knowledge forced [Henry] Ford into accepting a dual philosophy of labor: workers were ideally mindless automatons but were in reality persistent foes of capitalist command and control" (1997, 4), capturing the ambivalence which also applies to the characterizations of labor in the Mi Comunidad case. The combination of state paternalism and capital fostered a similar ambivalence within the program: the much-decried lack of a work culture *was the other side* of the coin of exactly that crucial quality of docility, thought to be particularly associated with *rural* women. The women of the urban areas are worriedly expected to, and do in fact, leave the low-paying maquila jobs once they have received the government-subsidized training.

A discourse of blame masked the exploitation of rural docility. As in cases where knowledge, especially of sex, is risky and potentially shameful for women to possess, there may be a lurking fear in the program that providing the women with training in a "work ethic" may actually lead to knowledge about the job's disadvantages. The key, self-contradictory challenges become how to inculcate a work ethic without creating high turnover and how to improve productivity, quality, and morale without spending additional money.

Through these state-directed diagnoses, the women workers became important, fetishized symbols for the program. The polyvalence of "las muchachas" included many meanings, often self-contradictory: both laziness and potential trouble; units of and impediments to managerial performance; dirtiness and closeness to nature; physical and mental stillness; heads of household and well trained yet backward and available; a material to be improved and yet something inherently impeding development—the problems of the program and of the nation, synonymous with quality itself. Like other symbols in the program—the statistics, the amount of work each maquila had or did not have, and the program rationales—the women workers fulfilled an important discursive function within the program and within the self-definition of its managerial participants.

The program directors' relative lack of attention to administrative detail and their deferral of their own authority as state representatives has already been noted at length, and even presented as a relatively positive aspect of government practices in Mexico. But this displacement of the program directors' own authority regarding labor in the program may have contributed to a rather unimaginative implementation of actual workplace conditions and policies. Whether or not these practices are inevitable in the maquila industry structure, let alone in the global market, it is clear that tackling and rethinking major, structural assumptions and contradictions of the program would not, and could not, be a priority for the directors, given the many other challenges they faced simply in managing the program and initiating new businesses.

Preexisting or structural tendencies became reinforced by the directors' fervent hope for the success and stability of each maquila. This act of hope required that all of the elements in the program worked hard, knew their place, and stayed in it. However, many tensions and possibilities for change arose from the anomalous position of the working women in the new family of the program. Like theories which seek to circumscribe and control the "wild facts" of social reality and personhood (Banta 1993), various work- and family-based controls over these women can never fully preclude or predict change.

REMAKING THE FAMILY

The uneasy fear of their restiveness or "trouble" if given too much self-esteem in a Saturday morning class, the disciplines within the maquilas which seemed so superfluous given preexisting controls on rural women, and the vagueness over wages all can be understood through an emphasis on the emotions of ambivalence within families, especially as they are impacted by migration. The differentiating touch of government authority within the "family" of the program began before the women were hired. They entered as members of real families but were ascribed a pre-existing position within another family structured by the state-citizen business partnership. Social justice and gender equity issues were not included in the early stages of planning. Indeed, community-based planning itself was not really tried, it was simply *simulated* by the involvement of people who *used to live there*. The act of leaving the community might have been seen as delegitimizing the authority of those who have left, or even empowering the female heads of households, as has happened in urban areas when women earn more than men (Del Castillo 1993) or in rural areas of Guanajuato when women's relative power grew within families during the Bracero program years (González 1972, 311). Instead, the status of the male migrants was raised in the program.

The emphasis on foundational capital recast the complex facts of male migration, shifting the meaning from guilt over male abandonment to a valorization of entrepreneurship and investment, a recognition and celebration of the dangers and hardships many of these migrants undergo in order to send money home. It is the men who have left the family, but through the program they were reintegrated into it and reinstated in their rightful positions as responsible heads of family. Yet it is the women who have remained behind, fulfilling multiple responsibilities and acting as strong and capable heads of household.

In the new family of the program, state and business authority were substituted for the absent men. Continued male vigilance over the women in the absence of their own husbands and other male kin was ensured; the program directors accepted and even encouraged the role that bosses played in maintaining controls over the working women. The maquilas seemed to have become a space where family members and government authorities could protect what Roger Rouse (1992) calls the "dangerously permeable" domestic boundaries. He claims that these boundaries are threatened by the phenomenon of migration and the absence of men as regulators of domestic space. Thus perhaps workshops in Guanajuato do, in this sense, reproduce domestic spatial arrangements, as Fiona Wilson argues. But the Mi Comunidad case also suggests that the double impact of migration and state involvement is reconfiguring conceptions and structures of family, work, and government authority, which are usually presumed to be separate and even opposed to each other. Although new forms of control may emerge from such permeations, new areas for questions and change may be just as likely.

The state government of Guanajuato acknowledged the important economic roles of women in a special issue of *Pa'l Norte* that featured an interview with a female investor/manager in a maquila. The role of capital has perhaps been more important in the program than gender ideologies. (This special issue of *Pa'l Norte* is also attributable to the avid feminism of one staff member.) More generally, it was a matter of course that the female workers were absent from the planning, operations, and emotional linkages of the program, as well as from the better jobs, for, it is presumed, such women could not be trusted. They complain all the time. They do not like to work hard. These and other remarks enabled the same kind of distancing shrug toward the women that the program directors gave toward statistics, facts, el Licenciado, and other aspects of their jobs. Challenges to the static, discursive role of the category "las muchachas" were deflected with a wide variety of common sense notions, which enabled the directors to defer action on several complex issues.

CHAPTER 8

Evasions

As familial boundaries of warmth and friendship were reproduced in the Mi Comunidad program, so too were various attendant secrets and shame, discretion and loyalty, protection and pride. The presentation of official data about the program was essential to continued funding; it constituted a successful professional task undertaken by the program directors. Program data was disseminated at state-level meetings and also distributed to all official visitors (journalists, academics, students, an election observer, etc.) who came for short periods of one day or less to learn about the office or the program. All were given a thick and rather daunting publication of the proceedings of a 1996 state-sponsored conference on migration. For many, the conference proceedings and a small sheaf of other papers (photocopies from a slide presentation about the program) were the sum total of information which they received. In addition, a chart listing the program maquilas was also distributed widely. These statistics and charts are faithfully reproduced in many published sources, including scholarship. Some sources reflected the glowing outsider view of the program; others simply presented this basic summary data without comment.

The chart outlines the locations of the Mi Comunidad maquilas and lists the names of the investors' communities, as well as the dates and stages of operation of each one. The place-names, locations, dates, amounts of money, and other details are carefully noted in a complex, indeed overwhelming and lengthy, chart structure. Several different undated versions of this chart were inside of several different folders. The chart presents numerous details about each maquila in a manner intended to be clear and comprehensive, condensing the very complex negotiations and situations of each case into one line of data. It claims a standardized, comparative nature for these diverse cases.

Figure 1 is a composite of several versions of this chart, omitting monetary amounts and actual place-names. Some versions specified worker gender; the total number of factories ranged from thirteen to twenty-two, depending on the version of the chart. Because the place-names used to refer to a new maquila location *did* change, and because there was no note

Figure 1. Sample (Composite) Chart of the Type Used to Present Mi Comunidad Program Data

Maquiladora	Socios contribution[a]	Government contribution[a]	Training help[b]	Plant built	Plant rented	Machinery received	Training	Residence of Socios[c]	Number of workers
1997									
A	$	$	CIMO	Done	No	Bought	Done		20
B	$	$	CIMO	Building	No	Bought	Done		6 M 12 F
C	$	$	CtyCC	Purchased	Renting	Bought	Done		5 M 40 F
D	$	$	CIMO	Done	No	Buying	Done		1 M 33 F
1998									
A	$	$	CIC	Building	Rented	Bought	Done		5 M 60 F
B	$	$	CIMO & CIC	Done	No	Bought	To be det'd		50 est.
C	$	$	CIMO	Building	No	Bought	Done		60
D	$	$	CIMO	Done	No	Bought	Done		40
1999									
A	$	$	CIMO	No	Renting	Bought	Current		about 50
2000									
A	$	$	—	—	Renting	Bought	Current		30
B	$	$	—	Building	No	Bought	To be det'd		50 est.
C	$	$	—	Building	No	Buying	To be det'd		50
D	$	$	—	Building	No	Buying	To be det'd	To be det'd	40
E	$	$	—	Built	No	Bought	To be det'd	To be det'd	—

[a] Actual charts include dollar values.
[b] Acronyms identify organizations that helped fund the program.
[c] Actual charts include place names.

of the date on which a given version of the chart had been printed, it was not possible to easily compare several charts over the course of a period of time in order to trace the progress of one or more specific maquilas. Insider knowledge was required to make the comparisons between some of these place-names. Also, some of the later entries did not list specific residences for socios, because these were part of the Northeast Project and were being initiated in different ways.

On my first visit to the office in June 1999, I too was given the thick volume of migration proceedings and these other documents. With time, I wondered if the charts were intentionally overwhelming, forestalling deeper analysis. One day I tried to make sense of several different, undated versions of a chart of program maquilas and asked Rosi to go through one with me. She made up a scheme on the spot, scribbling on the first eight an E for "está bien," or "doing well." Then she wrote P for "pending," which she elaborated as: construction was completed, "pero ya no" (i.e., not yet operational). One was cancelled and maybe another two were also. There were about five to eight question marks. One was listed as being "constructed" and buying machinery, but this was a deserted construction site we had visited one day. As Rosi went through the chart with me, summarizing the status of each business, her face and words expressed clearly the great variation and uncertainty about these place-names. With some she shook her head, glancing at el Licenciado's office, and said, "He thinks so, but I don't think this one will happen," or "I believe, no," on and on, with varying degrees of sadness, concern, or pleasure. The uncertainty of the process was acknowledged, but it was also a sad and troubling fact. As with other times when I learned of maquilas involved in problematic situations, the information was imparted with great sorrow, in sad whispers.

A factory once profiled as a model had been the site of distrust, nepotism, and allegations of embezzlement. At the time of my research, this factory was being run by the son of el Licenciado, in an outcome which was viewed with disfavor by the program directors. They whispered that yes, it was part of the program, "but it's not typical." Rosi said sorrowfully, "It's painful to say," when I asked innocently about the thick file. She told me that "[the son of el Licenciado] says what to do, and el Licenciado does it." A visitor to the office who was also involved in the case dropped his voice to a whisper to summarize it as "a series of irregularities." By 2002, the general bureaucratic and operational "limbo" of the Mi Comunidad program and most of its maquilas was being sadly admitted, although plans to maintain and strengthen the program were also continuing.

While awareness of wider uncertainties did not prevent the reproduction for outsiders of these charted possibilities, if someone like me was going to push for even more details, they might be revealed, but with a kind of painful sadness. I felt I had pried too far in questioning things, and, as if hearing an adult's whisper to a child in explaining a sad family secret, I felt vaguely guilty for even asking. On another occasion, I saw Rosi evade questions over a period of several days from a journalist about statistics and overheard their somewhat tense discussions about the validity of the data which Rosi was providing. Thus, the chart was officially useful, but also evocative of intense emotion.

THE BEAUTIFUL MAQUILAS

Another important program record was a photo album with pictures taken at many different maquila sites and events. Soco always took this album to meetings with outsiders, even when we met the director of the Institute of Women, a setting in which she must have sensed that her program would be regarded with misgivings. One maquila could be seen in the background of a photo, clearly unfinished. In the foreground Rosi stood looking sweetly pleased, next to the *mariachi* band hired to serenade her as a surprise for her birthday. When I asked about this maquila later, I learned that since the time the photo was taken a year earlier, no further progress had been made on the site. The smiles and waves of people standing in front of unfinished maquilas were poignant: photographed in their hopes for the opening of the business, an opening that still had not come. The beaming faces of the investors and government workers as they clustered closely together and were photographed from a distance looked small in front of the cavernous space of the maquila behind them, walled on three sides and with a roof, but open entirely from one side. Rosi smiled with remembered delight in recounting the fun of the surprise celebration. Her faith in the program and her personal fondness for the jefes and socios involved in it were the most important issues for her, not the actual status of the particular project.

One day the three of us stopped to inspect what looked to me like an abandoned construction site in the middle of acres of fields, where workers were bent over picking vegetables, wearing shirts tied around their heads against the afternoon sun. The site was once intended by its owner for a disco, but he was shifting to the idea of a maquila because the location was so remote. Despite her discouragement at its state, Soco nevertheless took several photographs of us standing in front of the structure. In the pictures we are standing close together, laughing and waving, arms around each other. *Something* existed on the site at least; the name of it remained stubbornly in the charts and statistics.

Soco also kept a stack of photographs from the maquilas, enlarged and mounted on white cardboard, on top of a shelf in the office to show visitors and to take along for displaying at opening ceremonies. A film made about the program and passed out to every participant at one maquila opening shows smiling, hard-working young women seated at their machines, as an attractive young female government journalist explains the workings of the program to viewers. Websites, official documents, and other publications also communicated pride and a sense of exciting opportunity regarding maquilas in the interior of Mexico. A publication by an association of clothing industry suppliers proclaims the prosperity and development ahead for Mexico through free trade in the clothing industry. One edition of *Pa'l Norte* shows two young women smiling as they work with a sewing machine, while the accompanying editorial praises Guanajuato for its location and the maquilas as one of the main avenues for investment of binational citizens who want to become businessmen. In one scene, the full complement of female workers stand by their machines in the film and shout out "We are working hard here in —!" But this maquila was the subject of trouble and grievously lower production just one year later.

The differences in scholarly focus regarding maquilas have their counterpart within the program practices. The straightforward rationale of job creation was seen as sufficient. It supported the claim of a "social service" being granted to the poor women of the isolated villages. This creation of jobs in and of itself was a source of pride; the *kind* of jobs was not the point. As crude as some of the physical conditions of the maquilas appeared to me, evocative of the history of the textile industry and early capitalism, yet government photographers and journalists were regularly shown around the maquilas in order to take photos for publicity, indicating that these factories were an achievement, not a shame, on a micro level. To realize this sincere sense of pride in these businesses was always an odd experience for me, accustomed as I am to the taken-for-granted notion of maquilas as terrible sweatshops. There is a great poignancy to the program, captured in numerous references during the film to "the dream" of building the maquilas. The earnest investors clearly believe in the benefits of the work, and the interviewed workers are alternately proud, nervous, shy, and humble as they describe their hopes to the interviewer.

Indeed, in relative terms these jobs of sewing are not the worst kind of work, and in some remote villages of the interior states, they are the only work available. It is clean, indoor work at which one does not have to bend over all day in the fields or be on one's knees; it also involves some chance of socializing with one's fellow workers. Although repetitive within a given product order, the styles and fabrics do change. The official, positive assertions are not merely ideological or false; they reflect realities for the people involved which must be taken seriously, even as one worries that the interior spread of maquilas is a sign of the "maquilization" of Mexico within the new international division of labor and that the polluted sprawl of the border areas will reach into the rest of Mexico (Peña 1997; Sklair 1993).

THE VALUE OF DATA

The emotion, confusion, and slight defensiveness regarding program data suggested that statistics and photographs were important symbols beyond their bureaucratic value. They mediated hopes and fears over the future of the program and deferred outside critique. The program directors already knew very well the vulnerable points of the program, and submitting these to even wider examination was personally painful, especially for the sensitive Rosi. They were also aware of the implications of maquila work. The "reworkings of physical presence" undertaken by bureaucrats (Greenhouse 1998) took the form in this case of intellectual or discursive acts of distancing. One staff member told me that Soco and Rosi were very invested in the program and did not want to think, and indeed could not, about its wider implications. In specific settings, the word *maquila*, which was usually used by the directors almost as exclusively as the words *las muchachas*, was replaced by other words for business, factory, or workshop, words like *taller* or *fábrica*. Soco explicitly noted to outsiders that the word *maquila* is associated with exploitation, so she preferred to use words like *empresa* (enterprise) or *negocio* (business).

At the meeting in the Institute of Women, Soco introduced the Mi Comunidad program as "businesses, well, in fact, maquilas," going on to assert that the government's first aim had been support for the business side, protecting the investment of the *paisanos*, and similar goals. In this setting, she emphasized the *economic* side of their work, not the social. This change from her statements in other settings reflected her awareness of the location of the meeting, an office where the needs of women were being dealt with more directly as social issues. There, she did not try to present her program as a social one. She also explicitly noted the concept of maquilas as exploitative, but she distanced her own program from that concept by saying the government was now in a position to become more involved in the women as human resources, even offering a kind of apologetic tone on how in the past they had not been able to do so due to "limited resources."

I think for both of the directors, the notion that the women received a paid training period was another key point which distinguished their program from others in maquila industry. This helps to explain why the act of quitting after the training was particularly resented by the directors and the jefes. From the point of view of Soco and Rosi, the people in real need of state assistance were those running the businesses.

As opposed to the single line of data for each maquila on the publicly distributed chart, individual files in the program's two filing cabinet drawers attested to the complexity and uniqueness of each case. Within some folders, there were copies of checks from the government, receipts for equipment, notices of inauguration ceremonies, and other documents that charted the relatively straightforward progress of several maquilas. The files provided a record of slowly increasing independence for some but trouble and failure for others. Some problems affected the maquilas right from the early planning stages, for example in raising funds and arranging details (for electricity, water, road paving, construction specifications, etc.) with local officials. The file of one unfinished maquila had records of meetings over funding for a school, and two years later, problems with water, electricity, and roads. These documents trace the history of multiple, interlocking needs in these home communities, possibly because local officials had not implemented basic services even when they had been funded by other levels of government. There were lengthy efforts by the distant socios to deal with these areas of need. Another file showed correspondence about debt collection, quality issues and defects, repairs needed, additional loans, and troubles with a landlord.

Records also showed a massive total "subsidy" from the government to support several maquilas in October 1999, indicating program-wide financial difficulties. Once Rosi told me that the government had paid the salaries of all the managers in the program for the entire previous year. The state government invested a great deal of money and effort to help small and medium-sized businesses succeed in Guanajuato, but in the case of the Mi Comunidad program, far from being ready to advance to other stages of operations, some of the maquilas seemed at risk for mere survival. As for the program itself, rather than fulfill Fox's goal of ten more maquilas annually after the ten of the initiation year (1996), in the start of 2000 there were still really only ten working maquilas, with several said to be "in the works" in various stages. The number of maquilas said to be in the program, and the number given to the documentary filmmaker, was twenty-six. Again, as noted, this uncertainty was more fully borne out by 2002, when the program as a whole was described as being in a suspended or pending state.

The fragility of the process made the businesses that *had* survived all the more noteworthy. In the government-made film about the program, the narrator notes that one of the maquilas is not currently in operation, but plans to reopen soon, although interviews and footage of it had already been included in the movie at that point. Slowly, one realizes that all of the footage related to this one particular maquila is presented in black and white, rather than color, and the edges of the screen have been slightly blurred, as if to suggest that although the achievement of this specific dream cannot be celebrated in the way that others are in the film, it still exists, only in a kind of fuzzy and gray, dormant version. The simple act of adding a place-name to the chart, and leaving it there, was a gesture of hope that in itself was valuable and indicative of the perennial optimism of the administrators. Although they recognized that the maquila process was tenuous and easily interrupted, they continued to hope that all of the dreams would come true. Even with the uncertainty of later restructurings, in 2002 Soco carefully showed me the entire catalog of products planned for the maquila of Las Cruces.

As I observed the varying presentations of the program, I wondered if there were simply no "true" answers to some of my questions about the maquilas, such as the notion of their profitability. Documents suggested large deficits in some accounts, and one jefe joked at a meeting that at the most his profits had been about 4,000 pesos (about U.S.$400). The others present wryly noted they had no money at all. Yet copies of undated slides from a presentation about the program state that the actual amount of investment into the "Integrated Maquilas" was U.S.$2,026,400 per year, with an average annual income per maquila of U.S.$225,155 and a 30 percent return on investment. The actual amount of work the maquilas had at any given time, and their production levels, were also subject to multiple interpretations, as noted. I could see that Soco and Rosi themselves were not always privy to certain details. I learned that not only were my own notions of what constituted a task with a specific beginning and end irrelevant in this setting where personal relations were highly valued, but that my notion of what constituted a *fact* to be learned about the program differed greatly from the kinds of facts which existed, and the contexts and reasons for giving them. Dates, amounts, locations—all were subject to negotiation and context. Yes, some maquilas actually existed, and so did sewing machines and workers. But others did not, or were no longer *really* a part of the program, or might not ever be, and yet were still listed on the official statistics and spreadsheets, or had loaned or borrowed machines and workers amongst themselves that they should not have really done, and so on.

BLURRING THE LINES

Taken as a whole, the many quality reports and consultants' bills in the office files, together with the optimistic data and shifting rationales, suggested to me a certain kind of optimism and hope, even gullibility, on the part of the directors in wanting to believe that various outsiders could provide solutions to the problems of the maquilas. At first I worried that I was the beneficiary of this kind of trust myself. But as I organized files and then watched them quickly become rearranged again, I saw that the most important things were not in the file cabinets. Some key documents were behind a curtain next to Soco's desk, which I joked was "the secret archive," or in her car. Facts and figures were in her assistant Rosi's formidable memory. Other things were intangible, like the close personal relationships and fond memories, which were protected from all outsiders. The appearance of openness to new ideas and to outside assistance was not an indication of gullibility but of a certain amount of cleverness and even wisdom. In describing the program to outsiders, both of the program directors were shrewdly able to assess the degree of detail they needed to go into about the program in any given context, judging the relative sophistication or education of any interlocutor. For example, with the rather intimidating documentary film crew (a group of tall, handsome men from Mexico City and their highly educated employers), the program goal was presented in its most basic "outside" form: to attract investment. Stripped of its emotional overtones about poverty, whether of remote villages or abandoned females, this is nevertheless an important goal, one at which the program was succeeding, and yet one which was relatively downplayed in most official presentations of the program.

Statistics and other presentations were a strategic necessity for the directors as bureaucrats validating and effectively maintaining the program and generating outside interest and investment income. Through them, the program directors expressed their vision of the future and were able to successfully produce themselves as bureaucrats. Statistics were part of a larger project of hopeful self-presentation in orientation toward the future as the place of improvement, the place where many problems will be resolved at last. Valuable in their very existence, data suggest progress and success. They speak of effectiveness, of the possibility of entry as equal partners into the complex global economy for the directors, all of the family members, and even for Mexico. To scratch the surface and ask more questions about this data *was* a bit prying, given such a scheme of hope and given the many ways in which the program directors were already working to support the program.

The directors sought to learn more from the academics and consultants they knew and to genuinely address the real problems they saw within the maquilas and in the program, while protecting secrets and details. Numeric data and program rationale had little bearing on the everyday practices of the program and the warmth of family relations within it. These evasions could easily be misinterpreted as dishonest. It would also be easy to suggest that this quality is related to what Rosi described as a "Mexican" need to gain approval. Indeed, one account of state bureaucracy in Mexico notes the "administrative value" of records as in a sense promoting an "image" of project results to superiors which does not reflect reality, while protecting the central bureaucracy (Arce 1993, 57–58). But such "promotion" strikes me as inherent to most organizational structures. Moreover, while shifts in the program rationale and data do prevent key problems from being addressed, I argue that these are not merely political uses of data, self-deceptions, or naivete.

PRACTICING THE STATE

Practices which deferred the authority of the program directors, as well as those which constituted a loyal, performative use of statistics and other images, also created a degree of autonomy for the program directors. Through statistics, Soco and Rosi positioned their official selves between the program and the world of their boss, the close, watchful office, and any other people with whom dealings were difficult or unpleasant. Their optimistic presentation of data may also have reflected skepticism about the worth of quantifying the important and deeply personal workings of the program, thereby preventing the incursions of outsiders.

Soco and Rosi escaped the tight office, with its gossip and back-biting and tiresome federal and state constraints, exploring and creating other spaces. They did so through the privilege of being themselves part of the "state," protecting their closest relationships, their own families, beliefs, secrets, and pasts. Thus, as officials, they were also able to maintain their most valued identities: daughter, wife, mother, and friend.

The program directors brought great seriousness and zeal to certain tasks, and spoke in very emotional terms about how much they cared for the program, working hard in many ways that could be considered both highly "professional" and very "emotional." But they also maintained a slightly bemused and distant attitude toward their work, and a certain resistance to pressures from their boss. For them, it truly was just a job. Indeed, each separately described to me a later disagreement with each other in terms of the need to maintain the integrity of their home life. They did not see themselves as a part of a deadly serious process of "embodying" the state. Rather, they were in a sense learning, even practicing, the process of being the state, a process that was continuously changing and contingent. They altered their self-descriptions and positionality on state authority itself, depending on the different contexts in which they found themselves, and the different tasks and responsibilities they faced.

As the global movements of capital and people begin to seem more incomprehensible and strange, perhaps the acts of wishing and hoping which constituted so much of Mi Comunidad practices, and the summoning of the magical power of statistics, mediate between the worlds of known reality and an "outside" of unimaginable wealth and power. Such wishes are not limited to this one case; they appear widespread and evident in the imagined "global economy." I suggest that they maintain the peculiar superstition that human complexity and unpredictability are best conceived as "rational agency." Such faith may even have the force of Herzfeld's (1992) notion of "secular theodicy," which invoked Weber.

In addition to the complex uses and meanings of data, it is important to note the program directors' use of a management concept which linked the family of the program to the "outside" world and transnational economy. Facing the vast scope of possible failures, the hopes of investors, and the reality of half-finished maquilas, keenly aware of problems in the program, Soco and Rosi relied heavily on the symbol of "quality."

DOCUMENTING QUALITY

State government documents, and later the federal PAN government's executive branch website, made frequent references to quality and ISO-9000, a set of international industrial standards. All-day quality meetings were regularly held by many state government agencies in Guanajuato, and thick binders of Total Quality documents from other workshops sprawled in the trunk of Soco's car. Quality was a theme in conversations Soco held with directors and garment industry dealers, as well as with job candidates. Written documents, letters, and memoranda showed that quality was a key reason for integrating nine of the maquilas in the Textile Association of Guanajuato in late 1998 and was part of other proposals as well. In the DACGE office, weekly quality and morale meetings were scheduled, but not always held. A lawyer on the staff had been hired primarily for the purpose of reinforcing quality; mostly she pressured us to go to weekly state-level quality meetings.

The emphasis in program events and documents on quality was echoed in the directors' comments and exhortations to the jefes, which is not surprising in the context of business and state government discourse. But within the familial intimacy of the program, this theme of quality also allowed the directors to subtly address, by carefully obscuring, certain sensitive "inside" problems in the maquila operations stemming from decisions made in the early planning for the program, from the very rhetoric of the program as a crossborder policy, and from ongoing assumptions and practices.

FAMILY SECRETS

I had realized after several meetings that there were always various father-son teams in attendance. The program had indeed created some opportu-

nities to acquire managerial experience, but these jobs tended to be re-
stricted to the male relatives of the men involved in the program as socios
or jefes. These young managers were those most at risk for leaving Mexico. The reality of kinship relations had ensured that the supervisory positions of the maquilas would tend to go to the young male relatives of the
people in the top levels of the program, but the patterns of familial intimacy in the program made this a sensitive topic, beyond the control of
Soco and Rosi.

Newspaper accounts praising the Mi Comunidad program explicitly
promoted the provision of work for one's relatives as a positive aspect to
the work-creation process. This has been seen by participants as a positive
virtue in Mexican administrative dealings because it creates conditions for
more trust (Grindle 1977; Soto Romero 1999), but for others such relations
are problematic. The corporate separation of family from work, based on
a belief in "impersonal" decision-making, is often more of an ideal than a
reality (Biggart 1996), and certainly in early industrial America was not the
case (Nelson 1975).

Privacy or discretion regarding the most important and unpleasant issues is an important part of boundary work, of maintaining smooth relations in a family, or of producing graciousness between citizen and state
in bureaucratic dealings. In the Mi Comunidad program, not all of the
family members who had been hired to run or supervise the maquilas
were well qualified. In the cases where the owner and manager were the
same, or where managers were better qualified, problems seemed less
marked, and less intervention by the government was needed. The fact of
unqualified management was related, although not in all cases, to the lack
of leadership, low product quality, and some of the other endemic problems in the maquilas, but this linkage was not typically stated. Instead, the
female workers were blamed, for example in the Monterrey report, which
pointedly omitted factors of importance to workers, such as salary and
work schedules, from its litany of program problems. The "poor" and
"lukewarm" responses of the workers were noted, but any enlightening
details of their responses were not presented. Indeed, the assertion by the
maquila supervisors that there was a lack of "work ethic" was listed by
the researchers as one of the "Major Business Problems" facing the maquilas, along with "worker attitude." This uncritical acceptance of the supervisors' assessment of the workers' unhappiness, coupled with the lack
of any data from questionnaires or interviews to illuminate the "poor and
lukewarm" responses, marked the document in my view as overly pro-
management and as solely in favor of stunningly costly solutions from
above.

The discourse of blame had become a bureaucratic habit. Soco's impa-

tience with the "male" attitudes she saw at work in Las Cruces was triggered only after a long period of frustration with this particular case. Yet
there were signs of change: although Soco sought to support and protect
the bosses of the program, she angrily denounced, on many occasions, her
own boss for his use of relatives in the program and for his efforts to force
her to assist them professionally. One afternoon we sat in the car in a street
bustling with strawberry and melon vendors, as Soco, between passionate complaints about el Licenciado's high-handed manner with her,
arranged things via her cell phone so that she would not have to help the
boss's son with some required paperwork.

This issue also burst into the program directors' everyday optimism in
a key meeting held by Soco, Rosi, and an enthusiastic consultant at a government agency which assists businesses. On our way to this meeting, we
three had driven to León squeezed into Soco's tiny car along with several
of her relatives, including her son, all of whom were going along for medical and shoe-buying errands (it was a school holiday). The consultant,
Miguel, whom Soco trusted deeply, responded to Soco's optimistic narrative about an expensive quality course for the jefes by baldly stating that
none of the bosses of the maquilas had the capacity to even benefit from
it. He said that "here in Mexico" this kind of boss does not know how to
run a business, but they have to learn to be productive quickly in the current world economy. He noted that the socios also needed to learn this and
be educated to the fact that they should not waste their investment on unqualified people. The fact that many of the maquilas were being run by
relatives of the socios hindered their ability to thrive because their pool of
managerial talent was limited from the start, he added. Soco averred the
importance of the family relations and how they govern these decisions:
that people look for the job to offer the nephew, brother, or cousin. Then,
showing her absorption of Miguel's remarks, she added that they did this
rather than starting with the post and looking to fill it with the best person. This was the most forthright expression of this fact of the program
that I ever heard; both Rosi and Soco discussed this issue more often after
this. It was even included in a draft about Miguel's plan as an issue relating to the lack of leadership, but was later deleted.

The ongoing studies of the lack of quality stalled more direct action, but
the issue was beginning to evade the controls of bureaucratic discourse
and practice, as evidenced in Soco's bursts of anger over Gerardo, the banter in ITG meetings, the shame over failed maquilas, and the bluntness of
Miguel's words. At this meeting with Miguel, I mentioned an idea which
I had already brought up on two occasions with the program directors.
Given the ongoing problem of a lack of qualified and adequate supervisors within the program, I had suggested the option of including the

women workers themselves as candidates in the labor pool for the supervisory positions. Soco and Rosi had immediately rejected this notion. Yet Miguel was very enthusiastic about it, noting how the knowledge of workers is being increasingly put to use in workplace innovations, problem-solving, and procedural improvements. This discussion did not lead to specific change.

THE LIMITS OF SOLIDARITY

The citizen–state interface in the Mi Comunidad program was shaped by Soco's forceful will and personality. Her recasting of truths about the program may have mystified and deferred uncomfortable realities, but it also supported her enactment of her own complex vision of fairness and success. Aware of structural problems in Mexico, and participative in a discourse of "lack" about the country, her sustained, fervent act of hope in wishing for the success of the program and its participants was framed by a vision of how to achieve this success, and who was likely to do so. Encouraging the managers, her primary clients, was one of her most important means of safeguarding the investment of the *paisanos;* she knew how easy it would be for the factories to slip back into the dust and weeds of an unfinished, empty concrete structure. She also strongly valued traditional roles within the family based upon a distinction between male and female emotional capacity. Thus it was that the "insider," family practices of the program, consonant with its goal of nurturing new businesses, produced culturally valued warmth and sociality at the managerial-class level. This warmth was inherently ambivalent because of the intersection of gender and class differences within the program.

Soco and Rosi were very close with other women who were involved in the program, such as a friend of theirs who is an official in a federal agency and one female maquila boss. But in general, as noted especially in the previous chapter, the program directors were dismissive toward las muchachas, women whom they considered to be in a distinctly different class. Middle-class values affected the "reworkings of bureaucratic presence" (Greenhouse 1998), distancing them from their weaker "sisters," who were thought to lack "culture" and who bore other attributes of lower value. Soco and Rosi's strength and power as women had not translated into a sense of camaraderie with the female workers. In their enactment of the state in this case, they forged ties of equality instead with men based on what they hoped would be shared middle-class values. Female authority, dissembled through metaphors of nurturance, extended the social work of the program in support of the male managers and investors only. Soco distances herself from "feministas" ("they hate men"), but she can easily do so, because she controls her own marriage and all extended family relationships, following in the footsteps of her highly engaging and domineering father. In planning the job descriptions and advertisements for the quality administration position in the ITG plan discussed above, Soco suggested to the jefes that they advertise for a man. She said that with family commitments, a woman would simply not be able to give the time commitment to the job that was needed. Of course, a woman must think of her children and her husband and other responsibilities first, and was thus compromised. All of the directors chuckled in agreement, while the sole jefa said nothing. As a friend to this very confident professional woman, I was surprised to hear her blunt statement, but I would not assume it was from *self*-doubt or alienation, although both women had expressed to me on other occasions their views of women as less rational and more emotional than men. Soco herself devoted vast amounts of time and energy to the administration of the program, while managing to be intensely involved with her doting husband, son, parents, grandparents, and a wide network of relatives and in-laws. Thus she knew full well that a woman *could* do the job. But she had already planned to reserve one of the two positions for Ana, a woman, so she was seeking to balance her a priori choice with a man. She could flatter the jefes a bit and let them feel as if they were having a say in the plan she was designing for them. In this case, she herself used a prevailing ideology about women's emotional nature to distance herself from other women and exert control over a work situation. In one sense, she subverted the very ideology she had evoked.

POSSIBILITIES

As in other instances of my fieldwork, participation in meetings provided useful insights into the complexity of gender issues in Mexico. Workshops on gender allowed me to witness (and at times engage) professional Mexican women grappling with these issues and debating with each other. There were many variations: an elaborate first anniversary celebration of the Institute of Women was held at one of the fanciest hotels in Guanajuato. Like fundraising events I had attended in a previous job with a charitable organization, the showy setting was oddly contrary to the key theme in speeches: the importance of reaching the most marginalized women (*las olvidadas de las olvidadas*). The first priority was protecting women from domestic violence; the second, female workers' rights.

Other workshops demonstrated the enormous potential for the dissemination of ideas about the construction of gender in society, as women of many different backgrounds worked together to define issues from scholarly texts. These topics were moving into the mass media and entertainment venues well. Once, several people from the office attended a performance by a feminist actress who spoke of sexual taboos and other such topics. Soco and Rosi were excited about the event, and Soco jokingly pantomimed how the older women in the audience had crossed themselves and kissed the crosses hanging from their necklaces. Another time Soco, with great approval, read aloud from and passed around the office an editorial about women written by candidate Fox, outlining his plan for including women in government and working to equalize their status in Mexico. She handed it to me with a special nod of gravity, for by then gender issues had been a common car-ride topic for us.

Yet of course, other patterns persist. Even the gender workshop coordinator, a woman, used the expression "Que padre," a phrase in Mexican Spanish that is equivalent to "Great!" and is distinctly the opposite from "Que madre," which is virtually untranslatable and obscene. When four of us women from the government attended a workshop in a distant city, the program directors participated in the two-day conference only for the first afternoon. At a state-government-run workshop on gender and poverty, Soco introduced herself to the group by saying that we were attending in order to find ways to help the women of the program. Later they claimed it had been interesting, then spent the night ridiculing the women of the office. Soco insisted we all describe how we lost our virginity. The two of them left as early as they could the next day for a wedding, in effect stranding a staff member and me (although making some arrangements on our behalf to get part of the way back to Guanajuato), on whom the irony of this happening at a gender conference was not lost. Soco was excited about a new outfit she had bought for this wedding, a dress and shoes that we had helped her shop for, and she was excited that she had been able to include Rosi in the invitation.

Although they were open to new ideas, there was only so far they would want to go down such a lonely and angry road, since for them the ultimate message of feminism was an anti-male one, as characterized by a strong, assertive female journalist in the office. Moreover, the ideas were issued in dull contexts: for example during a meeting held at an institute far out in the fields away from any nearby town, attended by mostly women, and plagued by flies, or in a small overly serious meeting held with a plain woman with no makeup. As emotional appeals, they fell flat, because Soco and Rosi believed and indeed knew, that they were *already* helping these women.

Soco rejected the efforts of others to control her as a woman, and used her "female" qualities instead to control situations within the office and the program. Deeply aware of the power of language, she shifted her use of words to describe the program, its intent, and so forth as needed. Given an opportunity to learn the analytical tools of feminism, she smilingly presented her most charming official self, but read the social situation at the workshop accurately as being a rather boring group of social workers with only two men present, and then discarded the experience completely, later using the discourse she learned at the gender workshop to promote her own involvement in it. The rationale for our attendance at the gender workshop was even listed in the monthly DACGE bulletin on staff activities: we had attended this workshop: "To acquire tools for understanding the sociological and productive situation of the women who work in the maquiladoras of the program." Our plan of "helping the women" was still unclear at that time, but as a clever strategist, Soco was already promoting our involvement in such an effort, and presenting this latest, flattering image of the program to the outside world.

The revolutionary possibility of Soco regarding the maquila women as sisters in a wider struggle for dignity has thus far been deferred. Perhaps this deferral was similar to the way in which she verbally displaced her own obvious and complete physical authority within the program and her life. Perhaps her own role in heading a program to strengthen local businesses was significant in itself. But her intellectual rejection of the new seminar-based information which directly pertained to the exact theoretical intersections of gender and class which were at work within her own program, was not inconsistent with her encouraging and kind manner toward me *personally* as a person who was also, in a much more indirect way, bringing up these kinds of issues. "Ah, this has really opened our eyes!" she assured me with sincerity, nodding at Rosi for confirmation, as we talked after the first day of the workshop. She wanted me to feel good about the fact that they were all attending the workshop; that desire of hers was far more important, and easier to achieve, than a more sustained effort to rethink the program through the new ideas themselves. For after all, those were only ideas. And she had a wedding to get to.

TYPES OF PLANNING

The work experience and intrinsic value of the workers were far from a top priority for any of the management. In fact, even thinking of these women as "human resources" (a problematic term in itself, long co-opted by corporate bureaucrats [Ferguson 1984]) was a *luxury* that the program management could only afford to acknowledge once other things were addressed. This kind of "no-frills" thinking about labor seemed to be vindicated by one particular case within the program.

One afternoon, we visited the construction site of an ambitious maquila project and took several photographs of large earth-moving equipment and teams of men working, digging, and soldering metal. We did not pose in the photographs this time, smiling or waving, for this was a serious project, where serious money was being spent. An engineer showed us the space for a large soccer field and a septic system that would cleanse the water and use it to irrigate nearby fields. Soco had proudly described this maquila and the large investment being made into it to me, and later to other officials. A newspaper article profiling the project, and the sad history of water shortages that marked the history of the town, was clipped and carefully filed along with the many others that describe maquilas of the program. Representatives of the socios traveled to Guanajuato to attend a meeting with a sewing machine salesman at which they negotiated an expensive deal for thirty-four new, rather than used, machines. The thoughtful young man who represented the fifty or so socios involved in this project made a point of carefully asking the salesman about the noise level of the machines and whether the workers would need ear plugs. Although they had already raised U.S.$220,000 for this plant, they planned to come up with even more for the sewing machines. At another meeting in June, the other jefes in the program joked about hesitating to go to the inauguration of such a fancy maquila, as it would make them ashamed of their own.

Then all was postponed. These hopeful and well-organized men, headed by a young and very sincere, serious engineering student, ran out of money and had to indefinitely postpone the inauguration of their maquila. The decision followed a series of events that almost seemed to prove the folly of trying to emphasize the social aspects of the maquila by going beyond the bare minimum: provision of a job. While both Soco and Rosi were sad as they reported the indefinite postponement of work on this site, I wondered if they secretly felt it was inevitable with such an ambitious project. Rosi said simply "They ran out of money because the construction was so expensive."

In reaching for a broader social impact, this project was an exception to the enduring developmentalist assumption that social justice, community-based planning, or gender equity issues are too "expensive" to include in the early stages of development planning.[1] This assumption is increasingly being questioned by scholars (Castañeda 1994). Albert O. Hirschman (1992) writes that his own argument thirty years ago for "sequential" problem-solving in policy and statesmanship, with its related "jeopardy thesis" (that one step forward may jeopardize earlier gains), is problematic for the simple reason that problems are *all too separable.*" In other words, it is easy and tempting to push ahead with certain issues and leave the more difficult ones aside, perhaps permanently. Feminists would argue that this has been the pattern with most nationalisms (McClintock 1991; Stoler 1989; Williams 1996).

The workings of sequential problem-solving were evident in the Mi Comunidad program in the processes through which the female workers typically came to be seen as not worth any investment beyond their initial training, let alone worth including in decision-making. The foundational value of male contributions to the program, and the equation of money with participation, were two important aspects of this process. When the businesses were finally established and operational, all of them were run along the lines of traditional business models, based upon hierarchized labor-management relations. Management functions included planning and inventory control, supervisory oversight of workers and of cost-profit concerns, and record-keeping. Laborers worked at simple, repetitive tasks determined by managers; in general, the work process in the maquilas of the border has become so fragmented that it is described as "hyperspecialized" (Peña 1997). In the small maquilas of the program, laborers were usually uninvolved in other work functions such as allocation of work load, scheduling of breaks, higher-level decision-making or input, and other tasks. In the larger maquilas of the border, "group chiefs" are often recruited from among the workers and assigned these slightly higher-level tasks, although Devon Peña charges that they are often harassed and manipulated. But in Guanajuato, the only time I saw female workers who were engaged in a task away from their sewing machines was when they stood at tables checking the finished products for quality prior to packing them; in other factories, this work was done by supervisors.

In these and many other ways, the implementation of the program fostered a definition of business or management knowledge as a limited, finite, male good.[2] Those representing the state within the program partnership were able, through their practices, to initially shape access to information and to construct knowledge as a static, preexisting and inheritable resource to be *received*, in which only some could share, and which emanated from *above* and *outside* of local contexts and processes. Soco and Rosi's own physical reality as women introduced an unpredictable aspect to this transfer, for they were not just conduits for the knowledge; they clearly possessed it through their university training and professional status and power—circumstances which outweighed their position as young females. But although they passed this information on as relatively powerful women, knowledge and its workings became gendered as "male" within the workplace and its organization of production. The investors and managers soon became a part of furthering this hierarchical knowledge process as they joined in the ranks of those in relative power. Knowledge could not be plural or multiple, could not grow, change, or be shared. In a teleological world in which it is imperative to "catch up," perhaps there is no time to include all voices in the construction of knowledge, policy, or social change.

SUMMARY

The unqualified male relatives in charge of some maquilas were not the only cause of the problems with quality, but silence over their role meant that the women workers were simultaneously blamed for these problems and barred from using their own very real, practical knowledge to improve production or quality. This kind of ambivalence can be traced in other cases of early industrialization, when control and knowledge were moved from the shop floor and the foreman to "professional or scientific" management (Nelson 1975). Thus, there is another side to the hopeful program statistics, the spaces made available for possibility and change, and the warm management relations. The concept of "quality" was used to blame the female workers for problems within the maquilas and for preventing the full realization of progress in the global market. Patterns of blame undermined and precluded deeper analyses of problems with quality.

Bureaucratic distancing within the Mi Comunidad program reflected middle class beliefs and stemmed from a male- and business-oriented vision of the future as the place of success. The desperate hopes for the program family, and the presence of two females in charge of it, precluded the discovery of commonality among all of the women of the program. In a sense, the directors' power was offset by statements and practices which affirmed that key foundations of authority would remain in place, even in the transition to the global market. But the subject of las muchachas as a management issue was beginning to arise in formal and informal ways, and there *were* spaces for change in the ways of casting the issue. In a meeting, Soco used the oddity of my presence to introduce the notion of the women as "human resources." She could present this idea as coming from an anomalous perspective somewhat outside of the program, rather than from herself, and make it a less threatening possibility to the jefes. Perhaps even to speak about the women in other ways during meetings marked a tiny change and suggests the constant presence of alternative directions for state policy and practice. Indeed, although by 2002 the program as a whole had been placed in a kind of temporary "limbo" under the authority of two different departments, both Soco and Rosi told me of their exposure to new ideas through university classes and through their new boss, suggesting changing directions for them in terms of their everyday work. Thus, while the fragile dreams of the Mi Comunidad participants were themselves being "deferred" within a context of wider awareness about program problems, many state government officials involved with the program were continuing its pattern of a tenuous balance between hope and doubt.

Stopping to Ask for Directions

Are the Mexican people capable of governing themselves?

T. ESQUIVEL OBREGÓN,
Mexican minister of finance, 1913

This book is in part an ethnography of travel. In our drives across the state of Guanajuato, we crossed and recrossed paths of memory and talk, connecting the different maquilas and their unique, internal social worlds. Close together and free in the small car, laughing, eating, debating, or singing, we were three comadres, inhabiting a world of adventure time. Travel was both an essential practice of the program implementation, and, in the context of this book, has been a key metaphor to describe the PAN vision which shaped the program. The business teleology of the Mi Comunidad program and the class mobility of its directors reflected a vision of Mexico in motion: traveling forward and progressing, wisely investing migrant remittances, and building new opportunities. Mexico's power was recognized and reclaimed by Vicente Fox as being grounded in its people, especially its absent citizens. Yet, within all of the valorizing and empowering discourse of the program, las muchachas were explicitly not heralded, not seen, not even engaged in speech. They simply received the gift of work from the state.

In program practices, the nurturing of the young businesses, and then knowing when to "let go" of them, was an important, "maternal" job. Middle-class physical freedom also was claimed as a female possibility. Even the wisdom of knowing how and when to stop and ask for help was, arguably, evidence of a "female" sensibility. But these empathetic and empowering practices were not extended to the female workers, whose very labor truly is essential to the program. The production of intimacy through everyday practice by the state government officials took an exclusive, differentiating form, creating experiences that program participants used to continually renew their own systems of meaning about work, the future, government, and personhood. These were inherently gendered and gendering experiences, shaped within middle-class values. Traditional and patriarchal forms of business and the family were presumed as normative within the program and good for Mexico—a presumption shared even by the young female administrators of the program. Yet these forms were themselves being changed by the very practices and relationships of the program, as well as by the wider phenomena of migration and the global assembly industry.

"Personal" dealings with the state in Mexico are virtually a cliché in scholarship. But a close look at the forms taken by "the personal" within specific gender and class contexts reveals important contradictions. As Carol Greenhouse (1998) has noted, "official categories do not monopolize the available terms of understanding, no matter how deeply 'inscribed' they are in institutions and preconceptions." Therefore, my perspective on "the state" as also comprised of the persons who embody it allows in this case a glimpse of the multiple, complex aspects of the managerial-level intimacy within the program.

The everyday production of inside intimacy and warmth might well reflect the "sometimes unwitting feminism of women's presence" within organizations and bureaucracies (Katzenstein 1998). Beyond mere presence, however, Soco's powerful will resisted most restraints, including those which were based upon gendered and generational power. Indeed, her practices suggest that "female" power, whether charming, maternal, or in other forms, can be every bit as calculating and dominant as that of any male. She tried on all the roles available to her as a middle- or professional-class, young Mexican woman, a wife, daughter and mother, and seems, in her deployment of them, to have subverted them all in their guise as authoritative claims about the limited singularity of female identity. Like the placement of strong, capable female heads of household into weak positions within the maquilas, Soco's youth and gender were inherent challenges to "traditional" authority. Confronting different types and situations of authority around her, she was usually able to tailor each one to her particular, contextual needs.

Soco's powerful, restless will, and to a lesser degree that of her stubborn, bright assistant, created circumstances within the program that reflected their unique forms of expressing and reacting to a set of expected social roles in Mexico that are based on gender and middle-class/professional work ideologies. Despite her smiling and deferential manner to the boss, she completely overruled him on certain issues. A charismatic leader, but one who was circumscribed by wider contexts of power, she ran the program in a way that made recruitment and enactment of it a positive experience socially, for herself and the managers, fulfilling her own vision of business success. That vision tended to correlate for the most part with the general developmentalist policy aims and Taylorist business model used in the program, but she was extremely flexible in recasting realities when these aims were challenged or they faltered. A wide variety of explanatory categories helped her in this process: rural life in Mexico, "the way some men are," the untrustworthiness of garment industry dealers, las muchachas, and so forth.

Soco's love of pleasure, fun, control, laughter, and conversation were given full rein within the administration of the program and were well suited to a job that required a great degree of zealotry, enthusiasm, and warmth, that of nurturing the young businesses and the older men through a difficult, risky process. Her boss surely recognized these qualities and, in his preoccupation with other dealings, gave her freedom to express them. In a sense, she reproduced conditions which might be described as "hegemonic," through valorizing the male contributions to the program while devaluing las muchachas. Gramsci understood such complexity in hegemonic processes, emphasizing the "ambiguities of consent," as well as the "variety and contrariety of experience" (Femia 1987; Gramsci 1971; Lears 1985; Sennet and Cobb 1973), rather than solely the "strategizing" that in so much of social theory passes for a discussion of personal agency.

Yet the Mi Comunidad case also calls into question the meanings of hegemony as a unidirectional force. For Soco also thwarted and undermined the authority of her boss, which suggests the small, localized, and individual interactions through which power, and maybe corruption, can be challenged and, perhaps, transparency in government can emerge—even from a personally based rather than a collective claim. She and Rosi also engaged in numerous practices which constituted a kind of deferral of their own power as state officials.

Taking seriously the role of "the personal" in government calls into question many scholarly assumptions about activism, civil society, and "the private" as separate from and opposed to the state. For example, the emphases on contestation, negotiation and "sites of struggle" are not as relevant for cases in which assumed, dichotomous realms are themselves continuously undermined by new partnerships or shared identities. Perhaps theorists have needed the state to be a solid, monolithic mass against which to pose society, the individual, and other constructs. Perhaps the very distinction so often assumed between state and society is itself a construct of power, maintaining order through modern, technical means (Bauman 1992; Mitchell 1991). But as the totalizing stance is questioned in so many of its forms, are the new perspectives to be reserved only for the continued, outside analysis of "the subaltern" or the proleteriat? Perhaps if the multiplicity, heterogeneity, and even occasional goodwill of government power is acknowledged more broadly by scholars, traditional positions of critique and complicity will be reconsidered in ways shaped less by polarizing scholarly habits than by efforts to foster dialogue.

These two state government representatives in charge of the Mi Comunidad program were far from insistent on standards of order, Taylorist efficiency, or the "synoptic" eye of the state "creating" homogeneity among citizens (Scott 1998). Continually late for meetings, they arrived slightly disheveled, juggling papers and folders, but always smiling, nodding, and waving with assurance. They often had to borrow pens and blank paper for meetings; the ends of their own clothing were frequently unraveled or held together with tape and pins and in a state of slight disrepair occasioning continuous giggling and laughter. Soco joked with the sewing machine salesman about just quickly reinforcing the hem of her suit jacket on one of the floor models, then rolled her eyes to me when he took her too seriously. Rosi could be stoic and even tough with the jefes on occasion, yet she cried during a meeting with one government official at the news of a change in funding for a quality proposal. They *did* bring the right papers with them to meetings, but that was nearly incidental to the overriding value placed on graciousness, personal warmth, emotion, and humor: the relationships with those around them in the present moment.

Through actions and words, the administrators displayed a laudable understanding of the constant possibilities for failure, seen by James Scott as a sign of wisdom in planning. This understanding was coupled with intense hope for the program and its success and expansion. However, this hope became one of the means by which problematic conditions were recreated. For the act of pointing out problems or asking about them was precluded or deferred, in a sense, by the program's implementation at the emotional level. If problems *were* resignedly admitted, cheery evasion or vague promises followed. To express or acknowledge the undercurrents of doubts, secrets, mistakes, and flaws was to trouble the surface of beautiful hopes. When one is working so hard to maintain an image of success and aptitude for a complex task, discussion of problems is almost rude. In this and many other ways, the program was run like a family in which the problematic behaviors and relationships within were protected from scrutiny by a variety of tactics: the brave smile, the gentle switching of the subject, the defensiveness or hurt when an issue was named aloud.

In this case, government power was embodied by two cheerfully disorganized women in motion, it was not structured and frozen into a stony building or an order-seeking organization, but *structuring* through talk, dreams, relationships, and the patterns which these bore, across wide geographic spaces and the space of dreams connecting the maquilas to their investors. Practices produced both sociality and solidarity, through talk and meetings and sometimes "arguing together about things that matter" (Zabusky 1995, 41).

The highly personal style of administration in the program, with its ripped hems and lost pens, vague statistics and documentation, signs of nepotism, and involvement in a problematic industry sector, may appear altogether highly "irrational" from the outside in two pejorative senses: inefficient and emotional. But this style may well prevent the more heavy-handed intervention of official power or function to forestall clientelism. Moreover, it may nurture the small-business class in a way that is important to significant political change in Mexico. Within a context of slowly decentralizing federal government power, Soco's response to the limits of her authority was notable. She handled the transition graciously within the parameters of the program's teleology toward business independence—rather than with blustering anger, control, invocations of the governor, or demands for personal or long-term rewards. As the managers of the maquilas became more autonomous from the government, they did show a capacity for developing as leaders of small- and medium-sized enterprises; small-business owners may be more inclined to resist government in areas like Guanajuato that have a "strong sense of history," and where people are suspicious of state presence (Wilson 1991).

The personal style of authority projected hopeful futures, eschewing the heavy hand of state control and explicit bribery and maintaining socially valued personal graciousness in the present. As Stacia Zabusky has noted, from a position "inside practice," one can "know, ethnographically" a social system, through its everyday reproduction: "actions, evasions and enunciations of value" (1995, 42), even when the social system is a culture created by a state government policy and when the ethnographer is at the "interface" between citizens and government (Long 1989). Here one also uncovers some of the meanings and gestures which question and reformulate hierarchical, monolithic, and traditional forms of authority (Greenwood 1988). Inside the everyday, there is a special vantage point from which to discern the uneven and ambivalent workings—the fits and starts—of the necessarily continuous project of democracy. The micro-level exposure of these processes is important for, in what are called the "fragile democracies" (Weffort 1993), there is often a contradiction between proclamations about the value of political democracy "as an end in itself" and those which urge "the voluntary renunciation of the rights of citizenship to achieve its consolidation" (Cammack 1994, 188). This contradiction makes the possibility of countries settling for "democracy without citizenship" an especially troubling one (ibid., 193). Perhaps simply not taking one's own power too seriously—enacting government power without a totalizing self-conviction or a singular vision of the future—is a form of embodying the state which merits theoretical and ethnographic attention if only to supplement more traditional emphases on unified, rationalized state power from above and resistance from below.

IN AND OUT OF FAMILIES

This narrative is like numerous others in the anthropological tradition of writing about journeys but differs in that its "discoveries" are not so much things that were new or exotic about myself or others. Nevertheless it bears a radical potential. For in sketching the liminal spaces which lie between macro and micro approaches to the reified entity of the state, whether constructed from the perspective of realpolitik, neorealist, institutional, or post-Enlightenment visions, I have argued for the wisdom of including "the personal" in discussions of government and the state, in both practice and analysis. The personal, "family"-based discourses and practices of this partnership between public and private capital allow one to understand the powerful emotions, ambiguities, and "irrational" particularities of policy implementation which often elude analysis. It is important to include in a discussion of government bureaucracy those emotional and *palpably* physical sensations that are associated with boundary work regarding the category of outsiders, however constructed. For differences in the physical experience and expression of the personal, insider intimacy in this case are indeed factors in the implementation of the policy: they *are* data, and not because they indicate "corruption" or "Mexicanness," let alone "irrationality." They reveal how processes of exclusion can be set in motion and maintained, even within the context of promise.

Ethnography conducted at the state–citizen interface reveals the "dynamic" of the state's "diffuse and heterogenous practices," including modifications of discourse and different contexts of negotiation (Nuijten 1995).[1] The Mi Comunidad program relied initially upon a discourse of family and investment and a male-centered, hierarchical approach to the process of forming the maquilas, reinforcing gender ideologies at work in the program. Insider secrecy and a discourse about quality and lack hid problems related to unqualified male leadership, while isolating and undervaluing the female workers. Discourses about the people of the Mexican countryside, feared for their "collectivity" as expressed in religious revolts from

early colonial Mexico through current activism in Chiapas, yet also excoriated for their "trait" of "nonsolidarity," were also quietly available to justify exclusivist patterns in the program.

However, state discourses *were* altered and challenged in practice, although not in ways which led to more inclusion for the female laborers.
The insider paternalism of the state was recast as the jefes worked to create a sense of separate unity and autonomy among themselves in practice,
redefining the meanings of "inside" in the program. Managers and program directors were open to discussion of some alternative ways of thinking about the laboring women.

Ideology as "meaning in the service of power" (Thompson 1990) is rel-
ativized here by a focus on the micro-level multiplicities and differentials
within power suggested by Foucault. These internal differences and shifts
in the very bases of power were expressed not only in contestations over
meaning but in the framings of decision making and the executions of action.

THE STATE IN MEXICO

To make sense of state power in this case—in terms of the very real presences and practices of cheerfully disorganized females—seems to me an
important and honest, albeit risky, endeavor. Such an effort seems important because it is rarely done from any perspective, and risky, given the
chance that I might echo or reinforce the "rational versus personal" assumptions of dismissive English-language developmentalist studies of
Mexican government and public policy (Grindle 1977; Riggs 1964). As I
have suggested in the use of several examples, this dismissiveness toward
Mexico lingers on in many forms, including business publications and
scholarship.

Research has often taken "government," or worse, governability, to be
inherent in Mexico, at times essentializing the PRI's monolithic nature
rather than seeking to excavate the role of PRI elites in setting the very
definitions and experiences of what politics and government mean. One
still finds "cultural" explanations for Mexican politics (Domínguez and
McCann 1996; Wiarda 1995). Radical political change or revolution in
Mexico always seems to be a possibility to writers and politicians, but
revolution, and thus the future, have been co-opted and quite literally institutionalized by the monolithic party-government through decades of
the practices of "permanent revolution" (Brandenburg 1964; Middlebrook 1995), as symbolized in the very name, the oxymoron adopted by
the Institutional Revolutionary Party. Moreover, cultural discussions and
critiques about Mexico have often become subject to nationalist, ideolog-

ical uses, as with the work of the Mexican *pensadores* (political essayists) (Lomnitz-Adler 1992).

In this book, I have sought to avoid both the judgment of the "irrational" nature of this personalized policy and an over-idealization of the warmth of the relationships. I do realize the irony and risk of appearing to privilege the notion of *personalismo* in a discussion of government bureaucracy in Mexico, but I also suggest that ethnographic narratives about those who embody the state can be much more than what Evans dismisses as "personal biographies or individual maximizing" (1995, 19). Far from epiphenomenal, details and contexts *do* matter in Mexico in many ways, one of which is precisely because in so many research models, the PRI has been taken to be synonymous with "the government" or the state. Understanding the contexts of individual biography is crucial to understanding the culture of government in Mexico, so as to provide additional ethnographic or historic detail for the long story of PRI rule. Seven decades of rule by a single party which has controlled all levels of government—including the most powerful, the executive branch—in which presidents pick their own successors, and which has appropriated many symbols of national heritage, fusing itself literally with Mexico, must be a major factor in any discussion of political or social life in Mexico. The Catholic Church has been a powerful partner in this long period of dominance, notwithstanding the anticlerical sentiments, policies, and events of Mexico's past. The decades of PRI rule have presumably affected many citizens' sense-making about time, luck, and fortune. PRI control over the meanings of government for citizens, including middle-class and professional individuals, is well beyond my scope, but is beginning to be more widely discussed and certainly merits further research, as this case study of Mi Comunidad suggests.

Some data has been gathered, at times unwittingly, through decades of scholarly focus on village life, presenting stories which speak more of local corruption rather than indigenous "beliefs." The very "sullenness" of the peasant (Edmondson 1960), alleged hostility toward national government, or other evidence of "deficient civic spirit" (González 1972, 331) must be described within the context of protection against the untrustworthy outsider or official. Arturo Warman captures the vagaries of local power in his description of the ways banks insist on the formation of one society for each communal land parcel (*ejido*), "preventing natural associations between friends and relatives who trust one another," then complaining that the members lack "solidarity" (1980, 237). There is still relatively little critical analysis of empirical evidence about local practices and whether or not they are pluralist, but some accounts suggest that local practices are, in fact, authoritarian (Zendejas 1995, 46). Bureaucratic culture in Mexico is said to be aimed at reconciling discrepancies "in a culture where change is normally associated with troublemakers" (Arce 1993, 60). Turning these "troublemakers" into citizens who can participate in the processes of self-government may require a thorough excavation of models of what it means to be Mexican, constructed from both the inside and the outside of the country.

The personal and the national are inevitably fused in the bureaucrats of a hegemonic nation, suggests Claudio Lomnitz-Adler (1992) in his unique discussion of Mexico. In the Mi Comunidad case, the bureaucrats did not represent the PRI, nevertheless, their roles raise issues about the categories of home and work, family and state, personal and public, as such categories are blurred in lived experience and in public policy. For as bureaucrats they are also Mexican citizens, as well as members of families and communities. Although the Mi Comunidad program was in fact *run by* government officials, there was also a sense of needing to evade laws. That sometimes meant laws at the *federal* level, which might be explained by party politics. But this sense of evasion seems borne out in numerous accounts of business and government in Mexico as "legalistic," where rules and regulations are said to be promulgated almost for their own sake. As one student of law noted to me, there is so much that is legislated in Mexico that one begins to simply disregard all of the laws.

For most theorists of government, this would imply chaos. But perhaps if definitions and practices of "government" are contingent and shifting, even among government officials and bureaucrats, the implications for democracy are truly fascinating and go well beyond this case. At the very least, the notion of the monolithic, rule-bound "state" is exploded, an intellectual project which has already begun among many scholars. In the questioning and/or evasion of laws or bureaucratic norms, there is of course a possibility for abuse of personal power and for self-enrichment at public expense, as there is in any public service case. Yet is there also a potential for new and completely unpredictable, and perhaps *more* democratic, forms of government practice? Moreover, how are the meanings of "the personal" and "the private" changed in cases where family and state are shown to be so closely intertwined? The assumed dichotomy of "the personal" and "the state," a dichotomy which is arguably related to other Western dualisms, and which is still promulgated through public policy curricula and evaluations of other countries' "corruption," is revealed as untenable. But in the blurring of state and personal, do the workings of power nonetheless take on predictable patterns? And as these realms blur, do people nevertheless construct them as solid and impermeable?

State and other organizational bureaucracies determine rules, tasks, positions, and procedures, but not "improvisations . . . the play of meaning within their spaces" (Zabusky 1995). This statement is particularly relevant for Mexico, and is applicable not just *within* institutional spaces but beyond them, for the proliferation of federal government bureaucracy, policy, and rules have fostered private spaces of evasion, "extralegal" dealings, and "alternative rules"(Grindle 1996; Nuijten 1995). There is in Mexico a vast "informal economy," subject to euphemistic, discursive practices by the PRI-state (Connolly 1985). Local attitudes and practices have often created manifestly contradictory results of federal policy (González Chavez 1995; Zendejas 1995). Mexico is one of many sociopolitical contexts in the world in which practices of legalism have become disconnected from ideas about law; clientelism has a long history. Even in the Mi Comunidad program, which was created and run by a PAN-controlled state government and which was explicitly *not* dominated by the PRI, relationships bore the markings of life under the PRI, because the party has for so long set the parameters of what government, society, and national identity mean in Mexico.

The arbitrariness of bureaucratic practice perpetuates clients' dependency, while an imposed atmosphere of external limits contributes to bureaucratic indifference (Ferguson 1984; Herzfeld 1992; Lipsky 1980). Where citizens are primarily clients of the state, perhaps *any* experience of fair and consistent government becomes a potentially empowering one, breaking or loosening ties of dependency. If citizens can also learn the language and practices of democracy even in the small ways illustrated in this case, they can begin to "speak to power" (Belenky et al. 1997; Wilson 1995) and to forge roles for themselves as participants in government.

This case suggests that both deep skepticism and contradiction, as well as fervent hope, flourish within one policy implemented even by an opposition government bureaucracy, indicating broader themes for studies of government and of Mexico. Future research might be profitably directed at the disentangling of the PRI from "the government," not only in policy practice, scholarly records, and ethnography, but in sense-making about luck, fortune, and time. The process by which authoritative declarations about the past delimit possibilities for the future (Bakhtin 1996), themselves shaping differentiated apprehensions of time and space, is just one archaeology which Mexican scholars will be able to take from their own literary traditions[2] for use in studies of government as something separate from the PRI-state. At the same time, they may discover local practices which already present important bases for democracy.

ANTHROPOLOGY AND PUBLIC POLICY

As is widely acknowledged, anthropologists have not always described the varying contexts of power, time, and history which intersect with culture, and thus have either ignored or undertheorized those official manifestations of power which constitute the state, as understood for example by political scientists and other scholars of government. In many highly detailed ethnographic micro-level studies of ritual, symbol, customs, language, and so forth, there has been a well-critiqued absence of certain macro-level phenomena, and thus a lack of context in which to understand local meanings and practices—let alone to theorize official power. This was certainly the case with regard to Mexico, where deeper analysis might have revealed the political nature of different constructions about "the peasant," a figure which is depicted as being at once sullen and individualistic (and thus *overly* "rational"), and also "corporate" and "collective," and thus perhaps a bit *too* "personal."

Anthropologists avoided linking peasant Mexican communities to larger structures (Mintz 1976, xii), and in doing so, reflected the developmentalist and Cold War concerns of their time (Kearney 1996). Although it is not entirely true that "the issue of hegemony is simply not treated in anthropology" (Hansen and Parrish 1983, 276 n.3), obviously ethnography and its related critiques have tended to be formulated from below. To be fair, some anthropologists may have felt their focus on marginalized people was in itself a politically important gesture. The role of political naivete in fieldwork decisions and ethnographic writing about Mexico has yet to be fully described; one might start with a study of knowledge production within the social context of political exceptionalism, a concept referring to the lack of a successful, mass-based worker's party in the United States (Lipset 1996). The complicity of anthropology within colonial projects remains under discussion, reviewed carefully by Joan Vincent (1990); John Gledhill (1994) urges the need to continue striving for the "decolonization of anthropology."

Eric Wolf argued eloquently for the inclusion of a sense of time/history and power in anthropology ([1959] 1974; and Wolf and Hansen 1972). He called for research into "the nature of power in Latin American politics" as a way to address violence and noted the need to determine "where power is to be found in such areas as the appointment of personnel, the formulation of policy, the administration of the functions of the state, and the adjudication of competing interests," including analysis of power in "personal and institutional" forms (1972, 242). Although there have been detailed, regional studies which look more closely at colonial encounters as more than a "single shock" (Roseberry 1993), systemic factors such as the role of the national government in shaping the current conditions within which village community members live have tended to be ignored. Indeed, although issues of class and the indigenous are mentioned in some ethnographies of village life, the complexities of national-level Mexican politics and government are still relatively unexplored, consigned to footnotes or very brief descriptions (e.g., of the PAN as "right wing" [Cook and Binford 1990, 234]).

The relatively apolitical focus within anthropology has changed significantly in recent decades, with numerous cross-cultural contributions.[3] Although "bureaucracies are as old as the state itself," anthropologists did not study them explicitly until academic and market pressures forced them to do so by dissipating their "monopoly" on non-Western cultures, according to the somewhat grudging introduction in Britan and Cohen's edited volume (1980), and the dire warnings in the last essay (Denich 1980). Since then, the early notion of "studying up" (Nader 1972) has been applied in various efforts, but the grassroots experience of the state—the view from below—has tended to be more heavily researched.

Scholars have used symbolic analysis and other concepts to move toward an anthropology of bureaucracy, but rather than make the bureaucrat "human," they either ultimately have reified "the bureaucrat" and "his" rule-making behaviors (Herzfeld 1992; Lipsky 1980) or have fallen back on judgments about other nations' bureaucratic irrationality. In a sense, Michael Taussig's (1980) work on devil beliefs, plantation workers, and tin miners or June Nash's (1979) study of miners complement some of the rich symbolic themes also found in Elliott Leyton's (1978) work on the interactions between bureaucrats and miners of Newfoundland, in which he not only notes the symbolism of "the mine disease" and the body within capitalist transformations, but also describes his own efforts to advise the policymakers at the workmen's compensation board. He suggests the "irrationality" and conflictive nature of bureaucracy and the "evils" of its dual position as an "enforcer of order on behalf of industrial power structure" and "creator of a depersonalized view of the world" (ibid., 136). But these points are not elaborated in many ethnographic studies, nor applied to policy in Mexico. The promise of Handelman and Leyton's 1978 volume on bureaucracies remains a rich possibility for application within anti-essentialist and participatory research projects.

Even current anthropologists who urge closer attention to the state emphasize the need to study "how power is acquired and transmitted in society as a whole" (Gledhill 1994) or to look at the "multiple sites" in which the processes and practices of states "are recognizable through their effects" (four of which are helpfully presented almost as a kind of preresearch checklist) (Trouillot 2001). Trouillot notes that the state's materiality resides in the way processes are reworked "to create new spaces for the deployment of power." Both of these perspectives seem overly broad and even over-theorized in application to my focus on state representatives as engaged in complex everyday encounters with citizens. It seems more than ironic that an article on public policy in Mexico in the *American Re-*

view of Public Administration would present a more relevant glimpse into the uneven workings of the state and thereby the possibilities of democracy: the uncertainty, fear, "transition through chaos," and simultaneity of advance and retrenchment that is being experienced in myriad local experiments with change (Cabrero-Mendoza 2000). This sense of process certainly evokes some of the classic emphases in democracy theory, such as the diversity and fragmentation of "muddling through" (Lindblom 1959) and the many conditions and norms involved in "polyarchy" (Dahl 1956).

Authors have suggested alternative metaphors to capture the "nonunitary" aspects of "the state," understood as the nation-state, but many of these perspectives have had a relatively more theoretical than practice-oriented aspect. Diane Nelson (1999) provides an extensive review of such works in her analysis of the fetishistic, productive, and magical aspects of the state in Guatemala. She asserts the state as "conditioning possibilities" for political work and being "re-territorialized" in its relations with subjects; she advocates a notion of "fluidarity" to capture these meanings. Fernando Coronil (1997) explores the mask of state unity as historical practice in Venezuela, noting that new social identities are developing that cannot be "mapped with antiquated categories." Indeed, these notions have a certain resonance in the case of the Mi Comunidad program and other state policies aimed at migration issues in evoking a sense of the flux and permeability in the new relationships which are being created.

Across fields, newer works on Mexico are also becoming more political, revealing the social construction of categories like "immigrants" (Gutiérrez 1996; Reisler 1996) and race/ethnicity/class (Chance 1978; Cope 1994; Knight 1990; Martin 1996; Rodríguez O. and Vincent 1997). The complexity of meaning and lived experience across and between *both* urban and rural sites is also evident in more recent works (Behar 1993).

Newer research and theoretical debates on Mexico remain coalesced around migration, a position which seems to have encouraged the lack of detail about national and local politics. Denise Dresser (1993) details the efforts of two Mexican political parties to build constituencies in California, with some details on Mexican domestic politics. Although English-language anthropology of Mexico has tended not to explicitly theorize the state either as a nation-state or as a function of PRI elites, this may be changing; recent work explores the transterritorial nature of both citizen and nation-state identities due to migration (Boruchoff 1998; Pries 2001) and to participation in contexts shaped by global capital (Kearney 1996; Rouse 1992).

As in other fields, anthropologists are questioning the nature of the state as confined to a territory (T. Turner 1997) and exploring other bases of personal identity, for example in Rwanda (Malkki 1995). Some texts in anthropology, cultural studies, and other disciplines which are written from anti-essentialist perspectives, to use Chantal Mouffe's (1993) helpful term, and which do address state power, are nevertheless "de-humanized," which can also still mean de-genderized. In conflating the multiple levels of state authority to a site or arena for struggles over meaning, or in privileging the sweeping, inscribed time-space vistas of "the imagination," the vastly more complex and even alarming roles and presences of government are trivialized; some authors even risk misapplying current understandings about time, space, or agency in relatively thin efforts to trace discursive strategies and "negotiations" in the past (Alonso 1995; Dore and Molyneux 2000). Moreover, as Hilary Rose (1994) notes, the antirealist or postmodernist school of feminism is "politically weakening" for any overall project of empowerment, let alone of women, because it reduces all truth claims to fictions that one can only "choose to disbelieve" but not fight outright as patently false.

Absent a critical focus on state structures, efforts to reduce the state or citizenship to a metaphor, a consumable identity, or a collective fantasy are not useful in application to Mexico. Indeed, they are very problematic given the PRI's long involvement in defining national truth. Perhaps the more widely found avoidance by anti-essentialist writers of an explicit argument about human agency is laudable, but human consciousness *should* engage and baffle us, and we should write out of that bafflement. Human complexity, creativity and unpredictability are causes for celebration. A sense of wonderment about these matters has permeated the works of earlier anthropologists (Evans-Pritchard 1979; Geertz 1973; Leach 1979; Lévi-Strauss 1966; Malinowski 1922; V. Turner 1967; Van Gennep [1908] 1960), despite other problems of these texts. This sense can and should remain explicit in our work and writing, but it must also be linked up to a serious analysis of the realities of power, which shape the conditions for human complexity and possibility and which also reflect that human complexity in their workings. A bricolage (a favorite word in anthropology) of feminist insights, in-depth political details, and newly recast, humbler structuralist models, combined with a methodological emphasis on practice and dialogue, may be most useful for ethnographies which seek to explore and critique the many levels of modern governments.

One thoughtful, grounded anti-essentialist work in anthropology is Claudio Lomnitz-Adler's 1992 *Exits from the Labyrinth*, which is both politically important and theoretically ambitious. He analyzes national culture as also a regional phenomenon, theorizing the "cultural heterogeneity that arises in spaces of hegemony" and grounding notions of "intimate culture" and a "culture of social relations" in detailed ethnographic analysis of mestizo–Indian relations in Huasteca Potosina and local government in Morelos. He notes the lack of detail available about the gubernatorial level of politics in Mexico, but nonetheless forges a multileveled perspective on national or state (federal) culture in Mexico that reaches into the intimate culture of homes and communities. For Lomnitz-Adler, national culture in Mexico is explicitly not produced in the home; it is based in institutional experiences. Learning the hegemonic culture is "one of its main demands," he writes, and "knowing one's place" is the fundamental requirement for sharing "a sense of reality" (i.e., for hegemony). The state itself "is the main available source of recognition of place." Within this form of hegemonic culture, change is always from the center, thus the middlemen are important; their motives are both "egotistical and comprehensible." Thus it is that "nationalism" becomes a "culture of personal interest": corporatism undermines "intimate culture" at the same time as it redefines and recognizes only certain intimate cultures as belonging to an image of "national society." These intimate cultures become themselves ideologically packaged and exchanged for personal benefit. This effort to balance many complex themes and to emphasize both regionalism and the penetration of Mexican nationalist ideologies offers, like Néstor García-Canclini's (1995) discussion of the national media in Mexico and the "obliquity" of hegemony, a compelling and broadly based approach to state power and its many levels. The theorization of human agency remains relatively limited in its basis in individual calculations of self-gain.

Guillermo de la Peña's *A Legacy of Promises* is another important examination—also focussing on Morelos—of relationships between the federal government and rural citizens in Mexico. He writes, "Latin American society cannot be understood without the historical force of the state . . . pervading economics and politics, religion and kinship, ethnicity and class" (1981, 254), and calls for research into regional integrations and the *purposes* of power at the regional level, among other factors.

De la Peña observes that the slowness of the federal government to address land claim issues has been functional for the government as a way to maintain the dependency of local people. Dependency pervades relationships: citizens depend on local politicians, who depend on political patrons; national society itself is organized as a "pyramid of patron–client relationships which permit concentration of power at the top" (ibid., 246). The "rules of the game" in politics, land dealings, and so forth are "perceived as being a function of personal protection by a patron," a service either bought with money or gained through loyalty. Individual success is achieved through politicking. But rather than finding such relationships inherent to the countryside or to the peasant, he tries to situate the village-level complexity of social exchange, favors, and reciprocity within national political dealings, because at any point in the hierarchy of patron–client relations, "government representatives are present." Although he does not provide the depth of biographical detail that might illustrate these points more fully, his general argument is crucial for scholars of Mexico, for he clearly situates the sources of inequality and poverty *outside* of the rural areas: "regional poverty and limits to growth are a function of national distribution of power. . . . It is not lack of technique but lack of power, not lack of rationality . . . but lack of alternatives that makes local economy stagnant" (ibid., 260).

De la Peña's work reveals an important piece of the story of self-contradictory and fetishized notions of "the Mexican peasant." Interestingly, nationalistic and ethnographic constructions of the Mexican peasant are paralleled in international financial discourse; work into the nature of causation and coexistence between these levels of meaning is still needed. Part of my own effort to write against this level of discourse on Mexico is to seek, even in my micro-case, to go beyond notions of human agency as synonymous with "strategizing." The conceptions of human agency used in free-market economic theory were not intended to and should not provide the only basis of social theory or visions of human life, obviously, but even more importantly, the use of them in descriptions of Mexico risks further complicity in the construction of "the peasant."

Roberto Varela's 1984 work on local politics in Morelos through a metaphor of energy systems as related to demographic change contains many fascinating details. In describing the different ways in which local hierarchies emerged and power was reproduced among certain privileged castes, he excoriates the PRI but avoids what he calls the "terreno pantanoso" (swampy, or tricky, ground) over which research cannot advance: the levels of integration between local, state, and federal power as told through biography. This job, he wryly notes, would require a novel rather than a social science analysis; his work suggests the importance of studying the letters of complaint written by peasants and *ejidatarios* as an important form of protest.

Intuitive and anecdotal are words used to dismiss the inclusion of living people in cases, but in this analytical move one "tidies up" the chaos of social life too much, perhaps at a cost which can no longer be justified. Anthropologists can be at the forefront of recording and translating alternative visions of government and cross-cultural variations in the enactment of the state by its stubbornly *human* representatives. Our project should be one of writing, carefully, against those who would decry all variants as irrational. In doing so we may discover that we have much to learn from local variations in the functions, meanings, and practices of government across cultures, in building on anthropological knowledge about differences in personhood, and in seeking a basis for social theory that incorporates participants in projects which control power.

THEORIES OF THE STATE

The state understood as a relatively neutral bureaucracy or organization is the subject of analysis by many scholars of public policy and organizational studies. These fields share a tendency to use extremely broad concepts such as culture, symbol, and power without engaging the critical theoretical contexts and the complexity of meaning which surround these concepts as they are developed within other fields like anthropology and political science. Without this critical context, organizational theorists' use of concepts like gender stereotypes, contingency theory, and even capitalism (Morgan 1986; Perrow 1986; Pondy et al. 1983) must remain relatively superficial. Some analysts of public policy and bureaucracy at least acknowledge the structures of capitalism in international settings or note state interventions as unwelcome, although often without offering conclusions which are explicitly linked to theories of the state. Even when employing promising approaches like ethnography or the notion of "critical points" between states and citizens, authorial conclusions tend to remain linked with rational actor assumptions and other problematic models and methods (Arce 1989, 1993; Britan and Cohen 1980; Long 1989; van den Zaag 1992; de Vries 1997; Zendejas and de Vries 1995). Research which has been preoccupied with judgments about the rationality of the peasant or the farmer thus misses the ways in which practices of the marginalized, far from "inherent," constitute a response to the specific and personally perceived history of intervention in Mexico. Clearly, such assessments must be made within the context of specific historical and political details.

Studies from both sides of the border on the public sector and bureaucracy in Mexico, notwithstanding some interesting, almost random insights, have thus tended to be developmentalist, "cultural," and comparative. Using idealized, universal assumptions about rationalization and efficiency which Mexico, and indeed any country, fails to reach, early authors discovered and prescribed a need to "improve" Mexican practices (Benveniste 1970; Grindle 1977; Purcell and Purcell 1977; Riggs 1964; Wionczek 1963). Current work on the costs and consequences for countries of corruption in government at least acknowledges the widespread nature of corruption (i.e., as outside of the Third World [Rose-Ackerman 1999]).

The power of the PRI is criticized by scholars of public policy, but many analyses reproduce stereotypes about Mexico as a whole. For example, the New Public Management systems put in place by President Ernesto

Zedillo as a Program for Modernizing Public Administration for 1995–2000 are described by one analyst as part of a political design "to reinforce the PRI's position that fundamental change was possible within what was essentially a centralized, hierarchical one-party system," at the same time as the author repeatedly invokes author Carlos Fuentes for insights into the "enigmatic character" of Mexico (Klingner 2000). One author notes Mexico's need for "strong economic medicine" as opposed to the "mature" U.S. and Canadian economies (Rose 2000), while another asserts that "compared to other developing countries, Mexico has quite a modern and developed tax system" (Solano 2000). These twists in prose suggest a complex of other meanings about Mexico.

Superficial labelings like "personal government" take on the rigidity of many framings of culture: as an ahistorical and essential, fixed attribute. Moreover, many authors discover that "ideology" exists only outside of the United States, and that even though corruption exists "everywhere," somehow it is at its worst in Mexico. This kind of thinking is not limited to scholarship, but is to this day echoed in many accounts and financial publications about Mexico.

Some note that the PRI-state itself is a cause of problems in governance in Mexico, including that of cynicism (Grindle 1988, 1996, 1998). Merilee Grindle's work on Mexico over nearly thirty years provides an interesting example of intellectual trajectory: from the serious analysis of the "personal" workings of clientelism, undertaken from the perspective of rationalism, to an extremely dense, abstract theoretical model of the PRI in its dominance of administration and a hope that elites can learn from the long-suffering and capable citizenry. As a researcher coming upon a case which could be "explained" by many of the same ideas and theories which Grindle used in her 1977 study, I was struck by the reproduction of certain patterns within Mexico, and within scholarship. Clearly, personal practices had not been "grown out of" in Mexico; perhaps they are successful in their own right, within specific values and contexts, not "rational" or "irrational," but part of everyday sense-making within individual lives and relationships.

The complexity of social change bedevils most efforts to simplify events and to see them in straightforward causal relationships; simplifications may worsen certain problems or preclude the perception of other possibilities. Don Handelman (1981) suggests that policy reflects the fact that there are some "tacit structural anomalies" which have no bureaucratic "solution." Perhaps any effort to analyze policy must begin by acknowledging what he refers to as the overlapping of different frames and meanings and the "pervasive dilemmas" which arise in the course of categorizing people. Ethnographic and symbolic analysis can enrich, or "enliven," social science analysis of government and the state (Verdery 1999), generating alternative interpretations and including a sense of history, local differences in power and process, and multiple meanings. However, such analysis must also be committed to piercing the "veil" of mystified and fetishized power (Taussig 1980, 1997), looking behind the masks which defer critique (Barthes 1972; Bourdieu 1977) and which deny futures to selected people. For policy is also implemented *by human beings*, through everyday practices, with inherent discontinuities that signal spaces for change.

POLITICAL THEORY

English-language historians of Mexico have long been much more explicit about power and the PRI in Mexico (Anderson 1976; Brandenburg 1964; Hamilton 1982) and about the role of U.S. imperialist pressures on Mexico (Weston 1972) than anthropologists have been. At the same time, Mexican anthropologists and other intellectuals have been more openly critical of the PRI and the elite in Mexico than their English-speaking counterparts (Bartra 1977, 1987; Bonfil Batalla 1996; Lomnitz-Adler 1992; Lomnitz et al. 1993; Warman 1970). However, some Mexican intellectuals—for example, Octavio Paz and Carlos Fuentes—are said to have been co-opted by the PRI. Jorge Castañeda suggests they are "token opponents brought into the fold" (2000, xiv).

Political scientists have addressed government in Mexico as bureaucratic-authoritarian; the size and extent of Mexican federal bureaucracy and its close relationship to the ruling party have forced political scientists to look seriously at bureaucracies and to theorize the Mexican state as a corporatist system (Middlebrook 1995; Purcell and Purcell 1977; Stevens 1977). But writers in political science and other fields which study power, government, and the state have tended to research and write about quantifiable and macro levels, through a focus on domestic or transnational political institutions (like political parties, judicial or legislative bodies, and nongovernmental organizations); on decision-making by elites or masses of voters; or on a given series of events within the context of wider economic and legal systems. Within political science, many works are characterized by teleological assumptions; problematic models of human agency, framings of questions, and usage of data; reductive notions of comparative or generalizable results; and methods of research and writing which emphasize positivism and prediction.

These aspects trouble anthropologists for many reasons; such studies seem to leave out, flatten, dismiss, or "black box" precisely the things of most urgency to us—such as differing values and symbolic meanings, local contexts, constructions of gender, differences in kinds of authority, the role of everyday practices, the force and complexity of emotion and identity, let alone the presence of the researcher and its effect on data, with the attendant ethical implications of knowledge and power. Thus, there are sweeping theorizations, detailed political histories, and skillful economic reviews, often framed at the comparative macro levels and sometimes from within competing ideologies as regards the free market, but tending to dismiss everyday experience in ways which have precluded the understanding of change.

Max Weber wrote that the "modern state" was characterized by "administrative and legal order subject to change by legislation," involving binding authority over members and "a compulsory association with a territorial basis" (1947, 156), an emphasis still used in textbooks about government: "Government is composed of institutions and processes that rulers establish to strengthen and perpetuate their power or control over a territory and its inhabitants" (Lowi and Ginsberg 2000, 9). This definition has been applied widely in cross-cultural modeling at the macro and global levels of analysis, which tend to be preferred and which have generated many useful works on Mexico. But since so much in Mexico is political, all forms of data and surveys—so favored by academics and experts in democratization—are suspect, in my opinion. Citizens understand well just how important individual context is: standing openly in a village answering the questions of a well-dressed urban male outsider who is taking a poll, who may or may not be a member of the PRI.

Mexico has reached one minimum definition of democracy, as "a system in which parties lose elections" (Przeworksi 1991, 10). But in ongoing discussions of Mexico and other "new" democracies, it seems that analysis of public policy or government must itself be processual, reflexive, and critical, sensitive to the context of historically dominant structures and discourses and to past constructions of knowledge about the topic itself.

There are many different meanings of "the personal" in governance. In Soco and Rosi's enactments of government responsibility, they enter into circumstances which have already been shaped by multiple experiences of governance in Mexico, whether experienced directly by the jefes, for example, or through exposure to discourses on the "mythic venality of public officials in Mexico" (Brandenburg 1964). In these settings, the sense of cheerful ironic distance from oneself, even when one is "the state," was a refreshing and important aspect in this case of what should and could constitute professionalism. Cleverly satirical skepticism, in the middle of deadly serious matters, is indeed a large part of President Fox's appeal.

Such a stance on the part of representatives of the state may constitute the best defense against the dominance of a hyper-efficient machinery of state-craft.

Competing claims and charges among academics about who is "Other-ing" whom, and why, can mask the deeper epistemological and political issues at stake. These issues have to do with the role of scholarship and so-cial order, theory-making, and stances toward rationality itself as a con-cept. The increase in cross-disciplinary studies of "identity politics" may suggest that the macro-level, highly quantified, game-theory-based mod-eling which precluded English-language scholarly awareness of the demise of communism in Europe is being understood as limiting. Protest movements both domestically and across borders, and bases of identity (formerly dismissed as epiphenomenal) such as ethnicity and religion, are beginning to be studied more widely by political scientists and scholars of democratization, although mainstream work remains highly quantified.[4]

As scholars reevaluate their own approaches—political scientists and international relations scholars in the light of their manifest inability to "predict" the fall of Communism, and anthropologists in the light of their own lengthy and sustained self-critique, both groups within the context of widespread changes in academia, publishing, and international intel-lectual relations—they can learn a great deal from each other. Reading pa-tiently across disciplines and delving into the study of middle grounds may be fruitful: exploring the liminal and uncertain areas that lie between macro and micro preoccupations, between classic social science and radi-cal deconstructionism, between control and irrelevance. The exciting and radical possibilities of combining the force and focus of critical anthro-pology and participatory practices with the detailed contextualization of national and local politics afforded by political scientists remain relatively underdeveloped.

The work of anthropology should be in directing the attention of re-search subjects themselves toward the relevant theories which can enrich their own understandings and their own roles in such processes. Because anthropology is a field in which the self of the researcher is acknowledged as "the instrument of knowing" (Ortner 1995), its practitioners are in a po-sition to understand and address epistemological issues—for example, those relating to acquisition of knowledge and experience—which arise in the individual, multiple experiences of power/authority within citizen-state encounters. Perceptions and the labeling of differing sensations as emotions, messages from others, chemical imbalances, moments of inhabitation by other beings, and so forth are culturally produced (Bourdieu 1990; Rosaldo 1980; Sangren 1991). Our efforts to understand *across* and *through* those differences in knowing and feeling can displace an exclusive methodological reliance on visualism.[5] Anthropological fieldwork is the sustained effort to understand these differences, undertaken through the sharing of experiences together, and ongoing dialogue about them.

Similarly, perceptions and ideas about the state and the human project of government, in all their enormous cross-cultural variety, can inform theoretical overreliance upon a monolithic State which is so far from actual experience. Ethnography of the "reworkings of physical presence" can be fruitfully combined with Teresa de Lauretis's early emphases on feminism as "a politics of experience, of everyday life" (1986, 10), and as "politics working for change" (Franco 1989, xxii, in a discussion of de Lauretis).

The position and insights of ethnography, directed at the state in Mexico as also something comprised of "state marketing boards, property law, protectionist institutions, the army and national guard" (Roseberry 1993), and the persons who staff these agencies, has great promise for new understandings in de Varela's "swampy terrain." For the liminal area between the state and the citizen, where each sees and recognizes the other in itself, may also hold a key to more justice in democratic government.

POWER AND THE PERSONAL

Néstor García-Canclini's (1997) notion of "oblique" power relations permeating the fabric of human lives is a wonderful metaphor in a book that analyzes work in the international garment industry. But another powerful image related to fabric, which incorporates the reality of the machinery of state and business, is the diamond-shaped point of a sewing machine needle, a new, advanced kind of needle, which a sewing machine salesman excitedly described to us in detail in his office one morning as we waited over an hour for three representatives of the investors in a maquila to arrive. The salesman first drew for us a diagram contrasting the shape of the point of this new needle to the older, more squared point. He then dug in the bottom drawers of his file cabinet to emerge with several thick binders of documents about this shape and its superiority in the way it cut through the criss-crossed threads in a piece of fabric, in order to penetrate them and bring another thread through them, reemerging as a result of its revolutionary design in a way that keeps the integrity of the fabric strong, that does not weaken it or cause it to be more susceptible to tears.

To design and market a needle with such care, for an industry of ready-made garments which is based in part on the presumption that each T-shirt or pair of slacks is destined for almost immediate replacement by another pair, so that the longevity of the fabric itself is not truly at issue, was not the only instance of self-contradiction at this sewing machine store. For the salesman also wanted to be sure to express the utmost importance of buying *new* sewing machines for many reasons: less noise, less dust in the workings, but also for the *longevity* of sewing machines in general, that they last and last. The new machines, so long-lasting, are valuable for that reason, but given the context of a sewing machine dealership, that reasoning does not and cannot mean that *used* machines are valuable. Similarly, in the low-skill work of the global economy, new workers are more valuable than older ones: they can be paid less, and the experience of the "used" workers is no longer of value (Braverman 1974; Fuller 2000; Peña 1997).[6]

Where state power becomes fused with the future, through metaphors of death and the body (Taussig 1997; Verdery 1999), or in the intentional confusion between individual and nation that is part of the magic of elections (Dunn 1980), or through the personal loyalties and practices of officials in Mexico, it can take on a normative sense suggested in a twist on the grammatical concept of "the future perfect." This concept was described in a political sense, but in another context, by Julia Kristeva (1981); it is borrowed here to capture the uses and control of the future by the powerful. "Imaginary Mexico," or the dominant social and political elite, has long denied the fact of Mexican heterogeneity by stigmatizing certain populations (most notably the indigenous) which are seen as holding Mexico back from what "should have been" and, indeed, from democracy (Bonfil Batalla 1996). To the extent that the elite in Mexico have tried to deny multicultural realities and to propose a national culture that is "a permanent aspiration to stop being what we are" (ibid.), the Mi Comunidad case of state government power is important in its marked absence of personal, political use of and control over a narrowly defined future, a "future perfect" for the few. While not a fully inclusive vision, yet in its very contradictory and complex nature, there were many possibilities for change.

LOS DOS (BOTH)

This book is a close study of the ways in which state government and local business combined to produce and reproduce paternalistic relationships through the *Mi Comunidad* program, through powerful symbols which are specifically related to the social construct of the family, while intervening in actual kinship relations. The needle of the state pierces the fabric of a family through its oblique practices, becoming, by virtue of its special design and implementation, a nonthreatening, indeed helpful, member of the new, recast family. For it is only in machines that the eye of the needle is also its point of entry into the fabric. In sewing by hand, the two functions are separated. The worker stitches together a simple garment, sitting at the sophisticated machine produced in the high-tech economies of Japan or Korea. The "eye" of the state, observing and documenting, photographing the rural, female Mexican worker, pulls its thread through individual lives with its tight, oblique stroke. But as this case proves, the eye of the state winks and flickers sometimes, the needles break, and the eyes of the female workers do look back.

In a simple reply made by a treasured friend, a Mexican citizen, patriot, intellectual, and librarian, I learned a lot about democracy in Mexico. My husband (a professor of government) and I were excitedly asking about a series of events in which the PRI was seeking to discredit Porfirio Muñoz Ledo, a long-present politician in Mexico on the relative left within the PRI who was seeking to establish his own candidacy. The PRI was alleging Muñoz Ledo's corruption at a time when he was in a powerful ministry position in Mexico. "Which is true?" we asked eagerly. "Was he corrupt, or is the PRI just trying to undermine his authority?" Our friend smiled his wonderfully gentle, inimitable smile and replied simply: "los dos" (both). For both to be true was to him a bit obvious perhaps, and more than that, completely comprehensible as such. To be both cynical about politicians and at times about each other after decades of control and corruption, and yet to retain a sense of the fantastic possibility within nations and people, may simply be a part of personal perspectives toward time, the future, and government in Mexico. Perhaps this quality lies outside of foreign models, unchartable, like the brain. As Mexicans pause to consider alternative directions, this quality, and their complexity of prides and needs, demands respect and attention.

Documents Written by the Author concerning the Mi Comunidad Program

To: [The DACGE Director]
cc: [Soco and Rosi]
From: Dolores Byrnes

After these months of research and work with the My Community program, I offer the following observations that I hope can be a part of the process of future planning. Thank you for permitting me to work with you; it has been a great honor.

Executive Summary
This program has enormous potential to improve the quality of life of the workers who are involved in it. Nevertheless, this potential will not be realized and the costly problems of job turnover, absenteeism, low quality, etc., will continue without a new emphasis on the contexts of *gender* in this case, and even more, on the employees as *human resources*. Without this new emphasis, the program takes the risk of exploiting its female workers and maintaining their marginal, subordinate situation in society.

Work in the Maquilas
In the world economy, maquila textile work is one type traditionally held by women, and frequently associated with abuses of the workers' rights. For example, among the 3,000 maquilas of the border, there are many cases of poor working conditions (illegal and unethical). To avoid these defects, we need to create in the My Community program an explicit focus on *gender*.

Toward Change
The bosses, investors, and planners of My Community can confront *effectively* the different personnel problems of the maquilas (absenteeism, low morale and quality, turnover, etc). To initiate these changes, we must begin with the awareness of and habits of thinking about these workers. Here are nothing more than some suggestions. First, it is necessary to un-

derstand the aspects of gender which affect this program and its businesses:

1. *The women's lives.* Everyone should understand that the female workers (women, not "girls") live without domestic help, thus their tasks at home continue whether they work in the maquila or not. There is a majority of households headed by women in the poorest regions of the state. It is estimated that rural women work 17–18 hours each day with domestic chores: cleaning clothes, preparing food, caring for children, gathering firewood, etc. Thus, they do not lack "a work ethic." They are not lazy, they are very hard-working. But, at times they lack effective *motivation* within the maquilas.

2. *This work is not charity.* Their low-paid labor and their disadvantaged position in the labor market have been a basic part, but silent supposition, of the program. Now is the time to recognize this fact. Yes, they receive training, scholarships, and the opportunity to work. But they also give much in their jobs: their time, energy, skills, etc. They are not objects of charity. We must create a work atmosphere in which a contract exists between the place of work and the women as human resources: the two sides are both *partners* in the business, it is not a case of paternalism nor of friction.

3. *The idea of progress.* Sometimes the women leave for other work. This result is almost inevitable with this type of work. To retain them, the bosses should think of them as *human resources*, working to understand why they leave and trying to change their conditions. Or at least, we can see these exits as a thing of pride, not a problem, because they are improving their opportunities.

Second, we should refocus the objectives of the My Community program. For example, we can direct the program explicitly to the field of training for women, and as a site for the development of leadership skills among them. In the maquilas, profit is not and should not be the first objective: this was not the original objective of the program. Already there are many governmental supports for these small businesses and the government is in a position to create new jobs, thus it is not working in "the free market." Therefore, why be limited by a vision related to labor-management that is derived from old, classical models? Some practical steps could be:

1. To make more flexible work schedules;
2. To convert sites to disseminate information about family violence, health, etc.;
3. The government must demand compliance with all work laws;
4. In each maquila, create a roundtable of management and representatives of the workers that meets regularly to discuss important topics and possible changes in the maquila.

Conclusions

It is necessary to change the models of thinking inside the operations of the My Community program. We need a new model for the new economy, a model of participation and dialogue between workers and managers, not one of mistrust and fear. With an emphasis on the female workers and their potential, this program gains the opportunity to develop the skills of the women in other capacities. My Community can be a model of development of human resources in the countryside, for other states and businesses.

DOCUMENT FOR USE BY THE DACGE STAFF
IN FUND-RAISING, JUNE 2000

Project for the Human Development of the Women of "Mi Comunidad"

The government and many other organizations have determined that there are various institutions through which changes can be made in the situation of women here in Mexico, especially in Guanajuato. The business sector is one of the institutions that can make a difference for the most disadvantaged women, not only by offering work to alleviate poverty, but by offering the opportunity to improve the quality of their lives and their future consciousness.

Obviously, the feminization of poverty is an enormous problem. Our program has been directed at the problems of migration, but with experience, we can see that there are more needs at which we should direct our energies. These women, upon whom the program depends greatly, live in difficult circumstances, with excessive occupations, but without real power. It is not certain that their conduct in the maquiladoras is owing to a "lack of a work ethic." What happens is that they live in a specific context that we need to better understand. It is a question of *education*, for them and for their bosses.

We are planning some form of intervention and dialogue that we can use in the maquilas. Our objectives are:

1. To consult agencies involved with women in Mexico;
2. To design a clear, relevant program for our context;
3. To implement the program in all of the maquilas;
4. To include this program in the beginning and the planning of our maquilas.

This program of human development should be directed at the following themes, among others:

1. Awareness of desires and needs;
2. The body and health;
3. Free will and self-esteem;

4. Discovering and increasing skills;
5. Human relations and those in the family, roles, etc.;
6. Leadership.

After the June conference, we can arrange more details of the program, working with the bosses and the women.

Confidential Questionnaire Designed for the Female Workers of the Maquilas, June 2000

To begin an educational, participative program, we need your opinions and ideas. Please, take a few minutes to complete this form. Thank you for your cooperation. You can use the other side of the page if needed.

Attentively,
The consultants of the Mi Comunidad program.

1. If you could change something in your life, what would it be?
2. What are your special skills/abilities?
3. Do you have enough time each day to do all that you have to do?
Yes___ No____ It depends_____
Why or why not?
4. If you could ask for some help of your government, what would it be?
5. For the big decisions in your life, with whom do you consult?
6. Would you like to attend a course on Saturdays held for women?
Yes___ No____
Which hours would be best for you to attend such a course?_____

QUESTIONS ADDED LATER BY SOCO:

7. Do you have control over the money you earn in the maquila?
8. Do you have relatives in the U.S.?
9. How old are they?
10. Do you have children? _____ How many? _____

THANK YOU FOR YOUR HELP!

Summary of Research on the Mi Comunidad Program by the Author, March 2001

EXECUTIVE SUMMARY

After using several months to analyze the My Community program and its implementation, I would like to share with you my ideas, obviously limited and partial, to continue our dialogue about the program. I hope they will be useful, and perhaps generate some written responses from you as well as new ideas for the program.

MISSION

The program mission, as within the DACGE office, is very broad and ambitious. The program has great hopes at its basis and complex objectives that change with social changes in Guanajuato. On one side, then, it can be considered a very *flexible and dynamic* program: it is said to be intended to (1) decrease the rates of migration; (2) generate jobs in the poorest regions of the state; (3) support the women "who remain"; and (4) attract the investment of countrymen in the U.S. All of these challenges are important and difficult, each one its own dimension. Thus, on the other hand, these objectives altogether are almost too large and even self-contradictory. There is a risk that they present a burden on the people involved in the program.

IMPLICATIONS OF THE COMPLEX, MULTIPLE HOPES

The intense hopes of the program directors for the survival of the businesses are expressed in many ways: in their commitments and practices each day in support of the bosses and investors, in their words of concern for the financial "health" of each maquila and for the ITG [Integradora Textil de Guanajuato, or Textile Association of Guanajuato], in their long and arduous trips across the state. It seems also that the complex and multiple hopes within the program mission have several implications:

1. The enormous intellectual and social energy which the directors bring

to their tasks represent an important support in Guanajuato: to sustain small and medium-sized businesses of the state without reproducing conditions of "paternalism," personalism, and total control that have been a part, frequently, of the relations between state and citizens in Mexico. Thus, the program has success simply in its form as a state intervention in the lives of the maquila bosses.

2. The difficulties which interrupt the progress of the maquilas—from initial obstacles of construction, water, infrastructure, etc. up to the problems of product quality, absenteeism, turnover, sales, etc.—are a part, perhaps inevitable, of the process. Projects throughout the world also suffer these challenges and problems. In their styles and wisdom, the directors demonstrate that they well understand the process of "entrepreneurship" and the needs of the managers: including precisely the characteristic of facing difficulties, learning different options, making decisions, and trying to resolve problems. As women, they bring skills and perspectives that are a very important part of social change in Mexico, in their very questions about masculine authority for example.

3. But, simply because of the *type* of program structure (hierarchical), and the structure of the maquilas, as well as the practices of support for the bosses, the women who sew (las muchachas) and their communities do not have a voice or form of participation in the program. They are not considered of value except as available and cheap labor, even "captive labor." Unfortunately, there are many stereotypes about "women of the country" that justify their exclusion outside of "the community" of the program and which maintain their position as "a problem." This results in their blame for *all* problems, without resolving at times other causes, such as unqualified bosses.

CONCLUSION

The intense hopes, inevitable program difficulties, and broad objectives of the program constitute great pressures on the program directors. In this situation, they focus on the basic needs of the program: business needs are recognized by the state as important and primary, in part because they appear to be resolvable and temporary. At the same time, the needs of the women are not given importance: they represent *irresolvable* problems. Their future potential is not a part of program planning. In the absence of their husbands, these women continue "below" in society, below in their salaries and schedules, outside of the possibility of contributing their opinions, talents, etc. to the future of the program, to Guanajuato, and to Mexico. It is my hope that with time, the program can also include their needs beyond simple levels of training and a job.

The directors have a radical position within the larger society. As women with relative power, they can advance the idea of the woman as capable and intelligent, and can change patterns between citizens and the state in Mexico. Also, they can introduce practices and attitudes which generate dignity and respect for the female workers, not just jobs.

Notes

INTRODUCTION

1. In-bond assembly plants/*maquilas* are businesses which assemble finished products from parts produced elsewhere, paying little or no duty at export. *Maquiladora* is a commonly used synonym for *maquila*. For more information, see chapter 6.

2. Some readers will already be familiar with the concept of *compadrazgo*, or "ritual godparent-hood," from extensive work on patron–client networks and their role in social and political life (Blank 1974; Campbell 1964; Foster 1953; Mintz and Wolf 1967; Pitt-Rivers 1958).

3. Election fraud has become commonplace in Mexico over the decades of PRI power. It is widely believed that Carlos Salinas de Gortari did not win the election in 1988, although he was awarded the victory. Whether the 1988 fraud was just "to win" or "to pad," elites have lacked "the political will to know" (Castañeda 2000). Brandenburg describes postelection outcries thus: "Accusations of fraud are intended to suggest the authenticity of an organized opposition of free and elective suffrage" (1964, 149). See also Lomnitz et al. (1993) on the rituals of the 1988 campaign. It should also be noted that the "Revolutionary Family," which dominated the elite since the time that its "first head," Francisco Indalecio Madero, was elected president in 1911, and the PNR, or Partido Nacional Revolucionario (National Revolutionary Party, the precursor to the PRI), officially predate the PRI in power.

4. The timeless "Mexican village" and the "closed corporate community" were the subject of important but relatively apolitical and ahistorical texts (Foster 1948, 1965; Lewis 1951; Redfield 1930, 1941; Wolf 1955) which are *still* cited, sometimes exclusively, as a basis for other generalizations about Mexican rural life, as in a 1987 "ethnosurvey" of migration by Massey et al. The very unit of analysis used in the political anthropology of Mexico was set by participants at a 1949 seminar, who decided that the generic term *community* would be more convenient than the more historically specific term *municipio* suggested by Sol Tax (Vincent 1990, 291). Even outside of anthropology, English-language scholarship has been divided along the "folk–urban" dichotomy theorized by Redfield and has tended to focus either on rural village life or urban strategies of survival in Mexico City, deemphasizing other cities in Mexico. In fact, this dichotomy seems to be present within federal policy itself, with its "persistent urban bias" (Grindle 1988), but it is the lack of attention to the *connections* between

urban and rural sites which has precluded deeper ethnographic analyses and understanding of this characteristic.

5. Douglas 1966 is the foundational work on the impurity of disorder or "matter out of place," with many important applications across disciplines, including vivid work in history (Rotter 2000) and anthropology of bureaucracy (Greenhouse 1998; Herzfeld 1992). Diane Nelson (1999) develops Judith Butler's notion regarding how bodies "matter." Insiderness is useful also to capture the still relatively underexplored "clubbiness" or "homosociality" of some male relationships to other males within positions of dominance (Allison 1994; Hearn and Parkin 1983; Korda 1972). Personally, I had already had experiences of the intensity of the interface between bureaucracy and the body, for example on the day my brother's last name was gone from a white erasable board in a Dallas intensive-care unit, indicating his death, or when I noticed the little check marks on the medical chart about another brother. These marks quantified the provision by ICU nurses of "emotional support" to us, his family, about his new condition of quadriplegia.

6. Victor Turner (1974) analyzes the Hidalgo uprising as a "limen" between colonial history and the Mexican nation, reviewing in detail the events, religiosity, etc. of the story and its role in Mexican mythology.

7. The Bajío region, which includes Guanajuato, was the site of the Cristero uprising, a 1926–1929 civil war in which 100,000 are estimated to have been killed. The army killed another estimated 5,000 supporters from 1929 to 1935 after a "treaty" was signed (Meyer 1976). The revolt was against the anticlerical policies of President Elías Plutarco Calles, founder in 1929 of the PNR, the forerunner to the PRI.

8. The Mexican government has tended to be dominated by the executive branch; thus power is reproduced in part through the predetermination of each new nominee for president by an "inner elite" (i.e., by the "Revolutionary Family" and, later, by the PNR/PRI) (Brandenburg 1964). The process of preselection was established by President Lázaro Cárdenas (1934–1940), has become highly ritualized, and is known as either *el dedazo* (the finger tap) or *el destape* (the unveiling), as detailed by Jorge Castañeda (2000).

9. Among numerous others, the ideological choice of "visualism" (in written metaphors and as a distancing technique in anthropology) (Fabian 1983), the "objectification of the subject" (Bourdieu 1990), the problem of "inscribing" the Other (Clifford 1988; Derrida 1976; Marcus and Fischer 1986), and the "colonizing" of the native through the needs of "expansionist . . . white anthropology" (Warman 1970) remain crucial issues of practice for anthropologists, because they deal with the differences in power and knowledge which affect fieldwork and ethnographic writing, not to mention the lives of "subjects." Anthropological discomfort with understanding through inscription is well-founded and, hopefully, ongoing. Abu-Lughod, for example, justifies her writing in terms of the goal of "tactical humanism" (1993) or of altering stereotypes, a goal also relevant for this case, given the negative stereotypes of Mexicans. Writing "from the body" is seen as a crucial act for women because it challenges "speech which has been governed by the phallus" (Cixous 1983, 285).

10. Of course, no one is "all-understanding," and such a research ideal is no

longer valid. Durkheim's depiction of the "objectivity" in social science methods as dependent on points of reference that are variable and "perpetually shifting in relation to each other," remains useful in fieldwork ([1895] 1938, 44).

11. On writing from the body, see Cixous 1983, and a critique in Flax 1987; on the body in relation to citizenship, see Jones 1990 and Mouffe 1993; regarding knowledge, see Keller and Grontkowski 1983 and Rose 1994; and in ethnography, Comaroff 1985. On power and the state, see Foucault 1979, 1980. On inscribing the body, see Bourdieu 1980 and Certeau 1984. On the importance of the everyday, see Smith 1987.

12. Docility is a key concept in studies of textile manufacturing and gender, as are the alleged "nimble" fingers of female workers. Both concepts serve to justify gendered job profiling as well as hiring and firing practices (see, e.g., Bradley 1989; Glucksmann 1990; Hafter 1995; Milkman 1987; Tsurumi 1990), but other practices may explain women's presence in this industry (Pearson 1986). Sklair (1993) reviews the literature and debates.

13. For example, González Casanova refers to the "idealism" of Mexican anthropology and its "humanistic" rather than "anticolonial" stance, which chose not to see "the Indian problem" as a *political* one (1970, 102), but it is not until much later that this hint is taken up by English-speaking anthropologists, e.g., in application to the creation by the discipline itself of "the peasant" (Kearney 1996).

CHAPTER 1. PERSONAL PRACTICES

1. Concepts derived from anthropology *are* used in writing about public policy (see Yanow 1996 for a thoughtful work) or organizational culture, but most lack a context of the wider meanings, critical theory, and practices associated with concepts such as "culture" (see, e.g., Trice and Beyer 1990, whose only citation for the concept of "rites" is their own work). Anthropologists' work on organizations includes the study of bureaucracy and symbolism (Britan and Cohen 1980; Herzfeld 1992), but has been rarer.

2. There is even a term (*acarreo*) given to the PRI practice of making people attend meetings by either deducting from their pay or by giving them meals or small gifts (Ramos Escandón 1994). This concept is also associated with PRI campaign rituals like filling a square with people to cheer in support of a presidential candidate (Lomnitz et al. 1993).

3. Evans's (1995) work on "embedded autonomy" uses "midwifery" to refer to state encouragement of entrepreneurship. The concept is relevant to the Mi Comunidad program but is limited by Evans to general "techniques," such as reducing risk and uncertainty and a vague notion of "intimate connections" between state and entrepreneurs that is neither fully elaborated nor linked to its obvious gender contexts.

4. All conversations among the three of us were in Spanish, but at times Rosi liked to speak to me in English, sometimes to test out her own use of English, other times to speak privately to me in front of those who did not know English.

5. "Political religiosity of a paternalistic variety, promoted by the entrepreneurs and linked to the factories," has also been noted in Nuevo León (González

Casanova 1970, 45). Many nineteenth-century textile mills also had chapels and schools (Keremetsis 1973). I saw a large and well-tended chapel on the grounds of a mining cooperative which held daily mass at 8:00 A.M. Such use of religious symbols at work, however, can backfire if workers then claim corresponding rights to attend church during the workday (Wilson 1991, 139). With visits to other maquilas, I saw that these details—an eating place, attention to drafts, or a tended shrine—indicated a certain amount of concern on the part of managers that was not present in all of the work situations. Whether such gestures translated into something perceptible as value to the workers, I could not tell.

6. I had hesitated to be seated with the other "officials" present, but Soco whispered that my name would be announced as a part of the ceremony and that it would make the trainees feel better if we were involved. It was thus that even a small child from the United States became included as one of the visiting "dignitaries."

CHAPTER 2. BUSINESS DEALS

1. The topic of land reform in Mexico, including the efforts to redistribute the *ejido*, or communal lands of the indigenous, is addressed in many works, including historic accounts by Benjamin (1996), Cornelius (1996), Eckstein (1966), Rus (1983), Silva Herzog (1964), Simpson (1937), Singer (1988), and Wasserstrom (1983), and close looks at policy, for example by Zendejas and de Vries (1995). On the indigenous in Mexico, some important works include Bonfil Batalla 1996, Coello et al. 1977, Friedlander 1975, González Casanova 1970, a *Nexos* special issue in 1999, Pare 1977, Ruiz 1997, Van Young 1990, and Wade 1997.

CHAPTER 3. SOCIAL WORK

1. Among the many instructive works on macro-level relations between the state and the private sector in Mexico, including protests and activism by representatives of capital, are Hamilton 1992, Heredia 1992, Pozas 1993, Teichmann 1995, Ugalde 1994.

2. Some relevant works include Jaggar and Bordo 1989, Jones 1990, and Ruddick 1989.

3. From United Nations and Planned Parenthood estimates, also cited by Steven Morris in "Abortion: Why the Religious Right Is Wrong," February 1997 (www.ffrf.org).

CHAPTER 4. THE DACGE OFFICE

1. Policy analyst Merilee S. Grindle (1977) noted this word, arguing that it reflected bureaucratic efforts to create a group of loyal subordinates around officials as part of other career advance strategies and "exchange alliances." This word is also in common use in national-level Mexican bureaucracies and politics (Lomnitz et al. 1993). I discuss these contexts in the conclusion.

2. On the 1988 campaign, see Lomnitz et al. 1993. For an excellent history of the founding of the Democratic Current, later the PRD, see Bruhn 1996.

3. This was much like the virulence toward Ralph Nader's third-party candidacy in the 2000 U.S. presidential election. A similar derogation ("egocentric") was applied to Cárdenas.

4. The Army is also represented in the PRI structure. President Lázaro Cárdenas played a decisive role early in PRI history in establishing these structures, excluding other groups, and institutionalizing the channels for citizen demands. See Stevens 1977 for a very useful review.

5. Two useful works on this topic are Benjamin 2000 and O'Malley 1986.

6. By 2002, the functions of the DACGE office had been divided. The staff members dealing with the Casas Guanajuato and directly with the families of migrants had begun working from a location on the other side of town, near the Alhóndiga. The new director of the DACGE office was a very smart, well-informed woman who had worked in the legal system in Los Angeles and who was passionate about the forms of support needed by migrants to the United States. Official stationery noted that DACGE was under the Department of State Government. Meanwhile, the Mi Comunidad program had shifted by 2002 to a kind of limbo between the DACGE office and another department, the State Commission on Support to Migrants and Their Families. Soco and Rosi work in this new office, dealing with economic matters and migrant communications, also headed by a woman, and located across the street from el Palacio. Still subject to many plans for the continuing and future use of its existing infrastructure, the program was described as having failed in many respects due to the fact that its participants were simply not "businesspeople" (*empresarios*). These changes are discussed further in the following chapters.

CHAPTER 5. *PA'L NORTE*

1. Coronil (1997) also captures this sense of national and oil wealth in writing of the Venezuelan state as a "landlord" of natural resources, describing wealth and sovereignty as being "sucked away."

2. This letter also referred to the *ejido* he represented as "a real and true representative of a marginal and poor Mexican *ejido*" (Arce 1989, 34). The author does not explore this phrase, but I read this rural man's words as a sophisticated understanding of the political importance of "authenticity discourses" in Mexico. Peasant claims framed in terms of being the "true people of Morelos" are said to be a clear response to the appropriation by bureaucrats of the image of the revolutionary hero Emiliano Zapata (Lomnitz-Adler 1992, 29).

3. Such purchases are, oddly, dismissed as "unproductive" by at least one economist (Massey et al. 1987).

4. There may be a parallel here to "sequential estimation of worth" as hypothesized by Fiona Wilson, whereby "male loom work" is seen as carrying greater value in the workshops because of its primacy in the production process and its relation to the resource allocations within the family/household, which reflect age and gender hierarchies (Wilson 1991, 137–38). Although Wilson does not explore this point in detail, she notes that value accrues to work in a kind of "inferred value."

CHAPTER 7. *LAS MUCHACHAS*

1. Many thanks to William French for indicating these wider meanings in a very helpful review of this work.

2. Giving a "voice" to women and other marginalized people is a common theme in scholarship, but Belenky, Bond, and Weinstock (1997) actually *do* this through their work. They also write of the importance of listening as empowering to low-income women. They explore how finding a "voice" indicates participation in the construction of knowledge. Lynn Wilson (1995) explores the earned right to speak and thus participate politically in the islands of Palau through the female networks of power which are being undermined by U.S.-based definitions of democracy. Nancy Ferguson builds on Foucault's notion of "radical deafness" to characterize administrative discourse and to emphasize how clients must learn to speak bureaucratic language in order to assert themselves as a "case" (1984, 82, 143–44).

3. One parallel is in Martha Banta's description of a 1908–1909 report investigating the garment industry in New York City: "Brief, random descriptions that 'read' the factories as indices of the immigrant women workers' characters stand out against the background of the generally utilitarian prose. . . . Toilets are in a bad state, but 'nothing more could be expected from the careless class of people employed'" (1993, 109). Or, from a 1986 study of workshops in Guanajuato: "The [workshop] owners make workers entirely responsible for their own health" (Wilson 1991, 139).

4. In an example from a very different setting, Deborah Rubin (1996) describes how the government in Tanzania has encouraged entrepreneurship and fostered a discourse of equality, but women are a special target through the value of their labor in support of male economic actors, *not* for their own intellect.

5. For women in Mexico, who were not fully granted the right to vote in all states until 1953, recasting the symbolic role of mother into one of political empowerment has constituted a route to justice (Martin 1990; Ramos Escandón 1994).

6. Another parallel to Taylorism, which sought to bring "order, rationality and efficiency out of the disorder, the irrationality, and wastefulness of the times," to "tidy up" the "ungovernable" in business, government, the household, in short "in the conduct of everday life" (Banta 1993, ix).

CHAPTER 8. EVASIONS

1. Taylorism, which urges men to "do better," also "says stop to the expensiveness that pulls inferiors (women, children, and lesser races) back into the past" (Banta 1993, 173).

2. Although George Foster's (1965) "image of the limited good" in Mexico is problematic for its omission of wider political contexts—erring in attributing the scarce resources model to peasant mentality rather than seeing how this scarcity could be created and manipulated by those in power (Sahlins 1972)—it finds an intentional echo here in my thinking about the workings of knowledge, which can be controlled by those in power and thereby constructed as a limited

resource, rendering the sharing of resources within library and information centers all the more crucial (Dosa 1974).

CONCLUSION

1. There are interesting theoretical discussions of what Schaffer (1975) called "the organisational connection" between officials and clients and "the ground roots of politics in the routine encounters of institutional life." From those who address "the state" as, in E. P. Thompson's words, "the institutional expression of social relationships" (cited in Taylor 1985, 147), there are calls for social histories which take account of the "interactions of state institutions with local society and politics at the point of face-to-face contact between people" (ibid.) and for policy studies which note the "complex and multiple effects of interactions between state agencies and different social groups and classes" (González Chavez 1995, 320). Work on interpersonal encounters in Mexico across power differences includes Clendinnen 1987 on colonial Yucatan; and on modern, rural agricultural policy Zendejas and de Vries 1995 and Long 1989.

2. Thanks to Davydd Greenwood for long ago pointing this out.

3. Among the examples of an ethnographic focus explicitly in relation to power are works on individual subordination to hegemonic ideas in Britain through the very effort to repudiate them (Willis 1981), on the reproduction of privilege within elite groups in France and Mexico (Bourdieu and Passeron [1964] 1979; Lomnitz and Pérez-Lizaur 1987), and on traditions of female speech and responsibility in Belau which contest imposed meanings of democracy (Wilson 1995).

4. Work on social movements includes Tarrow 1998 and Katzenstein 1998 in political science and Burdick 1993 in anthropology, to name three very diverse examples out of a burgeoning field.

5. But an exclusive theoretical reliance on "the body" may signal a retreat to a different kind of authoritative privileging or claim of "primacy" that is just as important to avoid as the exclusively textual and intellectual claims (Sangren, personal communication with the author). See Keller and Grontkowski 1983 for a helpful historical review of the visual as a "male logic"; Cixous 1983 on phallologocentrism; Flax on the problem of "writing from the body," because the body is "presocial and prelinguistic" (1987, 632).

6. Here we also saw a vast machine capable of simultaneously sewing multiple patterns, which was displayed with a long fabric stitched with repeated images of a voluptuous reclining woman with vaguely "Asian" features, clothing, jewelry, and hair design. Since all of the machines shown were built in Asia, I assumed the display pattern was set by the manufacturer. This cloth, to promote a machine destined to be used by low-paid women, was to me a powerfully condensed symbol of the double oppression of localized sexism and transnational capitalism.

Bibliography

Abu-Lughod, Lila. 1986. *Veiled Sentiments: Honor and Poetry in a Bedouin Society.* Berkeley: University of California Press.
———. 1993. *Writing Women's Worlds.* Berkeley: University of California Press.
Adler. See Lomnitz-Adler.
Allison, Anne. 1994. *Nightwork.* Chicago: University of Chicago Press.
Alonso, Anna María. 1995. "Rationalizing Patriarchy: Gender, Domestic Violence, and Law in Mexico." *Identities* 2:1–2, 29–47.
Ambriz, Agustín. 2000. "Para atraer el voto femenino, el PRI mexiquense recurre." *Proceso* no. 1231, 4 de junio, 30–35.
Anderson, Charles W. 1963. "Bankers as Revolutionaries." In *The Political Economy of Mexico,* edited by William P. Glade and Charles W. Anderson, 103–85. Madison: University of Wisconsin Press.
Anderson, Rodney. 1976. *Outcasts in Their Own Land.* DeKalb: Northern Illinois University Press.
Arce, Alberto. 1989. "The Social Construction of Agrarian Development: A Case Study of Producer–Bureaucrat Relations in an Irrigation Unit in Western Mexico." In *Encounters at the Interface,* edited by Norman Long, 11–52. Wageningen, the Netherlands: Agricultural University.
———. 1993. *Negotiating Agricultural Development.* Wageningen, the Netherlands: Agricultural University.
Arellano-Gault, David. 2000. "Challenges for the New Public Management: Organizational Culture and the Administrative Modernization Program in Mexico City (1995–1997)." *American Review of Public Administration* 30, no. 4 (December): 400–414.
Arnold, Linda. 1988. *Bureaucracy and Bureaucrats in Mexico City, 1742–1835.* Tucson: University of Arizona Press.
Babb, Florence. 2001. *After Revolution.* Austin: University of Texas Press.
Bakhtin, Mikhail. 1996. *Speech Genres and Other Late Essays.* Austin: University of Texas Press.
Banta, Martha. 1993. *Taylored Lives.* Chicago: University of Chicago Press.
Barrett, Michèle, and Mary McIntosh. 1991. *The Anti-Social Family.* 2d ed. London: Verso.
Barthes, Roland. 1972. *Mythologies.* New York: Hill and Wang.
Bartra, Roger. 1977. "The Problem of the Native Peoples and Indigenist Ideology." In *Race and Class in Post-Colonial Society,* 421–44. Paris: UNESCO.
———. 1987. *La Jaula de la melancolía.* Mexico: Editorial Grijalbo.

Bauman, Zygmunt. 1992. *Intimations of Postmodernity.* New York: Routledge.

Bazant, Jan. 1977. *A Concise History of Mexico.* New York: Cambridge University Press.

Behar, Ruth. 1993. *Translated Woman.* Boston: Beacon Press.

Belenky, Mary, Lynne Bond, and Jacqueline Weinstock. 1997. *A Tradition That Has No Name.* New York: Basic Books.

Benjamin, Thomas. 1996. *A Rich Land, a Poor People.* Albuquerque: University of New Mexico Press.

———. 2000. *La Revolución.* Austin: University of Texas Press.

Benveniste, Guy. 1970. *Bureaucracy and National Planning.* New York: Praeger.

Biggart, Nicole Woolsey. 1989. *Charismatic Capitalism.* Chicago: University of Chicago Press.

———. 1996. "Family, Gender, and Business in Direct Selling Organizations." In *Working in the Service Society,* edited by Cameron Lynne Macdonald and Carmen Sirianni, 157–83. Philadelphia: Temple University Press.

Blank, Stephanie. 1974. "Patrons, Clients, and Kin in Seventeenth-Century Caracas: A Methodological Essay in Colonial Spanish American Social History." *Hispanic American Historical Review* 54, no. 2 (May): 260–83.

Bonfil Batalla, Guillermo. 1996. *México Profundo.* Austin: University of Texas Press.

Boruchoff, Judith. 1998. "The Road to Transnationalism: Reconfiguring the Spaces of Community and State in Guerrero, Mexico and Chicago." Chicago: Hewlett Foundation Working Papers Series.

Bourdieu, Pierre. [1980] 1990. *The Logic of Practice.* Stanford: Stanford University Press.

Bourdieu, Pierre, and Jean-Claude Passeron. [1964] 1979. *The Inheritors.* Chicago: University of Chicago Press.

Bradley, Harriet. 1989. *Men's Work, Women's Work.* Minneapolis: University of Minnesota Press.

Brandenburg, Frank. 1964. *The Making of Modern Mexico.* Englewood Cliffs, N.J.: Prentice Hall.

Braverman, Henry. 1974. *Labor and Monopoly Capital.* New York: Monthly Review Press.

Britan, Gerald M., and Ronald Cohen, eds. 1980. *Hierarchy and Society.* Philadelphia: Institute for the Study of Human Issues.

Bruhn, Kathleen. 1996. *Taking on Goliath.* University Park: Pennsylvania State University Press.

Burdick, John. 1993. *Looking for God in Brazil.* Berkeley: University of California Press.

Cabrero-Mendoza, Enrique. 2000. "Mexican Local Governance in Transition: Fleeting Change or Permanent Transformation?" *American Review of Public Administration* 30, no. 4:374–89.

Cammack, Paul. 1994. "Democratization and Citizenship in Latin America." In *Democracy and Democratization,* edited by Geraint Parry and Michael Moran, 174–95. New York: Routledge.

Campbell, J. 1964. *Honour, Family, and Patronage.* Oxford: Oxford University Press.

Cárdenas Sánchez, Enrique. 1998. "Mexico's Private Sector, Then and Now." In *Mexico's Private Sector: Recent History, Future Challenges,* edited by Riordan Roett, 19–36. Boulder: Lynne Rienner.

Carrillo, Jorge. 1980. "La utilicización de la mano de obra femenina en la industria maquiladora: El caso de Ciudad Juárez." Unpublished report. Centro de Estudios Sociológicos, Colegio de México, Mexico City.

Castañeda, Jorge. 1994. *Utopia Unarmed: The Latin American Left after the Cold War.* New York: Vintage Books.

———. 2000. *Perpetuating Power.* New York: The New Press.

Castro Escudero, Teresa. 1995. "El problema militar y la consolidación de la democracia en América Latina." *Estudios Latinoamericanos* num. 3 (enero–junio): 33–54.

Cebada Contreras, María del Carmen. 2000. "Emigración Guanajuatense a Estados Unidos." *Comercio Exterior* 50, num. 4 (abril): 354–60.

Centeno, Miguel Angel, and Sylvia Maxfield. 1992. "The Marriage of Finance and Order: Changes in the Mexican Political Elite." *Journal of Latin American Studies* 24:57–85.

Certeau, Michel de. 1984. *The Practice of Everyday Life.* Berkeley: University of California Press.

Chance, John K. 1978. *Race and Class in Colonial Oaxaca.* Stanford: Stanford University Press.

Chávez, Leo R. 1992. *Shadowed Lives.* Orlando: Harcourt Brace.

Chock, Phyllis Pease. 1998. "Porous Borders: Discourses of Difference in Congressional Hearings on Immigration." in *Democracy and Ethnography,* edited by Carol J. Greenhouse and Roshanak Kheshti, 143–162. Albany: State University of New York Press.

Cixous, Hélène. 1983. "The Laugh of the Medusa." In *The Signs Reader,* edited by Elizabeth Abel and Emily K. Abel, 279–97. Chicago: University of Chicago Press.

Clendinnen, Inga. 1987. *Ambivalent Conquests.* New York: Cambridge University Press.

Clifford, James. 1988. *The Predicament of Culture.* Cambridge, Mass.: Harvard University Press.

Coello, Manuel, Sara María Lara, and Humberto Cartón. 1977. "Capitalism and the Native Peasant Population (the Chol People in the State of Chiapas)." In *Race and Class in Post-Colonial Society,* 355–76. Paris: UNESCO.

Comaroff, Jean. 1985. *Body of Power, Spirit of Resistance.* Chicago: University of Chicago Press.

Connolly, Priscilla. 1985. "The Politics of the Informal Sector: A Critique." In *Beyond Employment,* edited by Nanneke Redclift and Enzo Mingione, 55–91. Oxford: Basil Blackwell.

Cook, Maria. 1996. *Organizing Dissent.* University Park: Pennsylvania State University Press.

Cook, Scott, and Leigh Binford. 1990. *Obliging Need.* Austin: University of Texas Press.

Cope, R. Douglas. 1994. *The Limits of Racial Domination.* Madison: University of Wisconsin Press.

Corchado, Alfredo. 1995. "PRI Faces Threat in Bitter Race." *Dallas Morning News*, 27 May, 1A.

Cornelius, Wayne A. 1996. *Mexican Politics in Transition*. La Jolla: University of California, San Diego.

Coronil, Fernando. 1997. *The Magical State*. Chicago: University of Chicago Press.

Corro, Salvador, and Rodrigo Vera. 2000. "Cabildes, presiones e intrigas en el Vaticano alcanzaron su objetivo." *Proceso* num. 1209 (2 de enero): 8–13.

Cortina, Regina. 1989. "Women as Leaders in Mexican Education." *Comparative Education Review* 33, no. 3:357–76.

Cross, Harry E., and James A. Sandos. 1981. *Across the Border*. Berkeley: Institute of Governmental Studies.

DACGE. 2000. Premio INTRAGOB Reporte. Guanajuato: DACGE (Dirección General de Atención a Comunidades Guanajuatenses en el Extranjero).

Dahl, Robert. 1956. *Preface to Democratic Theory*. New Haven: Yale University Press.

Dávila Capalleja, Enrique Rafael. 1997. "Mexico: The Evolution and Reform of the Labor Market." In *Labor and Markets in Latin America*, edited by Sebastian Edwards and Nora Claudia Lustig, 292–327. Washington, D.C.: Brookings Institution Press.

de la Garza, Rodolfo O., and Gabriel Szekely. 1997. "Policy, Politics, and Emigration: Reexamining the Mexican Experience." In *At the Crossroads*, edited by Frank D. Bean, Rodolfo O. de la Garza, Bryan R. Roberts, and Sidney Weintraub, 201–25. Lanham, Md.: Rowman and Littlefield.

de la Peña, Guillermo. 1981. *A Legacy of Promises*. Austin: University of Texas Press.

de Lauretis, Teresa. 1986. "Issues, Terms, and Contexts." In *Feminist Studies: Critical Studies*, edited by Teresa de Lauretis, 1–19. Bloomington: Indiana University Press.

Del Castillo, Adelaida R. 1993. "Covert Cultural Norms and Sex/Gender Meanings: A Mexico City Case." *Urban Anthropology* 22 (fall–winter): 237–58.

del Refugio Ortega, Laura, Margarita Ortega González, and Diana Alvarez Fernández. 1999. *Diagnóstico de la situación de la mujer en Guanajuato*. Guanajuato: Consejo Estatal de Publicación.

Denich, Bette. 1980. "The Bureaucratic Scholarship: The New Anthropology." In *Hierarchy and Society*, edited by Gerald M. Britan and Ronald Cohen, 165–75. Philadelphia: Institute for the Study of Human Issues.

Derrida, Jacques. 1976. *Of Grammatology*. Baltimore: Johns Hopkins University Press.

de Vries, Pieter. 1997. *Unruly Clients in the Atlantic Zone of Costa Rica*. Amsterdam: CEDLA.

Dillon, Sam. 2001. "Profits Raise Pressures on U.S.-Owned Factories in Mexican Border Zone." *New York Times*, February 15, A3.

Domínguez, Jorge I., and James A. McCann. 1996. *Democratizing Mexico*. Baltimore: Johns Hopkins University Press.

Dore, Elizabeth, and Maxine Molyneux. 2000. *Hidden Histories of Gender and the State in Latin America*. Durham: Duke University Press.

Dosa, Marta. 1974. *Libraries in the Political Scene*. Westport, Conn.: Greenwood Press.

Douglas, Mary. 1966. *Purity and Danger*. New York: Praeger.

Dresser, Denise. 1993. "Exporting Conflict: Transboundary Consequences of Mexican Politics." In *The California–Mexico Connection*, edited by Abraham F. Lowenthal and Katrina Burgess, 82–112. Stanford: Stanford University Press.

Dubbs, Steve. 1996. *The Logics of Resistance*. Ph.D. dissertation, University of California, San Diego.

Dunn, John. 1980. *Political Obligation in Its Historical Context*. Cambridge: Cambridge University Press.

Durkheim, Emile. [1895] 1938. *The Rules of Sociological Method*. Chicago: University of Chicago Press.

Eckstein, Salomon. 1966. *El Ejido Colectivo en México*. Mexico: Fondo de Cultura Económica.

Economist. 2000. "Survey/Mexico: Revolution Ends, Change Begins." October 28, 3–16.

Edmondson, Munro S. 1960. *Nativism, Syncretism, and Anthropological Science*. Publication 19. New Orleans: Middle American Research Institute.

Evans, Peter. 1995. *Embedded Autonomy*. Princeton: Princeton University Press.

Evans-Pritchard, E. E. 1979. "Witchcraft Explains Unfortunate Events." In *Reader in Comparative Religion*, 4th ed., edited by William A. Lessa and Evon Z. Vogt, 92–98. New York: Harper Collins.

Fabian, Johann. 1983. *Time and the Other*. New York: Columbia University Press.

Fajans, Jane. 1997. *They Make Themselves*. Chicago: University of Chicago Press.

Falk, Pamela S. 2001. "Easing Up at the Border." *New York Times*, 15 February.

Femia, Joseph V. 1987. *Gramsci's Political Thought*. Oxford: Clarendon Press.

Ferguson, Nancy. 1984. *The Feminist Case against Bureaucracy*. Philadelphia: Temple University Press.

Fernández-Kelly, Maria Patricia. 1983. *For We Are Sold, I and My People*. Albany: State University of New York Press.

Flax, Jane. 1987. "Postmodernism and Gender Relations in Feminist Theory." *Signs* 12:4 (summer): 621–43.

Foley, Michael W. 1993. "Organizing, Ideology, and Moral Suasion: Political Discourse and Action in a Mexican Town." In *Constructing Culture and Power in Latin America*, edited by Daniel H. Levine, 227–66. Ann Arbor: University of Michigan.

Foster, George. 1948. *Empire's Children*. Mexico: Impr. Nuevo Mundo.

——. 1953. "Cofradía and Compadrazgo in Spain and Spanish America." *Southwest Journal of Anthropology* 9, no. 1 (spring): 1–9.

——. 1965. "Peasant Society and the Image of Limited Good." *American Anthropologist* 67, no. 2 (April): 293–315.

Foucault, Michel. [1970] 1994. *The Order of Things*. New York: Vintage Books.

——. 1979. *Discipline and Punish*. Harmondsworth: Penguin.

——. 1980. *Power/Knowledge: Selected Interviews and Other Writings, 1977–1984*. Edited by Lawrence Kritzman. New York: Routledge.

Franco, Jean. 1989. *Plotting Women*. New York: Columbia University Press.

Frazer, James G. 1965. "Sympathetic Magic." In *Reader in Comparative Religion*,

2d ed., edited by William A. Lessa and Evon Z. Vogt, 300–315. New York: Harper and Row.

French, William E. 1996. *A Peaceful and Working People.* Albuquerque: University of New Mexico Press.

Friedlander, Judith. 1975. *Being Indian in Hueyapan.* New York: St. Martin's Press.

Fuentes, Carlos. 1992. *The Buried Mirror.* Boston: Houghton Mifflin.

Fuller, Steve. 2000. *The Governance of Science.* Buckingham: Open University Press.

García Canclini, Néstor. 1995. *Hybrid Cultures.* Minneapolis: University of Minnesota Press.

García y Griego, Manuel. 1996. "The Importation of Mexican Contract Laborers to the U.S., 1942–1964." In *Between Two Worlds,* edited by David Gutiérrez, 45–85. Wilmington, Del.: Scholarly Resources.

Geertz, Clifford. 1973. *The Interpretation of Cultures.* New York: Basic Books.

Gherardi, Silvia. 1995. *Gender, Symbolism, and Organizational Cultures.* London: Sage.

Gledhill, John. 1994. *Power and Its Disguises.* Boulder: Pluto Press.

Glucksmann, Miriam. 1990. *Women Assemble.* London: Routledge.

González, Luis. 1972. *San José de Gracia.* Austin: University of Texas Press.

González Casanova, Pablo. 1970. *Democracy in Mexico.* New York: Oxford University Press.

González Chavez, Humberto. 1995. "The Centralization of Education in Mexico: Subordination and Autonomy." In *State and Society,* edited by John Gledhill, Barbara Bender, and Mogens Trolle Larsen, 320–41. New York: Routledge.

González-Martínez, Laura, and José Hernández Hernández. 1998. "Presentación." In *Coloquio internacional sobre migración Mexicana a Estados Unidos,* 3–8. Guanajuato: Gobierno del Estado.

Gramsci, Antonio. 1971. *Selections from the Prison Notebooks of Antonio Gramsci.* Edited and translated by Quintin Hoare and Geoffrey Nowell Smith. New York: International Publishers.

Greenhouse, Carol J., with Roshanak Kheshti. 1998. *Democracy and Ethnography.* Albany: State University of New York Press.

Greenwood, Davydd J. 1988. "Egalitarianism or Solidarity in Basque Industrial Cooperatives: The FAGOR Group of Mondragón." In *Rules, Decisions, and Inequality in Egalitarian Societies,* edited by James G. Flanagan and Steve Rayner, 43–69. Aldershot, England: Avebury.

——. 1991. "Collective Reflective Practice through Participatory Action Research." In *The Reflective Turn,* edited by Donald Schön, 84–107. New York: Teachers College Press.

Grindle, Merilee S. 1977. *Bureaucrats, Politicians, and Peasants in Mexico.* Berkeley: University of California Press.

——. 1988. *Searching for Rural Development.* Ithaca: Cornell University Press.

——. 1996. *Challenging the State.* Cambridge: Cambridge University Press.

Guerin-Gonzalez, Camille. 1993. "The International Migration of Workers and Segmented Labor: Mexican Immigrant Workers in California Industrial Agriculture, 1900–1940." In *The Politics of Immigration Workers,* edited by Camille

Guerin-González and Carl Strikwerda, 155–74. New York: Holmes and Meier.

Guerrero Reséndiz, Ma. Engracia. 1999. "El impacto económico de la migración." Master's thesis, University of Guanajuato.

Gutiérrez, David G., ed. 1996. *Between Two Worlds.* Wilmington, Del.: Scholarly Resources.

Hafter, Dayrl M., ed. 1995. *European Women and Preindustrial Craft.* Bloomington: Indiana University Press.

Hall, Linda B. 1995. *Oil, Banks, and Politics.* Austin: University of Texas Press.

Hamilton, Nora. 1982. *The Limits of State Autonomy.* Princeton: Princeton University Press.

Handelman, Don. 1981. "Introduction: The Idea of Bureaucratic Organization." *Social Analysis* 9 (December): 5–23.

Handelman, Don, and Elliott Leyton. 1978. *Bureaucracy and World View.* St. John's, Newfoundland: Memorial University.

Hansen, Edward C., and Timothy C. Parrish. 1983. "Elites versus the State." In *Elites: Ethnographic Issues,* edited by George E. Marcus, 257–77. Albuquerque: University of New Mexico Press.

Hearn, Jeff, and P. Wendy Parkin. 1983. "Gender and Organizations: A Selective Review and a Critique of a Neglected Area." *Organization Studies* 4, no. 3:219–42.

Heredia, Blanca. 1992. "Profits, Politics, and Size: The Political Transformation of Mexican Business." In *The Right and Democracy in Latin America,* edited by Douglas A. Chalmers, Maria do Carmen Campello de Souza, and Atilio A. Borón, 277–302. New York: Praeger.

Herzfeld, Michael. 1987. *Anthropology through the Looking Glass.* Cambridge: Cambridge University Press.

———. 1992. *The Social Production of Indifference.* Chicago: University of Chicago Press.

Himmelweit, S. 1995. "The Discovery of 'Unpaid Work': The Social Consequences of the Expansion of Work." *Feminist Economics* 1, no. 2 (summer): 1–20.

Hirschman, Albert O. 1982. "Rival Interpretations of Market Society: Civilizing, Destructive, or Feeble?" *Journal of Economic Literature* 20 (December): 1463–84.

———. 1992. "The Case against One Thing at a Time." In *Towards a New Development Strategy for Latin America,* edited by Simón Teitel, 13–19. Washington, D.C.: Inter-American Development Bank.

Hochschild, Arlie. 1983. *The Managed Heart.* Berkeley: University of California Press.

INEGI (Instituto Nacional de Estadistica, Geografia, e Informatica). 1992. *Encuesta Nacional de la Dinámica Demográfica* (Mexican national survey of demographic dynamics). Aguascalientes, Ags, Mexico: INEGI.

Jaggar, Alison, and Susan Bordo. 1989. *Gender/Body/Knowledge: Feminist Reconstructions of Being and Knowing.* New Brunswick: Rutgers University Press.

Jay, Nancy. 1992. *Through Your Generations Forever.* Chicago: University of Chicago Press.

Jones, Kathleen B. 1990. "Citizenship in a Woman-Friendly Polity." *Signs* 15, no. 4:781–812.

Kamel, Rachael, and Anya Hoffman, eds. 1999. *The Maquiladora Reader.* Philadelphia: American Friends Service Committee.

Katzenstein, Mary Fainsod. 1998. *Faithful and Fearless.* Princeton: University of Princeton Press.

Kearney, Michael. 1996. *Reconceptualizing the Peasantry.* Boulder: Westview.

Keller, Evelyn Fox, and Christine R. Grontkowski. 1983. "The Mind's Eye." In *Discovering Reality,* edited by Sandra Harding and Merrill B. Hintikka, 207–24. London: D. Reidel.

Keremetsis, Dawn. 1973. *La industria textil mexicana en el siglo XIX.* Mexico: Secretaría de Educación Pública.

Kirk, Betty. 1942. *Covering the Mexican Front.* Norman: University of Oklahoma Press.

Knight, Alan. 1990. "Racism, Revolution, and *Indigenismo:* Mexico, 1910–1940." In *The Idea of Race and Class in Latin America,* edited by Richard Graham, 71–113. Austin: University of Texas Press.

Kopinak, Kathryn. 1996. *Desert Capitalism.* Tucson: University of Arizona Press.

Korda, Michael. 1972. *Male Chauvinism.* New York: Random House.

Kristeva, Julia. 1981. "Women's Time." *Signs* 7, no. 1:13–35.

Leach, Edmund R. 1979. "Anthropological Aspects of Language: Animal Categories and Verbal Abuse." In *Reader in Comparative Religion,* 4th ed., edited by William A. Lessa and Evon Z. Vogt, 153–66. New York: Harper Collins.

Lears, T. J. Jackson. 1985. "The Concept of Cultural Hegemony: Problems and Possibilities." *American Historical Review* 90, no. 3 (June): 567–93.

Lévi-Strauss, Claude. 1966. *The Savage Mind.* Chicago: University of Chicago Press.

Lewis, Oscar. 1951. *Life in a Mexican Village.* Urbana: University of Illinois Press.

———. 1966. *La Vida.* New York: Random House.

Leyendas de Guanajauto. n.d. Guanajuato: Ediciones Casa Valadés.

Leyton, Elliott. 1978. "The Bureaucratization of Anguish: The Workmen's Compensation Board in an Industrial Disaster." In *Bureaucracy and World View,* edited by Don Handelman and Elliott Leyton, 70–134. Newfoundland: Memorial University.

Lindblom, Charles. 1959. "The Science of Muddling Through." *Public Administration Review* 19, no. 2 (spring): 79–88.

Lindquist, Diane. 2001. "Rule Change for *Maquiladoras.*" *Industry Week,* January 15, 23–26.

Lipset, Seymour Martin. 1996. *American Exceptionalism: A Double-Edged Sword.* New York: Norton.

Lipsky, Michael. 1980. *Street-Level Bureaucracy.* New York: Russell Sage Foundation.

Lomnitz, Larissa Adler. 1977. *Networks and Marginality.* New York: Academic Press.

Lomnitz, Larissa Adler, and Marisol Pérez-Lizaur. 1987. *A Mexican Elite Family, 1820–1980: Kinship, Class, and Culture.* Princeton: Princeton University Press.

Lomnitz, Larissa Adler, Claudio Lomnitz Adler, and Ilya Adler. 1993. "The Function of the Form: Power Play and Ritual in the 1988 Mexican Presidential Campaign." In *Constructing Culture and Power in Latin America,* edited by Daniel H. Levine, 357–401. Ann Arbor: University of Michigan Press.

Lomnitz-Adler, Claudio. 1992. *Exits from the Labyrinth.* Berkeley: University of California Press.

Long, Norman. 1989. *Encounters at the Interface.* Wageningen, the Netherlands: Agricultural University.

Lowi, Theodore, and Benjamin Ginsberg. 2000. *American Government.* 6th ed. New York: Norton.

Macdonald, Cameron Lynne, and Carmen Sirianni, eds. 1996. *Working in the Service Society.* Philadelphia: Temple University Press.

Malinowski, Bronislaw. 1922. *Argonauts of the Western Pacific.* New York: Dutton.

Malkki, Liisa. 1995. *Purity and Exile.* Chicago: University of Chicago Press.

Marcus, George E., and Michael M. J. Fischer. 1986. *Anthropology and Cultural Critique.* Chicago: University of Chicago Press.

Martin, Cheryl English. 1996. *Governance and Society in Colonial Mexico.* Stanford: Stanford University Press.

Martin, Joann. 1990. "Motherhood and Power: The Production of a Women's Culture of Politics in a Mexican Community." *American Ethnologist* 17, no. 3:470–90.

Massey, Douglas, Rafael Alarcón, Jorge Durand, and Humberto González. 1987. *Return to Aztlan.* Berkeley: University of California Press.

McClintock, Anne. 1991. "No Longer in a Future Heaven: Women and Nationalism in South Africa." *Transition* 51:104–23.

Memoria del Proceso Electoral. 1997. Guanajuato: Instituto Electoral del Estado de Guanajuato.

Mexico Business Monthly. 1999. "76% Growth of Maquila Plants." 9, no. 6 (July): 16.

Meyer, Jean. 1976. *The Cristero Rebellion.* New York: Cambridge University Press.

Middlebrook, Kevin. 1995. *The Paradox of Revolution: Labor, the State, and Authoritarianism in Mexico.* Baltimore: Johns Hopkins University Press.

Migration News. 2000. Vol. 7, no. 1 (January).

Milkman, Ruth. 1987. *Gender at Work.* Urbana: University of Illinois Press.

Mines, Richard. 1981. *Developing a Community Tradition of Migration to the United States.* La Jolla: Center for U.S.-Mexican Studies, University of California, San Diego.

Mintz, Sidney. 1976. Introduction to *Markets in Oaxaca,* edited by Scott Cook and Martin Diskin, i–xx. Austin: University of Texas Press.

Mintz, Sidney, and Eric Wolf. 1967. "An Analysis of Ritual Co-parenthood (Compadrazgo)." In *Peasant Society: A Reader,* edited by Jack M. Potter, May N. Diaz, and George M. Foster, 180–81. Boston: Little, Brown.

Mitchell, Timothy. 1991. "The Limits of the State." *American Political Science Review* 85, no. 1:77–96.

Mizrahi, Yemile. 1994. "Rebels without a Cause? The Politics of Entrepreneurs in Chihuahua." *Journal of Latin American Studies* 26:137–58.

Monroy, Douglas. 1999. *Rebirth: Mexican Los Angeles from the Great Migration to the Great Depression.* Berkeley: University of California Press.

Moore, Henrietta. 1988. "Gender and Status: Explaining the Position of Women." In *Feminism and Anthropology*, 12–41. Minneapolis: University of Minnesota Press.

Morgan, Gareth. 1986. *Images of Organization*. Beverly Hills: Sage.

Moser, Caroline O. N. 1995. "La planificacion de género en el tercer mundo: Enfrentando las necesidades prácticas y estratégicas de género." In *Una nueva lectura: Género en el desarollo*, edited by Virgina Guzmán, Patricia Portocarrero, and Virgina Vargas, 55–124. Lima, Peru: Ediciones entre Mujeres.

Mouffe, Chantal. 1993. *The Return of the Political*. New York: Verso.

Munn, Nancy. 1970. "The Transformation of Subjects into Objects in Walbiri and Pitjantjatjara Myth." In *Australian Aboriginal Anthropology*, edited by Ronald M. Bendt, 141–63. Nedlands: University of Western Australia Press.

Myers, Fred. 1991. *Pintupi Country, Pintupi Self*. Berkeley: University of California Press.

Nader, Laura. 1972. "Up the Anthropologist—Perspectives Gained from Studying Up." In *Reinventing Anthropology*, edited by Dell Hymes, 284–311. New York: Pantheon.

Nash, June. 1979. *We Eat the Mines and the Mines Eat Us: Dependency and Exploitation in Bolivian Tin Mines*. New York: Columbia University Press.

Nelson, Daniel. 1975. *Managers and Workers*. Madison: University of Wisconsin Press.

Nelson, Diane. 1999. *Finger in the Wound*. Berkeley: University of California Press.

Nexos. 1999. Special feature: "La cuestión indígena." *Nexos* 258 (junio): 53–68.

Nuijten, Monique. 1995. "Changing Legislation and a New Agrarian Bureaucracy." In *Rural Transformations Seen from Below*, edited by Sergio Zendejas and Pieter de Vries, 49–67. La Jolla: Center for U.S.-Mexican Studies, University of California, San Diego.

Obregón, T. Esquivel. 1920. "Are the Mexican People Capable of Governing Themselves?" In *Mexico and the Caribbean: Clark University Addresses*, edited by George H. Blakeslee, 3–4. New York: Stechert and Co.

O'Malley, Irene V. 1986. *The Myth of the Revolution*. Westport, Conn.: Greenwood Press.

Ong, Aihwa. 1987. *Spirits of Resistance and Capitalist Discipline*. Albany: State University of New York Press.

Orlove, Benjamin S. 1991. "Mapping Reeds and Reading Maps: The Politics of Representation in Lake Titicaca." *American Ethnologist* 18, no. 1:3–38.

Ortner, Sherry. 1995. "Resistance and the Problem of Ethnographic Refusal." *CCSH* 37, no 1:173–93.

Palerm, Juan Vicente, and José Ignacio Urquiola. 1993. "A Binational System of Agricultural Production: The Case of the Mexican Bajío and California." In *Mexico and the U.S.: Neighbors in Crisis*, edited by Daniel G. Aldrich, Jr., and Lorenzo Meyer, 311–67. San Bernadino, Calif.: Borgo Press.

Pare, Luisa. 1977. "Inter-ethnic and Class Relations (Sierra Norte region, State of Puebla)." In *Race and Class in Post-Colonial Society*, 377–420. Paris: UNESCO.

Paz, Octavio. 1961. *The Labyrinth of Solitude*. New York: Grove Press.

Pearson, Ruth. 1986. "Latin American Women and the New International Division of Labor: A Reassessment." *Bulletin of Latin American Research* 5, no. 2:67–79.

Peña, Devon. 1997. *The Terror of the Machine*. Austin: Center for Mexican American Studies, University of Texas at Austin.

Perrow, Charles. 1986. *Complex Organizations*. 3d ed. New York: McGraw-Hill.

Pitt-Rivers, J. A. 1958. "Ritual Kinship in Spain." *Transactions of the New York Academy of Science* (series 2) 20, no. 5 (March).

Plan Básico de Gobierno, 1995–2000: Compromisos con Guanajuato 96. 1996. Guanajuato: Gobierno del Estado.

Pondy, Louis R., Peter J. Frost, Gareth Morgan, and Thomas C. Dandridge. 1983. *Organizational Symbolism*. Greenwich, Conn.: JAI Press.

Portes, Alejandro. 1990. "From South of the Border: Hispanic Minorities in the U.S." In *Immigration Reconsidered*, edited by Virginia Yans-McLaughlin, 160–84. New York: Oxford University Press.

Pozas, María de los Angeles. 1993. *Industrial Restructuring in Mexico*. San Diego: Center for U.S.-Mexican Studies, University of California, San Diego.

Pries, Ludger. 2001. "The Approach of Transnational Social Spaces: Responding to New Configurations of the Social and the Spatial." In *New Transnational Social Spaces*, edited by Ludger Pries, 1–45. New York: Routledge.

Primera encuesta para emigrantes del Estado de Guanajuato: Resultados definitivos, 1995–1996. 1996. Guanajuato: Gobierno del Estado.

Przeworksi, Adam. 1991. *Democracy and the Market*. Cambridge: Cambridge University Press.

Purcell, John F. H., and Susan Kaufman Purcell. 1977. "Mexican Business and Public Policy." In *Authoritarianism and Corporatism in Latin America*, edited by James Malloy, 191–226. Pittsburgh: University of Pittsburgh Press.

Quiñones, Sam. 1998. "Mexican Emigrants Turn Dollars into Dream Homes." *Houston Chronicle*, 19 July.

Ramirez, Cirila Quintero. 2000. "Migration and Maquiladoras on Mexico's Northern Border." *Migration World* 28, no. 3:14–18.

Ramos Escandón, Carmen. 1994. "Women's Movements, Feminism, and Mexican Politics." In *The Women's Movement in Latin America*, edited by Jane S. Jaquette, 199–221. Boulder: Westview Press.

Redfield, Robert. 1930. *Tepoztlán*. Chicago: University of Chicago Press.

———. 1941. *The Folk Culture of Yucatan*. Chicago: University of Chicago Press.

RedNet News. 2000. "Se reúne gobernador de Guanajuato con comunidad guanajuatense radicada en Dallas." *RedNet News*, 30 October 2000 (www.rednetnews .com).

Reichert, Joshua S. 1981. "The Migrant Syndrome: Seasonal U.S. Wage Labor and Rural Development in Central Mexico." *Human Organization* 40, no. 1 (summer): 56–66.

Reisler, Mark. 1996. "Always the Laborer, Never the Citizen: Anglo Perceptions of the Mexican Immigrant during the 1920s." In *Between Two Worlds*, edited by David G. Gutiérrez, 23–44. Wilmington, Del.: Scholarly Resources.

Ries, Nancy. 2002. "'Honest Bandits' and 'Warped People': Russian Narratives about Money, Corruption, and Moral Decay." In *Ethnography in Unstable*

Places, edited by Carol Greenhouse, Elizabeth Mertz, and Kay Warren, 276–315. Durham: Duke University Press.

Riggs, Fred. 1964. *Administration in Developing Countries*. Boston: Houghton Mifflin.

Rodríguez O., Jaime E., and Kathryn Vincent. 1997. *Common Border, Uncommon Paths*. Wilmington, Del.: Scholarly Resources.

Rosaldo, Michelle Z. 1974. "Woman, Culture, and Society: Theoretical Overview." In *Woman, Culture, and Society*, edited by Michelle Zimbalist Rosaldo and Louise Lamphere, 17–42. Stanford: Stanford University Press.

———. 1980. *Knowledge and Passion*. New York: Cambridge University Press.

Rose, Hilary. 1994. *Love, Power, and Knowledge*. Bloomington: Indiana University Press.

Rose, Joseph B. 2000. "A Comparative Analysis of Public Sector Restructuring in the U.S., Canada, Mexico, and the Caribbean." *Journal of Labor Research* 21, no. 4 (fall): 601–26.

Rose-Ackerman, Susan. 1999. *Corruption and Governance*. Cambridge: Cambridge University Press.

Roseberry, William. 1993. "Beyond the Agrarian Question." In *Confronting Historical Paradigms*, edited by Frederick Cooper, Allen F. Isaacman, Florencia E. Mallon, William Roseberry, and Steve J. Stern, 318–68. Madison: University of Wisconsin Press.

Rotter, Andrew J. 2000. *Comrades at Odds: The U.S. and India, 1947–1964*. Ithaca: Cornell University Press.

Rouquié, Alain. 1982. *The Military and the State in Latin America*. Berkeley: University of California Press.

Rouse, Roger. 1992. "Making Sense of Settlement: Class Transformation, Cultural Struggle, and Transnationalism among Mexican Migrants in the United States." *Towards a Transnational Perspective on Migration*. New York: Annals of the New York Academy of Sciences, vol. 645 (July): 25–52.

Rubin, Deborah. 1996. "Business Story Is Better Than Love." In *Women out of Place*, edited by Brackette F. Williams, 245–69. New York: Routledge.

Ruddick, Sara. 1989. *Maternal Thinking*. Boston: Beacon Press.

Ruiz, Ramón Eduardo. 1997. "Race and National Destiny." In *Common Border, Uncommon Paths*, edited by Jaime E. Rodríguez O. and Kathyrn Vincent, 27–42. Wilmington, Del.: Scholarly Resources.

Rus, Jan. 1983. "Whose Caste War? Indians, Ladinos, and the 'Caste War' of 1869." In *Spaniards and Indians in Southeastern Mesoamerica*, edited by Murdo J. MacLeod and Robert Wasserstrom, 127–68. Lincoln: University of Nebraska Press.

Sahlins, Marshall. 1972. *Stone Age Economics*. Chicago: Aldine-Atherton.

Said, Edward. 1978. *Orientalism*. New York: Pantheon Books.

Sangren, Steve. 1991. "The Dialectics of Alienation." *Man* 26:67–86.

Schaffer, Bernard. 1975. "Editorial." *Development and Change* 6, no. 2 (April): 3–11.

Scott, James. 1998. *Seeing like a State*. New Haven: Yale University Press.

Sennett, Richard, and Jonathan Cobb. 1973. *The Hidden Injuries of Class*. New York: Vintage Books.

Shaffer, Mark, and Jerry Kammer. 2000. "Vigilante Ranchers Strike Fear in Heart of Migrants." *The News*, 22 May, 4.

Silva Herzog, Jésus. 1964. *El agrarismo mexicano y la reforma agraria.* Mexico: Fondo de Cultura Económica.

Simpson, Eyler N. 1937. *The Ejido: Mexico's Way Out.* Chapel Hill: University of North Carolina Press.

Singer, Marie-Odile Marion. 1988. *El agrarismo en Chiapas (1524–1940).* Mexico: Instituto Nacional de Antropología e Historia.

Sklair, Leslie. 1993. *Assembling for Development.* San Diego: Center for U.S.-Mexican Studies, University of California, San Diego.

Smith, Dorothy. 1987. *The Everyday World as Problematic.* Boston: Northeastern University Press.

Solano, Manuel. 2000. "Mexico." *International Tax Review,* July–August, 43.

Soto Romero, Jorge Mario. 1999. "The Building Blocks of Cooperation: Insights from Baja California." In *Institutional Adaptation and Innovation in Rural Mexico,* edited by Richard Snyder, 109–34. La Jolla: Center for U.S.-Mexican Studies, University of California, San Diego.

Stephen, Lynn. 1991. *Zapotec Women.* Austin: University of Texas Press.

———. 1996. "Too Little, Too Late? The Impact of Article 27 on Women in Oaxaca." In *Reforming Mexico's Agrarian Reform,* edited by Laura Randall, 289–303. Armonk, N.Y.: M. E. Sharpe.

Stevens, Evelyn P. 1977. "Mexico's PRI: The Institutionalization of Corporatism?" In *Authoritarianism and Corporatism in Latin America,* edited by James Malloy, 227–54. Pittsburgh: University of Pittsburgh Press.

Stoler, Ann Laura. 1989. "Making Empires Respectable: The Politics of Race and Sexual Morality in Twentieth-Century Colonial Cultures." *American Ethnologist* 16, no. 4:634–60.

Tarrow, Sidney. 1998. *Power in Movement.* Cambridge: Cambridge University Press.

Taussig, Michael. 1980. *The Devil and Commodity Fetishism in South America.* Chapel Hill: University of North Carolina Press.

———. 1997. *The Magic of the State.* New York: Routledge.

Taylor, William B. 1985. "Between Global Process and Local Knowledge: An Enquiry into Early Latin American Social History, 1500–1900." In *Reliving the Past,* edited by Oliver Zunz, 115–90. Chapel Hill: University of North Carolina Press.

Teichman, Judith A. 1995. *Privatization and Political Change in Mexico.* Pittsburgh: University of Pittsburgh Press.

Thompson, Ginger. 2000a. "Mexican Leader Visits U.S. with a Vision to Sell." *New York Times,* 24 August, A3.

———. 2000b. "The Desperate Risk Death in a Desert." *New York Times,* 31 October.

———. 2001. "Fox, on Tour, Stresses Mexico's Economic Importance for California." *New York Times,* 23 March.

Thompson, John. 1990. *Ideology and Modern Culture.* Stanford: Stanford University Press.

Tiano, Susan. 1994. *Patriarchy on the Line.* Philadelphia: Temple University Press.

Tiano, Susan, and Robert Fiala. 1991. "The World Views of Export Processing Workers in Northern Mexico: A Study of Women, Consciousness, and the New International Division of Labor." *Studies in Comparative International Development* 26 (fall): 3–27.

Toulmin, Stephen, and Björn Gustavsen. 1996. *Beyond Theory.* Philadelphia: John Benjamin Publishing Co.

Trejo, Frank. 1996. "Mexican Governor Urges Economic Political Reforms." *Dallas Morning News,* 21 March, 33A.

Trice, Harrison M., and Janice M. Beyer. 1990. "Cultural Leadership in Organizations." Department of Management Working Paper, University of Texas at Austin.

Trouillot, Michel-Rolph. 2001. "The Anthropology of the State in the Age of Globalization." *Current Anthropology* 42, no. 1 (February): 125–38.

Tsing, Anna L. 1993. *In the Realm of the Diamond Queen.* Princeton: Princeton University Press.

Tsurumi, E. Patricia. 1990. *Factory Girls.* Princeton: Princeton University Press.

Turner, Terry. 1982. "The Social Skin." In *Not Work Alone,* edited by J. Cherfas and R. Lewin, 112–40. Beverly Hills: Sage Publications.

———. 1997. "The Dithering Away of the State." Address at University of Chicago, March.

Turner, Victor. 1967. *The Forest of Symbols.* Ithaca: Cornell University Press.

———. 1974. *Dramas, Fields, and Metaphors.* Ithaca: Cornell University Press.

Ugalde, Francisco Valdez. 1994. "From Bank Nationalization to State Reform: Business and the New Mexican Order." In *The Politics of Economic Restructuring,* edited by Maria Cook, Kevin Middlebrook, and Juan Molinar Horcasitas, 219–43. San Diego: Center for U.S.-Mexican Studies, University of California, San Diego.

van den Zaag, Pieter. 1992. *Chicanery at the Canal.* Amsterdam: CEDLA.

Van Gennep, Arnold. [1908] 1960. *The Rites of Passage.* Chicago: University of Chicago Press.

Van Young, Eric. 1990. "To See Someone Not Seeing: Historical Studies of Peasants and Politics in Mexico." *Mexican Studies/Estudios Mexicanos* 6:133–59.

Varela, Roberto. 1984. *Expansión de sistemas y relaciones de poder.* Mexico: Universidad Autónoma Metropolitana.

Vaughan, Mary Kay. 1990. "Women School Teachers in the Mexican Revolution." *Journal of Women's History* 2, no. 1:143–68.

Vélez-Ibáñez, Carlos G. 1996. *Border Visions.* Tuscon: University of Arizona Press.

Venegas, Juan Manuel. 1999. "Convoca Fox a 'la gran revolución de finales de siglo.'" *La Jornada,* 10. de agosto.

Verdery, Kathryn. 1999. *The Political Lives of Dead Bodies.* New York: Columbia University Press.

Vincent, Joan. 1990. *Anthropology and Politics.* Tucson: University of Arizona Press.

Wade, Peter. 1997. *Race and Ethnicity in Latin America.* London: Pluto Press.

Wall Street Journal. 2000. "Mexican Factories' Growth Defies Tariffs," 6 November, A29.

Ward, Peter M., and Victoria E. Rodríguez. 1999. "New Federalism, Intra-Governmental Relations, and Co-governance in Mexico." *Journal of Latin American Studies* 31, no. 3 (October): 673–710.

Waring, Marilyn. 1999. *Counting for Nothing*. 2d ed. Toronto: University of Toronto Press.

Warman, Arturo, ed. 1970. *De eso que llaman antropología mexicana*. Mexico D.F.: Editorial Nuestro Tiempo.

———. 1980. *"We Come to Object."* Baltimore: Johns Hopkins University Press.

Wasserstrom, Robert. 1983. *Class and Society in Central Chiapas*. Berkeley: University of California Press.

Weber, Max. 1947. *The Theory of Social and Economic Organization*. New York: Oxford University Press.

Weffort, Francisco. 1993. "What Is a New Democracy?" *International Social Science Journal* 136:245–56.

Weiner, Annette. 1976. *Women of Value, Men of Renown*. Austin: University of Texas Press.

Weiner, Tim. 2001. "Mexico Seeks Lower Fees on Funds Sent from U.S." *New York Times*, 3 March.

Weston, Rubin Francis. 1972. *Racism in U.S. Imperialism*. Columbia: University of South Carolina Press.

Wiarda, Howard. 1995. "Constitutionalism and Political Culture in Mexico: How Deep the Foundation?" In *Political Culture and Constitutionalism*, edited by Daniel P. Franklin and Michael J. Baun, 119–37. Armonk, N.Y.: M. E. Sharpe.

Wight, Albert R. 1997. "Participation, Ownership, and Sustainable Development." In *Getting Good Government*, edited by Merilee S. Grindle, 369–413. Cambridge, Mass.: Harvard Institute for International Development.

Williams, Brackette F. 1996. "Introduction: Mannish Women and Gender after the Act." In *Women out of Place*, edited by Brackette F. Williams, 1–33. New York: Routledge.

Willis, Paul. 1981. *Learning to Labor*. New York: Columbia University Press.

Wilson, Fiona. 1991. *Sweaters*. London: MacMillan.

Wilson, Lynn. 1995. *Speaking to Power*. New York: Routledge.

Wilson, Patricia. 1992. *Exports and Local Developments: Mexico's New Maquiladoras*. Austin: University of Texas Press.

Wionczek, Miguel. 1963. "Incomplete Formal Planning in Mexico." In *Planning and Economic Development*, edited by Everett Hagen, 150–82. Homewood, Ill.: Richard D. Irwin.

Wolf, Eric. 1955. "Types of Latin American Peasantry: A Preliminary Discussion." *American Anthropologist* 57:452–71.

———. 1958. "La Virgen." *Folklore* 71:34–39.

———. [1959] 1974. *Sons of the Shaking Earth*. Chicago: University of Chicago Press.

Wolf, Eric, and Edward C. Hansen. 1972. *The Human Condition in Latin America*. New York: Oxford University Press.

Yanow, Dvora. 1996. *How Does a Policy Mean?* Washington, D.C.: Georgetown University Press.

Zabusky, Stacia. 1995. *Launching Europe.* Princeton: Princeton University Press.

Zendejas, Sergio, and Pieter de Vries. 1995. "Appropriating Governmental Reforms: The Ejido as an Arena of Confrontation and Negotiation." In *Rural Transformations Seen from Below,* edited by Sergio Zendejas and Pieter de Vries, 23–48. La Jolla: Center for U.S.-Mexican Studies, University of California, San Diego.

Index